SOCIOLOGICAL REVIEW MONO

Lost in Music

The Sociological Review

SOCIOLOGICAL REVIEW MONOGRAPH 34

Lost in Music

Culture, Style and the Musical Event

Edited by Avron Levine White

Routledge & Kegan Paul
London and New York

First published in 1987
by Routledge & Kegan Paul Ltd

11 New Fetter Lane
London EC4P 4EE

29 West 35th Street
New York, NY 10001, USA, and

North Way, Andover, Hants SP10 5BE

Set in Times
by Hope Services, Abingdon
and printed in Great Britain
by Billing & Sons, Worcester

Library of Congress Cataloging in Publication Data

ISBN 0-7102-1440-5

Contents

Acknowledgements

I would like to express my sincere thanks to all contributors for their patience in the preparation of the monograph. I would especially like to thank Caroline Baggaley for her consistent administrative and secretarial support throughout the entirety of this project.

The chapter by John Shepherd, 'Towards a sociology of musical styles,' first appeared in *Canadian Music Review* 1981, pp. 114–37. The chapter by Alan Lewis, 'The social interpretation of modern jazz', first appeared in *Canadian Music Review* 1981, pp. 138–65.

Contributors

John Blacking pioneered the systematic study of Ethnomusicology in the British Isles and is now recognised as a major world leader in the study of all the social aspects of music. He has been Professor and Head of Department of Social Anthropology at Queen's University, Belfast for many years and was previously Professor in Witwatersrand, South Africa. He has carried out extensive fieldwork and recording in many parts of Southern and Central Africa. He is an accomplished pianist and is also interested in dance, film, symbolism and ritual and the anthropology of the body on which he edited a seminal collection of papers for the Association of Social Anthropologists.

Harry Christian has also done research on professionalism and trade unionism among British journalists and on social change and rural schooling in Staffordshire. He is currently engaged in research on anti-sexist men's groups and masculine gender role change among men in Staffordshire. He was editor of *Sociology of Journalism and the Press, Sociological Review Monograph* No. 29, October, 1980.

Simon Frith is Professor and Research Director in the John Logie Baird Centre at the University of Strathclyde. He writes about Rock for *The Observer* and *The Village Voice*.

Dave Harker took a one year temporary job at Manchester Polytechnic fifteen years ago. He wasn't stopping, but is still there. Most of his published work has been given a hard time by reviewers, but this doesn't seem to stop him. His latest book is *Fakesong* (Open University Press, 1985).

Alan Lewis was formerly Professor of Sociology at Trent University, Peterborough and is still living and working in Canada.

John Shepherd has been Professor of Music at Carleton University, Canada since 1984, and was Executive Secretary of the International Association for the Study of Popular Music 1983–1987.

Christopher Small was born in New Zealand in 1927. He obtained degrees in science and music and after several years teaching there was awarded a New Zealand and Government scholarship to study composition in London, with the late Priaulx Rainier. In the course of subsequent teaching, in secondary schools and higher education, he became increasingly concerned with social and political aspects of music, on which he has written numerous articles and reviews, as well as

Music, Society, Education (John Calder, London, 1977 and Riverrun Press, New York, 1982) and *Music of the Common Tongue* (John Calder, London and Riverrun Press, New York, 1987). He retired from teaching last year and now lives in Spain.

Stephen Struthers studied Economics and Sociology at Cambridge and Sussex before undertaking postgraduate research on the Sociology of cultural production at the University of Keele. He now works in university administration in Birmingham.

Avron Levine White graduated from Boston University, Massachusetts and came to Britain to study sociological aspects of film and photography at Keele. After a Master's degree on film using *The Pawnbroker* as a case study, he shifted his attention to the social organisation of popular music in North Staffordshire in which he was heavily involved as a performer. He gained his doctorate on the Sociology of Musical Groups and became a community art organiser specialising in the experimental application of a video based approach to popular culture and media education. He moved to Cornwall to take up the post of film officer at Plymouth Arts Centre. He still lives in Cornwall and supports himself commercially, but continues to devote his spare time to music and the arts, their social analysis and legal implication.

Introduction

Avron Levine White

For some time the sociology of music has lacked both a core of literature and a unifying body of theory. It has an almost elusive anonymous character but nevertheless occasionally provides an interdisciplinary link between the humanities and social science. Although music for most individuals still remains a highly dramatic experience there is still no common language for its discussion or any real way of deciphering its impact on individuals or groups. If we look back to the popular sociological studies of the late 1960s and the 1970s we find that the work is primarily based upon 'effects' or 'reflection' theory; an analysis of music's capacity to 'reflect' political and social undercurrents or an examination of music's potential effect upon a listener's subsequent social behaviour. Simon Frith's *Sociology of Rock* (1978) and Denisoff and Peterson's *The Sounds of Social Change* (1972) are perhaps the most successful of these studies, providing a wide range of analysis of lyrics and social behaviour during the commercial 'pop' music boom.

At the same time, while all the analysis of hidden meanings, messages and general behavioural response to new musical experiences was being documented in various academic studies, there was a less popular but equally important network of studies about the community of musicians themselves and the changing technology of their craft. The seminal work in this field was certainly Howard Becker's 'The professional dance musician and his audience' (1951). Becker's perspective starts with the community of jazz musicians: their attitudes towards work, their aesthetic objectives and their relationship with audiences. Through this network of concerns, Becker explores some of the general pressures upon individual jazz musicians who must confront conflicting commercial and artistic goals. Since Becker's study, there has been a sprinkling of unpublished PhD theses on musical communities and related areas (see Etzkorn 1959; Schockett 1964; Delcour 1967; and Faulkner 1968).

A contemporary investigation complementing the style and scope of Becker's work on jazz is H.S. Bennet's *On Becoming*

A Rock Musician. What Bennet looks at successfully is the community of amateur and semi-professional musicians who play in local bands, their learning procedures and performance expectations.

There is clearly a divergence in the character of sociological study. Some researchers have as their objective the musical end-product which is viewed as a thing-in-itself reflecting and influencing groups of people by virtue of its availability and popularity. Other research objectives identify the actual process of production with all its labour relations and technological artefacts.

In other words, one either studies the matter in the abstract concentrating on the accessible factors available to the non-musician, namely, the lyrical content, the aural and social experience; or alternatively one studies the production process from the standpoint of a knowledge of musical technique. Both kinds of studies are in my opinion valid and productive; my only concern is that there has been rather more of the former variety of study than the latter.

For some years, ethnomusicologists have been arguing that an understanding of music and society requires an understanding of musical technique (practical ability strongly implied); that as anthropologists it is necessary to go into the 'field', to learn to play what we are listening to and to examine the structural pattern of the sound itself. From this knowledge we will understand music's integral meaning within the society in which it occurs. Obviously, this kind of research objective limits research practitioners to those who have special ability with music.

Nevertheless this emphasis on looking at musical practice and musical technique has produced some interesting results, particularly in weighing upon the impact of technology on the culture of musical production. An important sociological work which has registered the impact of this research direction is *Whose Music? A Sociology of Musical Languages* (1977) by J. Shepherd, T. Wishart, P. Virden and G. Vulliamy. In their book of essays they express a view of sounds as symbols in culture. Initially they establish important relationships between the 'underlying epistemology of the modern western world' and a 'sociologically based aesthetics of music'. Beyond this there is an attempt to blend musicological or technical study of music structure with the study of music as a functioning part of complex industrial society. In Trevor Wishart's article, 'Musical writing, musical speaking', he discusses the effect of technology on the accessibility of music in the learning situation. He also discusses the way technology makes possible the creation and transmission of musical ideas which are apprehended outside the scope of conventional musical notation. Essentially Wishart identifies the conflict between learning processes based upon analytic notation and those which in his terms 'are not mediated via notation but rather through aurally-based musical praxes, e.g. direct sound recording'.

> The 20th century discovery of the technique of direct sound recording has enabled musical praxes which are not mediated via notation (at least not in some overwhelming way) to be captured and distributed in their entirety and has hence shattered the hegemony of the notationalist view of music. In the tradition of jazz and rock musics, the filtering mechanism of a notation procedure has been specially bypassed and elements such as subtle pitch inflexion (especially deriving from the blues), complex rhythmic nuance, timbre control, and inflexion, and subtle control of dynamic balance, acoustics and acoustic balance (made possible in the modern electronic recording studio) have returned to the foreground of musical concern for people involved in these essentially aurally-based musical praxes. (Shepherd, Virden, Vulliamy, Wishart, 1977, p.137)

In other words, many of the African-based non-western influences on 'pop' music (e.g. African via black American) have been learned by ear. Inexpensive recording equipment and radios have made it possible for a culture of musicians to learn the craft from repeated listenings rather than notation.

More to the point and perhaps a little more concrete in analysis is Dave Harker's *One for the Money: The Politics of Popular Song*. In his chapter on 'Electricity' he gives a very useful synopsis of changes in the commercial operation of the music business as a result of technological developments in sound production. He also shows how it has limited the scope of many musical projects. Initially he discusses the first changes brought about by electronic amplification.

> Singers soon came to realise that the mike (microphone) and the amplifier enabled them to produce more noise than an amplified band. . . . Big bands came to be economic albatrosses, and were undercut by small groups and solo artists. In fact, we

> can date the rise of the solo performer in North America from the early 1940's.' (Harker, 1980, p.32)

But what is still of greater significance *vis-à-vis* the technological factor changing the parameters of the 'live performance' is the way that studio reproduction has reversed the conceptual expectation of 'realism' as it applies to 'recorded' and 'live' music. That is to say that whereas initially the 'recording' was expected to be a faithful representation of the original 'live' performance, now it is the 'recording' of the studio performance which is deemed to be the 'original' and the live performance is merely a substandard albeit visually complete copy. To wit:

> One of the long term consequences of technologically sophisticated recording was the relative demise of the 'live' performance group during the later 1960's and early 1970's. Those same technological developments which helped Britain by hire purchase, led to a significant democratization of music making, also led to the eventual removal of the commercially successful groups from live performance altogether. The Beatles' first LP cost £400 to produce. By the time of *Revolver*, however, their exploitation of the new electronics in the studio made reproducing the same sound on stage all but impossible. After *Sgt. Pepper*, which took four months and £25,000 to make, live performances were totally impossible outside the more sophisticated studios. (D. Harker, 1980, p.35)

Although there is now technology to ensure that the 'live' performance version matches the 'recorded' version, there is an ever-increasing cost factor which has inevitably led to the introduction of pre-recorded and computerised sounds in the 'live' performance. Furthermore, the more complex 'live' stage sound in the professional circuit has altered the standards for the semi-professional circuit and consequently severely restricted the number of groups able to compete even at this level. Even jazz has been affected. Although traditional jazz performance has remained relatively unaffected by the technology factor, there is nevertheless far more amplification introduced than in previous years, and certainly there are more bass players foregoing the string bass for the electric instrument.

In conclusion, then, this monograph will explore a variety of concerns which in all reflect two central dimensions of study which are, in my view, relevant to sociological investigation: first, that which is based upon the accessible end-product, and second, that which is based upon the process of musical production. Hence the monograph is divided into several sections, the first of which is entitled 'The social character of music'. In this section several authors examine the social, historical and economic parameters of musical style. The next section, entitled 'Words and music', deals initially with the social impact of lyrics in music throughout a particular social and historical period. The section entitled 'Convention and constraint in working life' looks more closely at the process of musical production and the legal structures controlling labour relations. The final section is called 'Recording music'.

Finally, it seems useful at this stage to distinguish between three areas of musical form, which in some respects share a common language, but which have entirely different historical, sociological and commercial points of reference. There is western orthodox music which includes classical, 'serious', orchestral and symphonic music. There is jazz which includes blues, ragtime, New Orleans, Dixieland, swing, bebop, cool and modern jazz. Pop includes rock 'n' roll, soul, progressive rock, funk, jazz/rock, disco-funk, new wave, punk rock, reggae, heavy metal, and futurist music. Although these categories are partially a product of commercial invention designed to facilitate the organisation and sale of records rather than the identification of musical idioms, they are, for the purposes of this monograph, accurate for the manner in which they are used throughout the various writings which will appear in this volume.

References

Bennet, H. S. *On Becoming A Rock Musician*, Massachusetts 1980.

Delcour, Jolly H. *Popular Music: a study in Collective Behaviour*, Unpublished Ph.D. thesis, University of Illinois, 1967.

Etzkorn, K. P. Musical and Social Patterns of Songwriters: An Exploratory Socialogical Study. Unpublished Ph.D. thesis, Princetown University, Department of Economics and Sociology, U.S.A. 1959.

Faulkner, Robert Roy, *Studio Musicians: their work and career and career contingencies in the Hollywood film industry*. Unpublished Ph.D. thesis; University of California, U.S.A. 1968.

Frith, Simon, *The Sociology of Rock*, London, 1978.

Harker, David, *One For The Money: The Politics of Popular Song*, Hutchinson Group, London, 1980.

Schockett, B., *A Stylistic Study of The Blues, as Recorded by Jazz Instrumentalists*, unpublished Ph.D. thesis, New York University, U.S.A. 1964.

Wishart, Trevor, 'Musical Writing, Musical Speaking,' in *Whose Music? A Sociology of Musical Languages*, Latimer New Dimensions, London, 1977.

THE SOCIAL CHARACTER OF MUSIC

Performance as ritual: sketch for an enquiry into the true nature of a symphony concert

Christopher Small

This essay will consider the symphony concert as a phenomenon within our society. I shall try to show that a symphony concert partakes of the nature of a ritual, a celebration, undertaken not fully awares, of the shared mythology and values of a certain group within our deeply fragmented society. The meaning of the ritual has changed profoundly over the past fifty years or so, even if its outward form remains apparently unchanged. This is of course not unusual for symbolic behaviour; Raymond Williams has pointed out how the word 'art', like other key words in our society such as 'class', 'culture', 'industry' and 'democracy', has changed its meaning and emotional resonance in the last hundred and fifty years,[1] and it is certain that many of those objects (including sound-objects) that we call artistic masterpieces have similarly changed their meaning even while retaining their outward forms. It is not just that a symphony by Beethoven, for example, has a different significance for us, to whom it is thoroughly familiar, even over-familiar, from that which it had for its first audiences, to whom it was fresh, surprising, even grotesque and frightening (we recall that Weber, who was a great musician and no fool, declared on hearing the Seventh Symphony that Beethoven was 'now ripe for the madhouse',[2] an expression of contemporary sensibility and experience and a metaphor for the cracking-open of social forms. The audience for the music, too, has changed its character in a way not always recognized; the nineteenth-century aristocratic and middle-class audience was full of confidence and fertile with ideas and invention, while today's audience feels itself beleaguered, its values and its position under attack. It is not inconceivable that a musical mind of the stature of Beethoven or Bach might appear today in our society, but it is hardly possible that his or her music could fulfil the same function for us as did Bach's and Beethoven's for their times, since, for the overwhelming majority of music lovers new music has nothing whatsoever to say to them; they remain apparently content with the familiar world of 'The Great Classics' (there is a world of meaning in that definite article, with its suggestion of something completed and closed). I believe this virtual freezing of the repertory to be an important phenomenon, and it will be a major purpose of this essay to investigate it.

What, then, is a ritual? I take it to be an act which dramatizes and re-enacts the shared mythology of a culture or social group, the mythology which unifies and, for its members, justifies that culture or group. According to Mircea Eliade, it celebrates the 'sacred history' of the culture – its creation, the coming of the civilizing heroes, their 'demiurgic activities' and finally their disappearance.

> The 'sacred history' – mythology – is exemplary, paradigmatic; not only does it relate how things came to be; it also lays the foundations for all human behaviour and all our social and cultural institutions. From the fact that man was created and civilized by supernatural Beings, it follows that the sum of his behaviour and activities belongs to sacred history; and this history must be carefully preserved and transmitted intact to succeeding generations.[3]

It is interesting that Eliade explicitly confines his comments to what are called 'traditional' or 'primitive' societies. 'Modern man's originality,' he says, 'his newness in comparison with traditional societies, lies precisely in his determination to regard himself as a purely historical being, in his wish to live in a basically desacralized cosmos.'[4] In other words, modern western man believes himself to have become divorced from (many would say, to have outgrown) the beliefs and ideas which shaped the lives of previous generations. Even Eliade is doubtful whether this is in fact so. I believe, and shall argue in this essay, that it is not true to any significant degree, that Eliade's comment in the preceding paragraph holds as well for modern western society as for any other, past or present. A symphony concert, as an important ritual of the power-holding class in our society, shows the modern westerner to be as much dependent on, and, to the extent that he suppresses any awareness of them, bound by his mythologies as any member of a 'traditional' society.

A symphony concert operates simultaneously on two levels. We can, as most of the audience do, content ourselves with the surface experience, contemplating the beauty of the music and the seemingly miraculous communication of ideas and emotions from one individual to another through the medium of organized sound; this is music, the abstract art, as it is celebrated by composers, performers and audiences alike and written about by critics and musicologists. But it is the second, the ritual level, generally unperceived or ignored since it is so close to us, that is the really important and interesting aspect of a concert, that gives us a clue to what it really is that keeps symphony orchestras playing and concert halls lit. To perceive a concert at this level we need to begin by examining it, not just as organized sound, but also as an event taking place within our society, at a particular time and in a particular place, involving a particular group of people.

In the first place, it is usual for the event to take place within a building that has been specially constructed or set aside, generally at considerable expense, for performance of and listening to music. Most often it is used exclusively for musical performances, although on occasion a church, the hall of a great house (themselves spaces that are built for ritual purposes, either religious or secular) or some other large space will be pressed into service. Either way, the desirable space is as nearly as possible soundproof, so that auditory connection with the outside world is cut off, while visual connection is also reduced to a minimum. Some kind of ante-room is desirable for the audience, where socializing (not possible during the performance) and the taking of refreshments can take place before and in the interval of the performance. Direct access from the outside to the performance space itself is not thought desirable (I have heard this given as a grave disadvantage of the otherwise admirable church-turned-concert-hall of St John's, Smith Square in London), presumably because, as in a temple, some transitional area is felt to be necessary between the world of every day and the space in which the central business of the event is to take place. It is also necessary to have a place by the entrance where tickets are bought and sold since, as we shall see, it is important to ensure that only those entitled to attend do so, and the passing of money is the symbol of this entitlement. In the performance space itself it is not thought desirable today to provide too much visual interest (earlier builders seem to have had no such inhibitions – further evidence perhaps of the changed function of a concert) since this is thought to distract attention from the real business of the event. The basic arrangement of the space is as formal as that of a traditional school classroom, which in many respects it resembles; both places reveal, before a word has been uttered or a note played, the nature of the communication that is to take place therein. The audience, the non-active participants in the event, are seated in more or less comfortable seats arranged in rows; the rows are generally curved to centre the sightlines on the middle of the performers' platform, to which the audience has no access. Unlike a theatre, a concert hall has no proscenium, so that at first sight the visual spectacle is somewhat diffuse and lacking in focus; closer attention shows that the players are also seated in concentric rows, whose centre, as with the audience's seats, is also on one spot at the front centre of the platform – the conductor's podium, which thus is at the point of intersection of the two foci of attention, the power centre of the entire proceedings.

The technology and logistics of a symphony concert are worth a moment's consideration. Each event involves a high degree of organization, both within the hall and outside it. Apart from the obvious complexities of booking artists, often members of the international jet set, often years in advance, of preparing publicity material and tickets, of planning programmes (a matter I shall discuss at more length later), apart from the obvious requirements of lighting, heating and maintaining the large building, there is required a sophisticated technological and organizational infrastructure by means of which all the 2,000-odd persons who attend, say, a Royal Festival Hall concert in London are informed of, obtain tickets for, and are brought to and taken from the event, some travelling a hundred miles or more for the purpose, with very few indeed free from reliance on some form of public or private transport.

Then there is the built-in proletariat of the concert hall, whose task is to keep the place running smoothly without any appearance of effort: booking clerks, ticket collectors and ushers, programme sellers, electricians and sound men, piano tuners, hefty men to shift the piano and arrange seats for the orchestra, bar and restaurant staff, and of course the cleaners, those ubiquitous but ever-invisible Nibelungen of the modern industrial state, without whose scandalously underpaid services not only concert halls and theatres, but also airports, offices and educational institutions would quickly clog to a standstill on their own detritus – all working as unobtrusively as possible to contrive the illusion of a magical world set apart from everyday reality where nobody has to work.

Clearly, such an event cannot happen spontaneously, either for the artists or for the audience; the very siting of such palaces as the Royal Festival Hall or the Albert Hall in London or the Fisher Hall in New York makes it highly unlikely that anyone just passing will decide on impulse to go in. Much planning, on both sides of the house, is clearly needed; in fact an observer at a performance would hardly gain the impression that spontaneous behaviour was called for from either performers or audience. Although, for the audience, conventions of dress have become much relaxed in recent years, there are still conventions of behaviour, both in the performance space itself and in its ante-rooms, which most people find binding. From the moment of entering the building one's behaviour changes, becoming more formal and inclined to be muted. Within the performance space itself this becomes even more marked; the arrangement of the seating does not, in any case, encourage interaction with any but one's immediate neighbours. And of course during the actual performance total silence and as nearly as possible total immobility are enjoined. Even to move one's foot gently in response to the music's beat is to invite condemnation as an ignoramus or a boor. Audible expressions of opinion during the performance are regarded as an offence, not just against the piece being played, but against the very event itself; histories of music make much of occasions such as the first performance of *Le Sacre du Printemps* or Schoenberg's Second String Quartet, when the audience did express its opinion forcefully during the performance, referring to them as 'scandals', and thus by definition deplorable. There is, however, one time when spontaneous or quasi-spontaneous behaviour is not only tolerated but positively expected, and that is at the end of a performance, either of an individual work or of a concert as a whole. Even here the range of behaviour is circumscribed, being confined to hand clapping and, in cases of extreme approval, shouts such as 'Bravo!' and rising in one's seat. But booing to signify disapproval is also tolerated at this time.

The behaviour of the performers is even more formal. Conventions of dress still remain more binding than for the audience; a uniform style is more or less universal for men, although some latitude is allowed for women. It is still almost universal for female orchestral musicians to wear black, although the actual cut of the dress is left to the individual; female soloists on the other hand are permitted (even encouraged?) to wear brighter colours, so long as the dress has the necessary formality and, if possible, glamour. The fact that some avant-garde groups wear, for instance, black trousers and coloured shirts or rollneck sweaters need not disturb us; the uniform remains, and all that is happening is that rollneck sweaters are becoming accepted for more formal purposes (this is a constant process in the history of fashion – today's high formal dress for men is an adaptation of Victorian hunting costume, while the movement up the social scale of blue denim would have astonished those gold prospectors of the '49 who first wore jeans).

The performers enter by a separate door and remain out of sight when not actually playing; they rarely if ever speak to the audience from the platform, and thus the audience never sees or hears them in anything other than their formal role. Despite the fact that the music they are performing is generally highly dramatic, it is considered bad form actually to show outward signs of emotion; the conductor or instrumentalist who engages in empathetic gestures with the music is often judged to have something of the charlatan about him. Singers seem exempt from this rule and are indeed expected to act out, with discretion, the emotions presented by the song; to look happy, sad, jocular or coy in accordance with the sentiments expressed by text and music. Whether this is just a carry-over from the opera stage is hard to say; I am inclined to feel that the reason lies in the concrete and specific nature of the emotional situations depicted in songs and arias, in contrast to the abstract and generalized nature of purely instrumental works. In any case, all these conventions serve to depersonalize the performers and to emphasize the universality and timelessness of the proceedings. In this there is a striking similarity to another, explicitly ritual, set of actions, those of the celebrant priest in a Catholic Mass, whose individuality is likewise concealed, by his robes, his stylized gestures and his artificial voice production. Here again it is the timelessness of the ritual that is important; the message is that priests (or musicians) may come and go but the Church (or the music) goes on for ever.

What then of the music itself, the occasion for this expensive building, this extensive staff of workers of magic, these musicians, this assembled audience? A symphony concert is usually planned to begin with a not too demanding piece, an overture perhaps, or some other lightweight work, ostensibly to allow performers and audience to settle down. Then follows a longer and more substantial piece, a concerto perhaps, or a symphony, after which an interval is taken, lasting generally about twenty minutes, at which time refreshments are taken in the foyer. There is no *physical* necessity for a break in the proceedings; people who know they are going to have to sit still for two or three hours or more, at events as various as a performance of *Das Rheingold* or a coronation, prepare themselves and manage without apparent discomfort. And certainly nobody need feel hungry or thirsty during such a short timespan. The truth is that the interval is not a break in the event at all but an essential part of it, providing opportunity for social intercourse with members of one's own reference group, to crystallize one's response to the event by discussion (intervals seem interminable to those with no one to talk to) and even to be seen as present by those whose opinions matter (by no means as discreditable a reason as many seem to believe). After the interval comes a further substantial piece, again usually a concerto or a symphony, making in all a duration of about one and a half to two hours. There are obviously many variations on this scheme – a work of great length such as Beethoven's Ninth Symphony or Mahler's Second may appear alone or preceded only by a short piece (even after a twenty-minute Mozart symphony it is common to take an interval), while an oratorio or passion may constitute the entire performance. Alternatively, the entire concert, usually aimed at a less initiated audience, may consist of an assortment of shorter, lightweight pieces, such as Sir Thomas Beecham used to refer to as 'lollipops' – a significant term to which I shall return later.

The musical works are, for the most part, the work of long-dead composers, who through the medium of notation are able to control the actions of orchestral musicians in our own time. Many of these works are termed 'immortal masterpieces', although in fact very few of them were created more than 250 years ago, a short time even by the standards of European history, and a mere flash when one considers that the first recognizable works of art that have come down to us were made probably 300,000 years ago. As Alejo Carpentier says in his remarkable novel *The Lost Steps*,

> Every time I saw the members of a symphony orchestra seated behind their music-racks I waited impatiently for the moment when time would cease to pile up incoherent sounds and fall into an organized framework in response to a prior human will

> speaking through the gestures of the Measurer of its Passing. The latter was obeying decisions made one century, two centuries ago. Inside the covers of the score were set down in signs the orders of men who, although dead inside some ornate mausoleum – or their bones lost in the dreary disorder of some potter's field – still held author's rights on time, imposing the measure of motion and emotion on future men.[5]

The musicians on the platform, then, have no creative role to play, only a re-creative one, to carry out, under the direction of the man Carpentier calls the Measurer of the Passing of Time, the instructions of long-dead humans, to produce sounds these humans had imagined in their heads and to give them life. This is a remarkable phenomenon, but even more remarkable to my mind is the fact that living, or even recently deceased, composers are sparsely, to say the least, represented in the repertory of regularly performed works. With very few exceptions, the repertory virtually froze around the time of the First World War (a disaster whose catastrophic effect on the morale of western middle-class culture still remains not fully appreciated), and little that has appeared since carries the appeal for the average audience of 'music lovers' that earlier music does; it carries the pejorative label 'modern music' and is viewed with the utmost suspicion. Those who advocate 'modern music' await its assimilation into the wider awareness much as the early Christians awaited the Second Coming, greeting each performance of *Arcana*, *Chronochromie* or *Jakobsleiter* as the first rays of a new dawn. But it does not happen and, in my opinion, cannot happen. The only music of the post-First World War era which has gained, or is likely to gain, anything like general acceptance is that which, like the later works of Sibelius or Rachmaninov, shows an immediate affinity with the world of nineteenth-century romanticism (this is by no means to devalue the work of these or comparable masters).

The virtual freezing of the repertory has had the consequence that a concert very rarely provides any genuinely new musical experience. The number of composers whose work is regularly represented in orchestral concert programmes is not large – around fifty at most, with a few others represented by perhaps one or two, often immensely popular, works (Bruch's First Violin Concerto and *Scottish Fantasy*, for example, or Dukas's *Apprenti Sorcier*) – which means that most concerts consist mainly of a limited number of works which get played over and over again, with minute variations in interpretation, and that audiences become extremely skilled in perceiving these variations and comparing them. They also become skilled at detecting deviations from the written text, either deliberate or accidental, and such deviations incur their severe disapproval.

In view of this situation it is astonishing that such an enormous volume of orchestral music has been composed since 1920 or so, and it is true that much of it does get played in concert halls by symphony orchestras, although mainly under the direction of second-string conductors rather than the superstars – the latter mainly prefer to continue honing and refining their performances of the existing repertory and show little interest in new music. One after another, composers have made their bids to have their works taken into the concert repertory, but remarkably few have succeeded, and of these, as I have said, almost all have been those who have retained strong links with the familiar world of nineteenth-century romanticism, or even of eighteenth-century classicism. For the rest, some works are performed occasionally – even if, like Stravinsky, Schoenberg or Varèse, their composers are considered to be great twentieth-century figures – while others are heard perhaps once or twice, are received with more or less respect, then disappear without trace. It is a tribute to the power of the creative impulse – with, no doubt, a shove or two from wordly ambition – that several generations of musicians have continued to compose, put their works before the public, and stake their claim to immortality of a kind. But the number of post-1920 works that have become as regular a part of the orchestral repertoire as are those of Beethoven, Brahms or Tchaikowsky is tiny indeed.

The orchestral musician, it seems, becomes inured to the experience of playing this small repertory of works over and over again – although the American critic Henry Pleasants believes that he will be – or become – 'emotionally and imaginatively stunted'. He says,

> He has no music of his own, nor can he play anyone else's music with the immediacy that it had for those to whom it was originally addressed, or expect from his listeners the same immediacy of response. Given such constraints as these, compounded by the stagnation of the repertory, it is a tribute to the Serious [sic] musician's skills, diligence and patience that he is not a duller fellow than he is, especially the orchestra

> musician, playing more or less the same notes in more or less the same way under the daily supervision of a variety of opinionated conductors year in and year out, or the itinerant virtuoso, condemned for the rest of his life to play a small bag of viable concertos by Mozart, Beethoven and Brahms.[6]

I do not wish to echo Pleasants's clear tone of condemnation of this state of affairs, being more interested at this point in understanding it. Nonetheless his comments do point up the extraordinary nature of this everyday phenomenon of the western concert world.

The human desire for novelty is not, however, dead, even in this situation, and it is met by the researches of musicologists into ever more obscure corners of the past repertory. The rediscovery of the Baroque in the 1930s and 1940s was, at least in part, a response to this desire, and there is no doubt that many neglected master composers from Monteverdi to Telemann were restored to the consciousness of concert audiences at this time. Again, Bizet's youthful and undeniably enchanting Symphony in C, now a regular concert item, lay, I am told, virtually unperformed until discovered in the 1930s; it is only one of many such. But such quarrying of the past for the semblance of new musical experiences must come, as with all strictly non-renewable resources, eventually to an end; although still possibly containing untapped fields for exploitation the resources are not unlimited, and already musicologists are becoming reduced to exhuming the works of ever more and more minor composers, or ever more obscure works by major composers, even making notional completions of incomplete or mutilated works (Mahler's Tenth Symphony and Schubert's Eighth come to mind) – anything that is new to the audience but bears the reassuring stamp of the familiar musical language and gestures. The search for novelty, frustrated in the one direction that could genuinely provide it, takes the form also of reassessment and reworking of familiar masterpieces (recent small-scale performances of Messiah for example) with a view to restoring 'authenticity' – whatever that is – or the digging out of early, often discarded, versions of others (Beethoven's *Leonora*, the early, and unsuccessful, version of *Fidelio*, recently recorded for the benefit of armchair musicologists). There are of course other reasons given for these researches, but I believe them to be mostly rationalizations of the raw fact that it is the human need for new experiences, unable to take its true direction, that provides the basic drive. A culture able to take full advantage of present creativity would not feel this compulsion to nitpick at its past.

I have discussed elsewhere[7] some of the technical features of symphonic music, and although I do not intend to reiterate that discussion here, there are one or two features of it that do bear comment. First, the music is highly dramatic in character, full of strong, even violent, contrasts of mood and emotion; its central technique, to which all others are subordinate, and which unifies all the music written between about 1600 and 1900, is that of tonal functional harmony, the arranging of chords in meaningful sequences by means of which the listener is led forward in time, his expectations being frustrated and teased but ultimately satisfied by the final perfect cadence in the home key (it is remarkable that there is scarcely a single piece written in the period that does not end in this fashion). There is no space here to expound the significance of tonal harmony, but, in a word, it is the essential field upon which is worked out that drama of the individual soul which is the symphonic work. We participate through the music in the experience of the composer, in his progression from doubt to affirmation and triumph. As Wilfrid Mellers says, 'In a sense, all our art has been an assertion of our post-Renaissance pride, for it has implied that other people care, or ought to care, about our experience.[8] And in so far as it passes from one individual soul to another through the medium of the orchestra and the concert hall, it celebrates the autonomy and essential solitariness of the individual in modern western society.

It is interesting that virtually all the most popular orchestral works, whether symphonies, concertos, symphonic poems or whatever, follow this dramatic progression from doubt and turbulence to triumph and even apotheosis of the soul (Tchaikovsky's Sixth Symphony is an exception of genius) with a period of respite and quietness between the turbulent beginning and the triumphant end; it is as if an old world were being dissolved and a new one brought into being. In its form the typical symphonic work suggests the representation of a passage rite, whose tripartite form has been remarked upon by van Gennep and others.[9] The sequence noted by van Gennep – (1) separation from the outside world, (2) seclusion and (3) celebration – represents, as Victor Turner suggests, 'the ultimate victory of life over death'. 'Herein', he says, 'is contained a dialectic that passes from life through death to renewed life'[10] – an excellent characterization of the symphonic process at work. The criteria by which the average listener judges a work of symphonic music are essentially dramatic; he cares little for the factors of logic, development, unity or variety by which critics seek to rationalize the process, but is concerned with the force of the struggle and the effectiveness of the triumph that is achieved in the music. The average listener is not for that reason to be scorned, since he is concerned with the ends of the music, while the critic is liable to find himself bogged down in means. But the drama remains an abstract one, taking place in the minds of the participants without the intervention of the body – a fact attributed by some observers, among them Harry Partch, to the Christian tradition's denial of the body (in a single robustly written chapter in *Genesis of a Music*[11] Partch dismisses virtually the entire western 'classical' tradition as hopelessly lost in abstraction, the arch-villains of the piece being – Bach, Beethoven and Brahms). In any case, the abstract-dramatic nature of the work can be judged from the storm of applause that follows immediately (too immediately on occasion) on the end of an admired performance of an admired work. To the majority of the audience the drama is as familiar as *Hamlet* is to a Shakespearian audience (theatregoing is of course equally a ritual activity – but that is the province of students of theatre), and holds no real surprises, but the excitement generated by the music seems to be no less real than if it were the very first time that the work had been played. Because of the abstract nature of the music it is not permitted to give physical expression to that excitement during the performance, and the whole response to the drama must be bottled up until the end, when it is likely to explode with a lack of moderation that would sometimes put a football crowd to shame.

What of the orchestra itself? The modern professional symphony orchestra is the very model of an industrial enterprise, a highly efficient body permeated through and through with the industrial philosophy, directed like all industrial enterprises towards the making of a product, namely a performance. Its social relations are those of the industrial workplace, being entirely functional and depending only upon the job to be done; players may know and care nothing about colleagues' lives apart from the job, and if, as in other jobs, friendships do develop these are irrelevant to the task to be performed. The written notes control the actions of the players and mediate their relationship. As in any other job, too, the rank and file are rarely consulted about the nature of the product to be made, but are required simply to play whatever notes are set before them, under the direction of as dynamic a managerial type as it is possible to engage. Time is money; the workers are highly unionized and generally unwilling to work extra time without extra pay, while the foreman (known as the leader) acts as middleman between rank and file and higher management. There is a distinct social hierarchy within the organization, with the string players accorded the highest status (white-collar, one might almost say), the brass and percussion having on the other hand a distinct blue-collar image, being generally regarded as jolly fellows, not over-sensitive and given to the consumption of large quantities of beer. The close association between the industrial mode of production and the symphony orchestra can be seen in societies that have recently been converted to industrialism (the industrial philosophy can of course be seen as overriding the ideological differences between capitalism, socialism, communism and most other isms); the formation of professional symphony orchestras and the appearance on the scene of a number of *Wunderkind* performers is often the first indication that such a conversion has taken place and become interiorized.

The rigid division of labour among instrumentalists in the orchestra (by no means a necessary condition of highly developed concerted music making, as can be seen, for example, in the Balinese gamelan, where each player is expected to take his turn at each instrument) is again in the interest of efficient production of a performance; each player is highly skilled on a single instrument or small selection of related instruments, and the skills of sight reading and rapid response are especially cultivated, while those of memory and improvisation are neglected to virtual extinction. The musicians' skills are such that mistakes in the notes are relatively rare, and total breakdowns almost unknown; in any case, the majority of the repertory is so familiar to any experienced orchestral player that he could almost play it blindfold. Among conductors, too, the ability to produce a competent performance in a short time is a highly desirable attribute, so that it is not surprising that the most successful conductors of our time tend to be cast in the same mould as industrial tycoons. More retiring or introspective types (Anton Webern was reputedly one such) who prefer to explore a musical work and let a performance emerge in its own time are, however fine their musicianship and deep their musical insights, left behind in the race for fame. (The recent rash of competitions for young conductors and instrumentalists also works in this direction, favouring those highly competitive personalities who are at their best in highly competitive situations

– it is in this way that a culture gets the musicians it deserves.)

What is the reason for this remarkable state of affairs, in which the majority of the music played by symphony orchestras is utterly familiar to both performers and audience, and yet still clearly has the power to attract and fascinate a large number of people? It has been much condemned but little understood, mainly, I believe, because we fail to perceive that a symphony concert, or indeed any musical performance, is not purely, or perhaps even primarily, an aural experience but a social ritual of profound importance to its participants, and the suspension of the passing of time implied by the freezing of the repertory is an important part of that ritual. I remarked in my book *Music, Society, Education* that modern man is starved of ritual; I now see that this is not really so. Rituals and mythologies are as much 'givens' of the human experience as is eating, and they play as important a part in the lives of modern westerners as they do in the lives of any 'primitive' people, even if we cannot always perceive them as such.

It is my belief that a symphony concert is a celebration of the 'sacred history' of the western middle classes, and an affirmation of faith in their values as the abiding stuff of life. As these values, and those of industrial society in general, come more and more under attack from both critics and the pressure of events, so the concert becomes more vital as a ritual of stability in an unstable world.

The lives and personalities of the 'great composers', their sufferings, their failures and their triumphs, their loves and their hates, all embodied quasi-autobiographically in their music, are paradigms for this belief, which is rehearsed every time their music is played before a paying audience in a concert hall. Beethoven's triumph over his deafness, the secure, death-obsessed Protestantism of Sebastian Bach, the barely controlled hysteria of Tchaikowsky, the warm, rational Enlightenment optimism of Haydn, Vaughan Williams's comfortable English agnosticism, Brahms's solid North German intellect and reticent sensibility, Delius's nostalgia for a world that never was, Richard Strauss's bourgeois vulgarity, Elgar's espousal of the imperialist extravagance of Edwardian England (comforting to an England currently in decline) and, perhaps most relevant of all for the late twentieth century, Mahler's outward success and prosperity and inner alienation and misery – all these and others are models for the experience of their audience, the performance of the music a ritual enactment of their mythology, an affirmation of the belief that the issues of the music are the important issues of life, and that things will not change.

The 'history of music' as perceived by the average music lover is seen in mythological terms, populated with heroes and their adversaries, tasks to be accomplished, the tricks of fate to be overcome, and destinies to be fulfilled. However obsessively, in the attempt to place them in historical time, musicologists may date and order the works, in the catalogues of Köchel, Deutsch, Longo or Hoboken, the works obstinately remain, in the minds of most music lovers, in mythological time, outside and independent of historical time altogether. No other attitude could produce a moment's credence to the claim that these works are 'immortal masterpieces'. The violence of the reaction of music lovers to any suggestion that the works of Beethoven or Bach may not be in the literal sense immortal but will one day cease to have any meaning for performers or listeners and will simply disappear from our consciousness testifies to the power of the myth. The ritual of stability in an unstable time cannot afford heroes who are alive in the present; with Theseus, Maui, Gilgamesh, Arthur and other civilizing heroes, 'the great composers' belong in the mythological past, and their works must live for ever.

Other elements of the symphony concert reinforce the idea of its ritual function. Eliade makes much of the idea of a 'sacred ground' on which the ritual takes place, an area set aside from the places of everyday living. As we have seen, just such a sacred ground exists in the concert hall, a place set aside at great expense for the performance of symphonic music, and for that alone (some music lovers feel that the Royal Festival Hall has been somehow violated when it has been let for a rock concert). Admittance to the sacred ground is gained by the purchase of a ticket (any ritual not involving the passing of money would ignore one of the most sacred functions of our society, whose mystical belief in money's absolute value and mysterious efficacy is enshrined in the policies of successive governments of the last decades).

Even the much-admired 'raising of performance standards' (that is, a demand for ever greater precision in the performance of the written notes and the development of digital dexterity to meet that demand) over the past decades speaks, for me, simply of a greater insistence on the accurate performance of the ritual, as with some American Indian healing rites, in which a single wrong word, sound or gesture can render the whole procedure invalid. The insistence is understandable; as our grasp of present events becomes ever more precarious, so we tighten our grip on the past with a magical ceremony for averting the catastrophic change we fear and for keeping things as they have been. Associated with the insistence on accuracy in the notes goes the quest for 'authenticity' in performance, and the research carried out to discover (we can *never* be sure) how the music sounded in the composer's own time. The 'sacred history' of our culture which, as Eliade says, 'must be carefully preserved and transmitted intact to succeeding generations' has become, as it never is for 'primitive' and especially for non-literate peoples (Duerden, for example, says that African societies 'not only remember creative events and forget destructive ones but deliberately refuse to adopt symbols which will last long enough to be destructive of the existence of these societies'[12]) fixed and rigid, leaving little or no room for creative development. This urge to preservation has an ally in the gramophone (indeed, one wonders if the recording of music would have become so ubiquitous in a more self-confident time – certainly Edison never imagined that his brainchild would be used for such a purpose); Stravinsky, for example, tried to capture his own performances of all his works on record so that succeeding generations would receive them intact. What Haydn would have had to say to that is a matter for conjecture, but it does show the extent to which the ritual function of music has changed since the First World War, and become the expression of something like desperation, as if the culture were trying to hold on to any possible semblance of stability. There are, on the other hand, other musical cultures within our society, mostly existing remote from its power centres, that don't give a damn about preservation, being too busy with the task of creation; this is true of much vernacular music, including the despised but vigorous and superbly self-confident disco culture. If those musicians think about the matter at all (and there is no reason why they should), they probably feel that there is plenty more where that comes from.

Since Lévi-Strauss the connection between music and food, both of which involve the transformation of natural materials into cultural products, has become something of a commonplace. Music and food are, in most societies, highly ritual matters, hedged around with rules and taboos, and it would therefore be surprising if there were not some such connection within our own society. Certainly the popular imagination has always perceived a connection, as can be seen from the widespread use of gastronomic metaphors in the discussion of music. One often reads of a 'feast of music'; over-enthusiastic attendance at a music festival can result in 'indigestion', while Sir Thomas Beecham referred to lightweight pieces of music used mainly for entertainment as 'lollipops'. I myself treasure a critic's comment some years ago which likened a concert by a famous American soprano to 'an entire meal of very delicately flavoured apple jelly'. The analogy is apt, as we shall see if we examine Mary Douglas's analysis of a meal. She points out that its very structure is a social code; a full meal, for example, is different from the less structured institution of 'inviting people for drinks'.

> There is no structuring of drinks into early, main, light. They are not invested with any necessity in their ordering. Nor is the event called drinks internally structured into first, second, main, sweet. On the contrary, it is approved to stick with the same kind of drink, and to count drinks at all is impolite . . . . The same lack of structure is found in the solid foods accompanying drinks. They are usually cold, served in discrete units which can be eaten tidily with the fingers. No order governs the choice of solids.[13]

She points out that drinks are a less intimate occasion than a meal; one invites people for drinks whom one would not necessarily invite for a full meal.

> Drinks are for strangers, acquaintances, workmen and family, meals are for family, close friends, honoured guests. Those we know at meals we also know at drinks. Those we know only at drinks we know less intimately. So long as this boundary matters to us (and there is no reason to suppose that it will always matter) the boundary between drinks and meals has meaning. There are smaller thresholds and halfway points. The entirely cold meal (since it omits a major contrast within a meal) would seem to be such a modifier. So those friends who have never had a hot meal in our home have presumably another threshold of intimacy to cross.[14]

Unlike drinks, a full meal is an intimate ritual and a highly structured affair, requiring internal contrast.

> A proper meal is A (when A is the stressed main course) plus 2B (when B is the unstressed course). Both A and B contain each the same structure, *a* plus *2b*, when *a* is the stressed item

> and *b* the unstressed item in a course. A weekday lunch is A, Sunday lunch is 2A, Christmas, Easter and birthdays are A plus 2B.[15]

The analogy with orchestral concerts is striking. Like a meal, a concert tends to begin with what Douglas calls an unstressed course – an overture, perhaps, or some other relatively lightweight work – followed by a stressed item – a symphony perhaps, or a concerto. It is generally felt that a symphony is heavier (more 'nourishing') than a concerto, and somehow of more moral/intellectual value (this idea of course dates only from the nineteenth century – Mozart certainly would not have agreed); this being so, it is usual to find the symphony forming the most stressed item of the concert and being placed, like the main course in a meal, as the penultimate item, while the concerto forms a kind of sweets dish which, while still stressed, is not viewed as being of quite equivalent importance to the main course. The situation may be reversed if, for example, the symphony is a relatively lightweight one and the concerto is, perhaps simply by reason of the fame of the soloist, considered more important. Each work, like the individual courses of a meal, contains internal stressed and unstressed elements. In the nineteenth century the conventions were different; meals and concerts alike were gargantuan affairs of many courses or items, reflecting perhaps the appetites of an exuberant middle class. Our own expectations of both meals and concerts are more modest, but the comparison may help us to temper our well-bred horror on reading that at the first English performance of Schubert's Ninth Symphony the movements were 'interspersed with song' according to the custom of the time, or that Beethoven's Fifth and Sixth Symphonies, Fourth Piano Concerto and Choral Fantasia all received their first performances, along with a number of other items, in a single concert in 1808!

Other structures are possible. A single large work – an oratorio, perhaps, or a large symphony or cantata such as Mahler's Eighth Symphony or Schoenberg's *Gurrelieder* – may constitute the whole of the concert, in much the same way as certain meals may consist of one large and complex dish such as paella – Douglas cites Chicken Marengo as a classic example. In such cases there needs to be enough internal variety and contrast of stressed and unstressed elements within the one dish, or work, to 'preserve the minimum structure' of the meal, or concert – which may explain, at least to some extent, the failure of certain large and admirable works such as *Gurrelieder*, which do not contain contrasting lightweight elements as well as elements of symphonic weight, to enter the regular repertory, while others which make just as great demands, such as Mahler's Second or Eighth Symphonies, do.

Of even greater interest from our point of view is a third type of concert, which consists entirely of what Beecham called 'lollipops'. Programmes with titles such as 'A Night in Old Vienna', 'Nights at the Ballet' or 'An Evening with Gilbert and Sullivan', consisting of a large number of easily assimilated shorter pieces – overtures, balletic waltzes, operatic excerpts and so on – resemble Douglas's ceremony of drinks rather than a meal; they are more homogenous in their material, less structured in their order, and are apparently designed to attract an audience which is not necessarily fully initiated into the mysteries of symphonic music (many dedicated concert goers would not be seen dead at such events). The overture-symphony-concerto structure is designed for initiates and is the central ceremony of the 'cultured middle class' reference group; the evening of 'lollipops', on the other hand, is more a matter of casual sociability than an intimate ritual. Both types of concert, however, celebrate shared beliefs and attitudes and help maintain those attitudes in the face of attacks from a hostile world. (The works of Webern, being of symphonic weight but lollipop length, have always posed a problem to programme planners and audiences alike; they subvert the ritual conventions of the symphony concert in much the same way as that science-fictional pill containing in one mouthful all the necessary nourishment of a meal would, were it ever to materialize, subvert all the existing rituals of eating.)

Symphonic music concerns itself with such a wide area of human experience, with joy, pain, happiness in and loss of love, with loyalty and treachery, with heroism and patriotism, triumph and apotheosis of the human spirit, that we are inclined to overlook the fact that there are vast areas of experience in which it does not appear to be interested at all, and that those are precisely the areas which fall outside the commonality of experience of the western industrial middle classes of the last two or three centuries. The first and most obvious of these is that of gross material deprivation. This is not to say that composers of the past did not at times suffer poverty, but so far as I know none of them actually starved. Poverty was regarded, if thought about at all, as a temporary condition, to be endured until fame, esteem and financial security were achieved; it was not a way of life as it is for the vast majority of the human race, and one finds in symphonic music no expression comparable to that in Blind Lemon Jefferson's lines:

> I stood on the corner and almost bust my head
> I couldn't earn enough to buy me a loaf of bread.
>
> Now gather round me people, let me tell you true facts;
> The tough luck has hit me and the rats is sleeping in my hat.[16]

The two great European masters who did die in poverty, Mozart and Schubert, were in fact no exception. Schubert, though undoubtedly poor, was supported by a circle of loyal and admiring friends, and died, almost accidentally, just as he was on the point of 'making it', at the age of 31. Mozart on the other hand, while he had a very clear notion of his worth as an artist, was in his personal life an almost insigificant figure who had no idea how to 'sell' himself or manage his resources; he did at times earn money in quite respectable amounts – very much more than his father ever saw – but constantly allowed it to slip through his fingers. Neither was born to poverty, nor did either accept it as his lot as Jefferson does in his blues. The popular notion of both masters' lives shows, in fact, the way in which the mythologizing tendency allows 'music lovers' to accept fictions which are quite at variance with the easily ascertainable facts.

Sexual love and desire, again dealt with quite explicitly in the blues, is the subject of only the most oblique of treatment (romantic love, on the other hand, is a major preoccupation); perhaps *Tristan and Isolde* comes nearest to confronting it directly, though even there it is subordinate to other, more general, philosophical issues, and the highly stylized treatment of love-making in the second act (there have been productions in which the protagonists do not even *touch* each other) lacks the raw and vivid realism that one finds in many other cultures, notably African and Afro-American. Political freedom and oppression are dealt with in abstract and heroic terms (*Fidelio* and the Ninth Symphony of Beethoven, or Berlioz's *Symphonie Funèbre et Triomphale*), never in terms of such gross realities as are actually experienced by the persecuted; Schoenberg's attempt to confront the matter head-on in *A Survivor from Warsaw* is considered tasteless, or at least flawed, the raw subject matter insufficiently assimilated into art. Likewise the experience of dispossession, of proletarianization, of racial discrimination and above all of total dionysian abandon and ecstasy (the finale of Beethoven's Seventh Symphony is often cited as an example of this, but in fact it is *about* ecstasy rather than *being* truly ecstatic, being tempered and moderated by the demands of the classical style for internal contrast and formal cohesion) form no part of the concerns of this music, lying as they do outside the experience, and thus the mythology, of the middle classes in western industrial society, with whose rise and apogee (and perhaps decline) what is loosely called 'classical' music is contemporaneous. (It should not need to be said here that to point out the non-universality of the values of symphonic music is not necessarily to condemn it, since all cultures define themselves as much by what they are not as by what they are; it is only our assumption of the superiority and universal validity of European values that blinds us to that obvious fact.) In any case it is ironic that the very surplus wealth that made industrial society (and symphony concerts) possible came to a major extent from the labour of those enslaved Africans whose descendants' music is today constituting the first major challenge to the dominance of classical music.

It need not, I hope, be emphasized that all musical performances everywhere partake to a greater or lesser extent of this ritual function and attest to shared beliefs and attitudes. Even within our society the ritual function is clearly recognized with certain types of vernacular musical performance, which are much studied from that point of view – rock music, for example, currently a favourite adventure playground for sociologists,[17] reggae and the blues, or even the singing of Mass in a Catholic church. If, therefore, in a symphony concert this function goes unrecognized it is because it is essential for its participants that this be so, since part of the industrial myth that it celebrates is, as we have seen, the idea that we have outgrown myth and thus ritual; as Eliade says, we like to regard ourselves as purely historical beings. For example: music lovers often complain about those who go to concerts, not for the music in itself, but because it is the socially correct thing to do. I can see nothing wrong in this; such people, attending concerts without a real understanding of the conventions by which the composer has sought to establish communication with his listeners, are simply staking their claim to membership of a particular middle-class reference group within our highly fragmented society. The 'genuine' music lover apparently feels that they are attending the ceremony under false pretences, but it seems to me that they are perfectly entitled to do so provided they can afford the price of a ticket (a ritual matter in itself in our money-devoted society) and are prepared to abide by the conventions of behaviour in the sacred space. Their actions are no more reprehensible than those of the Catholic who does not necessarily have to like or 'understand' the music of Palestrina to which the Mass is being sung, but does not for that participate any the less in the ritual. Of course, it is understood that full initiation into the ritual, which includes the ability to carry on informed discussion of the conductor's tempi, the soprano's vocal quality, the pianist's technique and so on, can occur only if the participant is fully experienced in the conventions and values of the culture, but, as with other societies of initiates, there is room for catechumens and permanent semi-outsiders as well as for full members. It is in this light, too, that we can understand those concert and opera performances which are presented as a matter of protocol for visiting heads of state; host and visitor are affirming a community of values (and the nature of those values – different values would be affirmed were they to attend a roller-disco or punk concert) which is necessary before serious business can begin to be transacted. It does not matter if, as is quite possible, both are thoroughly bored with the proceedings, since the display is more for the benefit of the public than for each other. In earlier times it would most likely have been Mass that they attended.

If the function of a symphony concert, then, is primarily ritualistic, and if the virtual freezing of the repertory since about 1920 is a result of that ritual function, what are we to make of those composers who since then have attempted to renew or revolutionize concert music – the so-called Second Viennese and Darmstadt Schools before and after the Second World War, or Varèse, Cage, Messiaen and a host of greater and lesser musicians? One thing is certain: in so far as the music continues to be presented in concert halls to paying audiences, the concert hall will impose its own conditions on whatever they do; there is no escaping it. There may be a revolution in forms, in sounds, in techniques, but it remains within the tradition and the set of conventions of gesture and behaviour, tied to the mythology of the industrial middle classes and to an unchanged attitude to the world.

And, indeed, it is clear when considering the work of those composers that nothing of any real importance *has* changed. The activity of music making remains the property of highly specialized experts – indeed, it would seem to have become even more arcane if the pages of *Die Reihe* and *Perspectives of New Music* and the activities of the Paris IRCAM are any guide. The composer still remains the architect of the musical work, dictating the actions of the performers by remote control, 'imposing the measure of motion and emotion' on them – and this remains as true of the most aleatory works of Cage and Stockhausen as of the totally controlled works of Boulez and others. The composer has arrogated to himself the function of arbiter of what the audience ought to like to an extent that would have horrified Haydn or even Beethoven. (Boulez has written, 'What do the feelings of some rag-and-bone man matter to me? My opinion counts a thousand times more than his; mine is the one which will last.'[18]) But then Beethoven, Haydn and their contemporaries knew on which side their bread was buttered, and had no complacent Arts Council or university music department to fall back on should their aristocratic patrons fail to like their music.

The contemporary musical work is still performed within the same kind of building, and under the same conditions, even, for the most part, by the same performers, as already described for traditional symphonic works, and it is disseminated in similar ways; the only change perhaps is that these works establish the ritual of a slightly different, if related, mythology. It is the myth of the technological fix, a faith in the ability to improve matters by a change in technique without a change in social structures and relationships. It is true that among even European avant-garde composers there seems to be some awareness that relationships within the concert hall *are* in need of change; thus, Berio places members of the chorus of *Passagio* (itself in its subject matter a plea for changed social relationships) among the audience to represent its views, while Pousseur in *Votre Faust* allows the audience certain options in deciding the course of the story – but both remain operas, performed in conventional spaces before paying audiences. Xenakis in *Terretekhtorrh* seats the orchestra among the audience – but this merely underlines, rather than destroys, their ritual separation from each other. Stockhausen in *Aus den Sieben Tagen* provides no written notes, merely verbal suggestions for improvisation – but it is said that the pieces work really well only under his direction. And Stockhausen, Kagel, Ligeti and others have satirized and even attempted to sabotage the sacred conventions and traditions of the concert – but, even when these do rise above the level of undergraduate pranks, they merely succeed, like blasphemies, in paying their tribute to the underlying and enduring mythology. I do not presume to criticize these fine musical minds, who I am sure are honestly seeking a new way for music, but I cannot help feeling that whatever happens in a concert is going to be inescapably subjected to the ritual requirements of the sacred space, which will subsume to itself everything, no matter how revolutionary or subversive in intention, which occurs there – and that it is no help to take over other spaces such as old railway-engine sheds or sports stadia (both interesting ritual spaces of industrial mass society[19]) and transfer to them the convention of the concert hall. The search by composers for renewal simply through new sounds, new techniques, like the search for new technologies as solutions to the problems created by the old, succeeds only in affirming, willy-nilly, those values whose bankruptcy those same composers have themselves proclaimed in the past. The profound wisdom of George Ives's famous advice, 'Don't pay too much attention to the sounds – for if you do you may miss the music',[20] becomes apparent here. New sounds do not make new music; only a new set of relationships can do that, as Ives senior knew well. He saw the old stonemason not just as the source of the raucous sounds that were being ridiculed but as a complete and loved man, in whose eyes one could see 'the wisdom of the ages'. It was in the whole man and not just in the sounds that the real music lay. The tonal explorations of the avant-garde, fascinating and beautiful as many of them undoubtedly are, are for the most part as strictly irrelevant to the spiritual problems of modern man as are the creations of contemporary epigones of the Romantic movement; they simply perpetuate, in the ritual of the concert hall, the separation of performer from composer, of performer and composer from audience, and above all the separation of the whole man from his music. Without an awareness of the ritual function of music, the 'researches' of Boulez and his colleagues of the Paris IRCAM remain a naive, gee-whiz celebration of the most superficial aspects of modern technology, and claims made by them and for them that they are attempting to come to terms with its problems and possibilities for the sake of the community as a whole seem no more credible than similar claims made by ICI, British Nuclear Fuels Limited – or Buckminster Fuller, whose 'rational madness' (to use Alex Comfort's telling phrase[21]) seems often to be mirrored in Boulez's writings about music.

It is often pointed out that to claim to have no politics is to proclaim, all unawares, the politics of the status quo. Similarly, I believe, to be unaware of the ritual nature of the act of performing and listening to symphonic music is to be entrapped by the mythology of a culture whose time is fast running out. As John Blacking has said, 'The chief function of music is to involve people in shared experiences within the framework of their cultural experience. The form that the music takes must share this function'[22] and, again,

> The rules of musical behaviour are not arbitrary cultural conventions, and techniques of music are not like developments in technology. Musical behaviour reflects varying degrees of consciousness of social forces, and the structures and functions of music are related to basic human drives and the biological need to maintain a balance between them[23].

We have not outgrown this condition, nor shall we; nor indeed does it even seem desirable that we should, since it is in human relationships that the richest source of creativity (above all in music, the social art *par excellence*) is to be found. If the music is felt to be in need of renewal, as many have felt, it is because our social relationships are in need of renewal – and this renewal is not impossible, even within the present situation. We have seen how the relationships within a symphony orchestra are strictly functional – the relationships of the industrial workplace. But every kind of musical ensemble establishes its own sets of relationships, both within itself and between itself and its audience. The Afro-American tradition, to take only one example, provides countless examples of more intimate and direct relationships, usually unmediated by any score, in which each member of the ensemble has a creative role to play – rock groups, reggae bands, country bands, jazz combos of many kinds from big bands to duos; this intimacy and directness reaches its apex perhaps in free jazz, where there is not even a set of chord changes to structure the musical relationships. In free jazz the most intense personal and technical discipline is practised, but freely and unforcedly; it can be at least as satisfying to its listeners as to its performers, all being caught up in a situation whose intensity can almost be described as erotic, and it is here perhaps that the true ritual nature of the musical act reveals itself, unencumbered by the layers of habit and consuetude that conceal from us the true nature of a symphonic performance. At its best, free jazz celebrates a set of informal, loving relationships which are experienced by performers and listeners alike, and brings into existence at least for the duration of the performance a society unlike that celebrated by the symphony concert, a society whose closest political analogy is perhaps with anarchism.

It is not my intention to conclude this essay with a polemic in favour of free jazz, or indeed, of any other specific way of making music (though I must confess that certain recent experiences in improvised music have given me more intense and satisfying experiences than anything in a concert hall); my intention is merely to show that other mythologies, other shared visions and other social relationships can be celebrated than those of symphonic music, in rituals of a different kind. It will, however, be clear that I do not believe that the act of performing symphonic music – or indeed western 'classical' music of any kind – is inherently superior to any other kind of musical performance – a belief that has profound implications for one's approach to music education. Whatever form of music making or listening we care to engage in, we may be sure that we are taking part in some way in a ritual which affirms the values we ourselves hold. One man's ritual may be another man's anathema, a fact attested all unawares by Cromwell's men as they smashed the medieval stained glass in one English church after another, as well as by the failure, after several generations of 'music appreciation' classes in English schools, to attract more than a small proportion of pupils to classical music; unless we grasp the essentially ritual nature of all our concert life we shall not begin to understand the forces that make it as it is.

Acknowledgements

I am deeply grateful to Edwin Mason and to John Baily for reading the manuscript of this essay and for making a number of perceptive and helpful comments.

Notes

1 Williams, Raymond: *Culture and Society 1780–1950*, London, Chatto & Windus, 1950, Penguin edition 1961, pp.13–19.
2 For some surprising early comments on the music of Beethoven and others see Slonimsky, Nicholas (ed): *A Lexicon of Musical Invective*, Seattle and London, University of Washington Press, 1953.
3 Eliade, Mircea: *Rites and Symbols of Initiation*, New York, Harper & Row, 1965, p. xi.
4 Ibid., p. ix.
5 Carpentier, Alejo: *The Lost Steps*, transl. Harriet de Onis, London, Gollancz, 1965, p. 18.

6 Pleasants, Henry: *Serious Music – And All That Jazz*, London, Gollancz, 1969, p. 79.
7 Small, Christopher: *Music, Society, Education*, London, John Calder, 1977, and New York, Riverrun Press, 1982 (Chapter 1).
8 Mellers, Wilfrid: *Caliban Reborn: Renewal in Twentieth-Century Music*, London, Gollancz, 1968, p. 2.
9 Van Gennep, Arnold: *The Rites of Passage* (1908), transl. N. B. Vizedom and G. L. Caffee, London, Routledge & Kegan Paul, 1960, p. 20.
10 Turner, Victor: *The Ritual Process*, London, Routledge & Kegan Paul, 1969, Pelican edition 1974, p. 34.
11 Partch, Harry: *Genesis of a Music*, 2nd edition, New York, Da Capo Press, 1974, Chapter 1.
12 Duerden, Dennis: *African Art and Literature: The Invisible Present*, London, Heinemann, 1975, p. 18.
13 Douglas, Mary: *Implicit Meanings*, London, Routledge & Kegan Paul, 1975, p. 255.
14 Ibid., p. 256.
15 Ibid., p. 259.
16 Quoted in Oliver, Paul: *The Story of the Blues*, London, Barrie & Jenkins, 1969, p. 38.
17 A remarkable book which studies the music of two despised subcultures, those of the bikers and of the hippies, with sympathy, insight and humour is Willis, Paul E.: *Profane Culture*, London, Routledge & Kegan Paul, 1978.
18 Boulez, Pierre: *Boulez on Music Today*, transl. Susan Bradshaw and Richard Rodney Bennett, London, Faber & Faber, 1971, p. 13.
19 See McKenna, Frank: 'Victorian railway workers', *History Workshop*, no. 1, Spring 1976, pp. 26–73.
20 Quoted in Ives, Charles E.: *Memos*, ed. John Kirkpatrick, London, Calder & Boyars, 1973, p. 132.
21 In a review of Fuller's *Utopia or Oblivion*, published in the *Guardian* in 1970.
22 Blacking, John: *How Musical is Man?*, London, Faber & Faber, 1976, p. 48.
23 Ibid., p. 101.

The social interpretation of modern jazz[1]

Alan Lewis

Introduction

The history of jazz, unlike that of classical music, has always tended to be viewed in social as well as musical terms. Although its origins are still unclear, it emerged as the folk art of a specific group of people, American Negroes, whose segregated social situation produced distinctive cultural patterns. Then again, in its popular commercialised forms of ragtime, dixieland and swing, the evolution of jazz seems obviously related to broad social changes associated with the development of mass consumption, mass media, and mass entertainment. The rapid changes in jazz musical styles here are clearly related to changes in entertainment venues, recording technology, and the processes of commercial organisation surrounding entertainment music. Popular music was – and is – a commodity, and has to be in tune with the times if it is to be saleable on a large scale. Since the 1940s the more esoteric traditions of jazz have been seen as the increasingly self-conscious high art development of the original set of folk musical traditions and elements, elaborated particularly in reaction against the pressures of commercialisation and white imitation. As part of this artistic development jazz evolved as a black instrumental music in which instrumental virtuosity in improvisation is its core. The rapidly changing character of the American black community, particularly the shift from an agrarian to an industrial basis, transformed the conditions of production and reception of this music and interacted with the processes of commercialisation.

The intensification of the 1950s civil rights movement and the ghetto riots and broader radicalisation of the 1960s have left their marks on the social interpretation of jazz. Three works in particular stand out as sociologically sophisticated attempts to connect the musical evolution of jazz with changes in racial relations and black political and cultural consciousness. *Blues People* by Leroi Jones,[2] the black poet and writer, appeared in 1963. Using a social anthropological perspective, Jones analyses the way the post-Emancipation exclusion of the American black from the social mainstream produces a cultural tradition resistant to assimilation, even though major elements of the dominant white culture are borrowed and used in producing that cultural tradition. Part of this cultural tradition has its roots in Africa and part in American experience, but it is entirely black, and not simply derivative of white American or European traditions. Black music – particularly jazz – clearly demonstrates the construction of a distinctive black culture which fuses African and European elements.

In 1969 a series of essays entitled *Black Nationalism and the Revolution in Music*[3] appeared, written by Frank Kofsky, a white historian and jazz critic. Kofsky argued that the black's status as a major part of the industrial reserve army, separated from the rest of the working class by special racist forms of exploitation and oppression, perpetuated a specific sense of national oppression on the part of blacks. This nationalism has had a long history, but is episodic in appearance because of the overwhelming power of white domination. However, black nationalism had grown continuously since the Second World War and ultimately exploded in the ghetto riots and black power movements of the 1960s. Black jazz musicians during this period are acutely aware of the cultural oppression of their people because of their own intense struggle for survival in an extremely competitive and exploitatively commercialised field of music. Hence they are either in the vanguard or express clearly in their music the nationalism which is slowly crystallising in the consciousness of the broader community of American blacks.

Two years later, Ben Sidran's *Black Talk*[4] appeared. In many respects this work recapitulated Jones's analysis using McLuhan's distinction between oral and literate cultures to specify the characteristics of the culture of blacks in America. Sidran sees black music as a developed expression of a more general oral foundation of black culture. For Sidran, black culture is founded on oral modes of communication and has produced advanced faculties of vocal expression and aural perception. Oral cultures are based on the spoken word and its oral derivatives, i.e. musical representation of basic vocalisations. In contrast, literate cultures are founded upon sight and printed signals, which operate as a distancing and abstracting medium of communication. In other words, oral communication is free from intervention of a medium while literary communication is dependent upon an intervening signal in space like print, stone inscriptions, punched cards, or pictures. Major consequences in psychological make-up, modes of emotional expression, and the organisation of social relations are held to derive from these two basic approaches to perception and organisation of information. In oral cultures music is of central importance – and in the case of American blacks has been the only possible outlet of cultural expression. Consequently, according to Sidran, black musicians have a very special status within the black community; as virtuousos of the oral culture they have been the vanguard group of black cultural expression, articulating changes in mood and perception in advance of the bulk of the black community.

Despite their differing theoretical bases, these works converge in their analysis of the relation between jazz and black social and political consciousness. Since the 1940s black jazz musicians have been in the vanguard of the American black's growing ethnic assertiveness or nationalism, and this has been expressed in the styles of music which have characterised jazz. I want to argue here that although there is considerable truth in this perspective, it is limited and misses a basic dynamic in the history of jazz. First I wish to present the argument for a strong relationship between jazz and black political consciousness since the early 1940s, and then I will turn to the limits of this argument.

Jazz and black political consciousness

The arguments of Jones, Kofsky and Sidran on the relationship between modern jazz and black political consciousness are threefold. First, jazz musicians, as *black* Americans, suffer gross discriminatory practices in the music business and, with very rare exceptions, experience extreme hardship in the pursuit of their vocation. Second, not only do jazz musicians suffer discrimination in salaries, contacts and work conditions, and experience exclusion from studio sessions, media work and the best touring circuits, but they are consistently denied credit for their own music. While black musicians have created a music lauded elsewhere as America's major cultural product, jazz has been treated as a minor entertainment music and largely relegated to bars. Where it is recognised it is most often identified with vulgarised and commercialised forms produced by white musicians who modify it to make it more acceptable to white audience tastes, and enjoy considerable commercial success in consequence. Third, in response to these circumstances black jazz musicians since the 1940s have developed a music which is increasingly assertive of its ethnic roots and singularity. Three phases of jazz history exemplify the development of growing black pride – the bebop innovations of the early 1940s, the hard bop and soul/funk movements in 1950s jazz, and the 'new wave' jazz of the late 1950s and 1960s. Each set of musical changes corresponds with changes in the political and social characteristics of the black community and its relationship with the dominant white social order.

Until the Second World War blacks had little power *vis-à-vis* whites and most blacks were fatalistic about chances for meaningful change. They did not control enough resources desired by whites to be able to bargain effectively. Nor could they coerce whites into making changes. They had nothing to offer to, or withhold from, whites other than their labour. But blacks were kept too close to the minimal subsistence level to use their labour power as an effective lever for change. They were forced to rely upon persuasion as a tactic. The NAACP engaged in lobbying and litigation, while the Urban League used education and persuasion. The outbreak of the Second World War provided blacks with a coercive lever since the US government needed to mobilise all of its internal strength to combat the Axis powers. Black non-cooperation with, or active hindrance of, the war effort was threatening enough to coerce white compliance with some black demands, such as creation of the Fair Employment Practices Commission and some desegregation of the armed forces.

The willingness of blacks to threaten non-cooperation with the war effort was itself rooted in the political and social experiences of the 1930s. Ultimately Roosevelt's New Deal had failed; the power of government did not change hands, nor did the economic structure of America open significantly to allow blacks occupational mobility and economic advancement. Rather, the New Deal seemed to salvage the pre-Depression economic structure with the large corporations emerging practically unscathed. It was, in fact, the 'forgotten man', the average lower-class American, who benefited least, and the black American who had to bear the added burden of racial discrimination remained fixed to the lowest rung on the socio-economic ladder. The Second World War, with its begrudging integration of industries serving government contracts, a fight against racist fascism on the western front combined with racist anti-Japanese propaganda on the Pacific front, opened up the possibility for black political leverage. While the civil rights politics of the largely white US Communist Party disappeared with its all-out support of the war effort, black leaders like A. Phillips Randolph and organisations like CORE adopted militant, non-violent methods of protest against discrimination and segregation. Although executive action imposed desegregation of defence industries and opened up jobs with improved economic status, racism persisted on a massive scale. At the height of the war, in 1943, a bloody race riot occurred in Detroit in which thirty-four people died. Earlier in the same year upgrading of black shipyard workers in Mobile, Alabama triggered a riot which required troops for its suppression.

The Depression had hit agriculture even more severely than it affected industry, causing a major flow of rural to urban migration. This was reinforced by the mechanisation of agriculture and the industrial boom arising from the war effort. After 1929, then, blacks came to the cities in ever-increasing numbers. The Depression had hit blacks very hard and this was true in their relation to the entertainment industry as everywhere else. 'Race' recordings designed specifically for black record buyers disappeared from the market in the early 1930s while racial criteria for job qualifications intensified in radio stations, ballrooms, dance halls and theatres. At the same time touring circuits for musicians and other entertainers were increasingly segregated as the more lucrative were monopolised by white performers.[5] The most vital regions of jazz creativity moved from New York and Chicago to Kansas City and the Southwest. In Kansas City the Pendergast machine supported a freewheeling, dance-hall-saturated city with a large black population where urban jazz traditions and rural blues mingled. A fusion occurred producing the Bennie Moten-Count Basie band blues and a new style of shouting blues singers. Both developments were associated with the rise to prominence of a new generation of sophisticated instrumentalists such as Roy Eldridge and Lester Young.

However, the position of the black jazz musician was undergoing considerable and rather peculiar changes. As jazz had expanded in the late 1920s and became incorporated as part of a broader entertainment industry, it had attracted musicians from more respectable, urban, middle-class origins. The Depression paradoxically reinforced this because only those musicians with the training and versatility to perform in pit orchestras and a variety of musical contexts could survive as professional musicians playing with jazz bands. A greater level of musical training combined with the shift in emphasis towards solo performance as the heart of jazz to establish individual instrumental virtuosity as the essential criterion of musical competence. But the Depression had ghettoised jazz and forced musicians with higher training and, to some extent, more middle-class background to perform almost exclusively for lower-class black audiences.

The 1930s also witnessed a new phase in the global acceptance of jazz. In its native land jazz was received with great hostility by critics and bodies associated with the high arts.[6] However, even in the 1920s Europe had proven to be not only as open as America in its acceptance of jazz as a popular entertainment music, but far more welcoming in terms of elite approbation. European classical musicians acclaimed (and misunderstood) ragtime and early jazz, while groups of middle-class people formed 'hot clubs' and 'rhythm clubs' of record-collecting *cognoscenti*. Ultimately France provided the first major jazz critics who attempted to develop aesthetic systems for interpreting and defining the music and evaluating its performers and their works.[7] Although these developments had little direct impact on the white American reception of jazz, there was sufficient transatlantic movement by jazz musicians for the different form of jazz appreciation in Europe to filter through the American scene and fuel the jazz musician's increasing sense of professionalism.

The final set of circumstances throwing the jazz musician into a state of uncertainty was the impact of commercial 'swing', the jazz-derived popular dance music which swept the popular music scene in the 1930s and early 1940s. Fletcher Henderson's arrangements for Benny Goodman and Jimmy Lunceford's work for the Dorsey brothers launched a new dance fad and band style. The commercialisation of a black jazz style, of course, ensconced white bands and their leaders in economically dominant positions. Their rapid commercial success quickly formularised the musical style and imposed a series of rigidly stereotyped demands on musicians throughout the entertainment field. It is likely that media penetration into the black community increased with black urban migration, and so forced black bands themselves to play a certain proportion of the most popular tunes. Side by side with these developments the jam session emerged – after-hours sessions where musicians and a few close associates gathered to listen to and to demonstrate virtuoso improvisational capacities through competitive performance testing stamina and imagination. The jam session is symptomatic of a period where the consolidation of jazz as an improvisor's art begins to clash with the dance band and other entertainment functions which economically sustain it.

The bop musicians of the early 1940s, building on the musical innovations of the 1930s, made explicit the perspective embodied in the jam session.[8] Jazz, the performers' art, was no mere entertainment music but an art to be ranked with the rest of the high arts.

> The music of Charlie Parker and Dizzy Gillespie represented a way for jazz to continue, but that way was not just a matter of new devices; it also had to do with a change in even the function of the music. Parker's work implied that jazz could no longer be thought of only as an energetic background for the bar room, as a kind of vaudeville, as a vehicle for dancers. From now on it was somehow a music to be listened to.[9]

In rejecting the entertainer image of the jazz musician the boppers also rejected the restricted and stereotyped roles available to blacks in American society.

Corresponding to these changes in the self-image of the jazz musician were a number of radical changes in musical style.

> Where tempos had been medium, they were now fast or slow. Where the first, third, fifth and seventh notes of the scale had been stressed, now the second and fourth were played up. Where the first and third beats of a measure had been accentuated, now it was the second and fourth. Where pairs of notes had been played extremely unevenly, now they were played almost equally. Where choirs of instruments had harmonised, now they were played in unison. Bop was, in the exact sense of the word a musical revolution. These men turned the jazz world upside down and sat on the top, thumbing their noses at their elders falling off the other side.[10]

The bop musicians' novel and aggressive assertions of their artistic status, and their uncompromising pursuit of a complex style of jazz, mirrored the new level of black assertiveness in the war and post-war period. Important gains had been made in jobs and income during the war, but these were now threatened by post-war economic slowdown. For most blacks, especially those in the Northern cities, the key question was one of safeguarding their newly achieved economic and social status. As early as 1945

NAACP lawyers began planning a legal assault on the segregation system. CORE, favouring non-violent direct action, began to launch freedom rides throughout the South in 1947 to test the enforcement of a US Supreme Court decision outlawing segregation on interstate buses. At the same time the Nation of Islam or Black Muslims, founded in 1930 and scarcely growing for fifteen years, began to increase in numbers after the war. From 1945, with four temples and 9,000 members, they increased to fifteen temples in 1955 and to thirty temples in 1959. While CORE and the NAACP were middle-class organisations directing their attacks against Southern segregation, the Muslims were strongest among working-class blacks residing in the urban areas of the North.[11] Both the Nation of Islam and other more orthodox Islamic groups gain adherents from the jazz community in the late 1940s and early 1950s.

Although the post-war period brought some reversals to the occupational and economic advances of American blacks, these were soon compensated for by the economic boom accompanying the Cold War and the Korean war. The Truman administration was more explicit than its predecessor in its support for civil rights and a real measure of desegregation in government services and the armed forces occurred. These developments reinforced the steady shift of blacks from the rural South to the cities of the East, Midwest and West. Outside the US independence movements in Asia and Africa had begun to erode European colonial domination. All these factors appeared to have heightened the confidence and increased the expectations of black Americans. The NAACP maintained its steady pressures for legal reform, while CORE and the Urban League undertook educational campaigns and various pressure group actions to further black advancement. After 1955 these organisations were joined by Martin Luther King's SCLC which became a major coordinator of direct action throughout the South. At the same time the Black Muslims continued to expand.

These various changes were reflected in diverse ways in the jazz scene. By the late 1940s several jazz musicians had adopted the Islamic faith and had publicly taken Muslim names. In the 1950s jazz musicians began to visit Africa, studying African music and even playing with tribal drummers. References to Africa appeared with increasing frequency in the 1950s, beginning with Miles Davis's 1954 recording of Sonny Rollins's composition 'Airegin' (i.e. Nigeria spelled backwards.) A blues turn was a marked feature of 1950s hard bop, the predominant black jazz style evolving out of bebop. Hard bop emphasised hard-driving, fiery, melodically complex improvisation and heavyweight, raw-textured tone colours which were in striking contrast to the characteristics of the West Coast post-bop style favoured by white jazz musicians.

The Northeastern cities such as Detroit, New York and Philadelphia which were the centres of hard bop were also major centres for the production of black popular vocal music, known by its trade name as rhythm 'n' blues. The latter was a fusion of several musical streams – 1930s band blues originating in the Kansas City region and developed by Louis Jordan, black gospel music, and various intermixtures of black and white rural music. A significant number of black jazz musicians, particularly saxophonists, began their careers playing in rhythm 'n' blues bands and many seemed to bring this experience into the jazz they played in the 1950s. In this decade, the use of blues chord progressions pioneered in Miles Davis's *Walkin'* session of 1954 became a distinctive style within hard bop. Blues- and gospel-tinged compositions and arrangements became the hallmark of Blakey's groups, the Adderley brothers, and much of Mingus's work, and was especially marked in keyboard players influenced by Horace Silver such as Ray Bryant, Les McCann, Mal Waldron, Bobby Timmons and Jimmy Smith.[12]

All these developments in the music seem to be symptomatic of a broader change of attitude, an increase in self-confidence and ethnic pride within the black community at large. The major domestic tactic adopted by the Eisenhower administration to sustain America's image and self-adopted role as leader of the 'free world' was the support of the desegregation measure ruled by the Supreme Court in April 1954. The resulting Federal intervention against Southern states which attempted to halt desegregation sustained the black community's optimism and rising expectations. Between 1956 and 1960 black protest declined until the February 1960 Greenboro, North Carolina sit-ins ushered in a new phase of militance. In the early years of the new decade sit-ins became a major and effective tactic because they disrupted business and caused a loss of profits. As the sit-in tactic spread through the South it met increasingly large-scale and violent white resistance. Publicity accopanying white violence stimulated support from the liberal white public and unified the black community in North and South. Northern support was expressed through picketing and boycotting of Northern affiliates of chain stores where there were sit-ins. The Congress of Racial Equality entered the Deep South for the first time and helped to organise and conduct six-ins. Throughout the early 1960s the civil rights movement changed rapidly. Tactics escalated in level of militancy. Boycotts and sit-ins were soon supplemented by hit-and-runs, mass marches, blocked streets, impeded construction vehicles and voter registration drives. While the NAACP continued its litigation and lobbying activities CORE, SNCC and SCLC specialised in non-violent direct action. Rising expectations, hardening anger at white resistance and organisational rivalry all contributed to increasing militancy as each organisation attempted to outdo the others.[13]

The movement achieved limited success. White liberal publics saw non-violent blacks making reasonable demands being brutalised for their efforts. This aroused sympathetic support, and the Federal government was pressured into intervening. Local businessmen urged concessions when disruption hurt tourism and drove away new industry. The civil rights movement broadened its base from its initial middle-class composition as victories raised aspirations and attracted working-class blacks. Dissatisfaction with the rate of change increased concomitantly with the growing belief that change was possible. Increasing numbers of less well-disciplined participants demanded more and faster change, turned towards more militant tactics, and reduced their commitment to non-violence.

This same period, the 1960s, was an especially fertile period for changes in the sound of jazz. Apart from the fact that a number of 1950s era innovators reached their creative peaks in the following decade (much as many of the pre-bop musicians attained creative peaks in the 1940s and 1950s), there was a proliferation of new approaches to jazz creation. Collective improvisation, which had fallen into disuse with the demise of Dixieland, was revived by Coleman, Coltrane, Mingus, Sun Ra and Cecil Taylor. Davis and Coltrane explored improvisatory methods based on modal forms rather than harmonically founded chord progressions. New instruments such as the fluegelhorn, flute and soprano saxophone and auxiliary percussion broadened the spectrum of jazz tones and textures. Towards the end of the decade non-European instruments were being used with greater frequency than ever before, and electronic instruments, amplification and electronic devices altering the sound of conventional instruments became increasingly common. In addition to using new instruments old instruments were played in new ways: high register playing on trumpets and saxophones became common; saxophonists cultivated more techniques to drastically bend their pitch and tone, sometimes playing several notes simultaneously, and at the same time producing a huge assortment of shrieks, squawks and wails. Instrumental proficiency increased and especially guitarists, pianists, bassists and drummers generally played faster and more precisely. New instrumentation and combo organisation were explored; the piano was absent from many recordings by Coleman, Shepp, Ayler, Rivers; a variety of duet forms were explored; several pianists recorded solo albums without the usual accompaniment of bass and drums; rhythm sections increasingly came to the forefront in ways previously assigned to reed and brass soloists. Compositional forms, melodic styles and improvisation altered radically as well. During the 1960s fewer compositions fitted the traditional twelve-bar blues and thirty-two-bar AABA popular song chord progressions. Rather tunes were more expansive, often modal, floating, often simpler and smoother with less pronounced syncopation and fewer notes than bop compositions. Sustained notes and silences often became just as important as rapid fire eight-note runs had been to bop and hard bop. While tunes were becoming simpler and smoother, rhythm section activity became more complex and turbulent, sometimes operating without strict metre or constant tempo. Much improvisation was based on far fewer chords than had typified bop and hard bop compositions, and for many performances the player invented his own harmonies while improvising instead of presetting them beforehand. In place of bebop's complex chord progressions and elaborately syncopated melodies, 1960s jazz saw an emphasis on colourful sounds and provocative rhythms, generating moods and textures, and exploring sound for sound's sake rather than for the sake of melody, harmony or swing feeling.

The jazz characterised by these changes originated particularly with the work of Ornette Coleman, John Coltrane and, despite his verbal hostility to much of the avant-garde, Miles Davis. The avant-garde jazz (known as the 'New Thing') movement of the 1960s, like the bebop movement of the early 1940s, was infused with strong ideological components. In contast to the earlier movement however, the New Thing experimentalist could draw upon more definite political elements with which to articulate the socio-political aspects of their aesthetic principles. Decolonisation of the Third World, generally arising from active liberation struggles, the radicalisation of the civil rights movements, and particularly the shift in definition of the civil rights issue from Southern desegregation to combating white racism wherever it may be found, the Chinese Cultural Revolution's providing an apparent break with the grey totalitarian tradition of Stalinism, and the anti-imperialist rhetoric of the opposition to America's Vietnam involvement all provided a rich source of social and political images and conceptions which the bebop movement lacked, operating as it did in the consensual atmosphere of the Second World War.

Again in contrast to the bebop movement, the New Thing musicians had articulate black critics in Leroi Jones and A.B. Spellman who drew the connections betwen shifts in music and broader changes in black consciousness and racial relations in a very effective way.[14] Among the musicians, tenor saxophonist Archie Shepp was the most insistent in connecting the style and substance of the new music with broader social changes.[15] However, the dominant tone of the new wave musicians' account of their musical aims and practices might be characterised as a form of spiritualism, even a form of black hippie ethics, rather than a primarily political ideology. Like the hippies, the New Thing players espoused an ideology which emphasised both individualism and collectivism equally. This perspective is captured perfectly in Rowell Rudd's statement, 'I was trying to get the music out of each guy in a kind of democratic or communal way so everybody could unload his stuff but with a balanced and communal form.'[16] The New Thing practitioners shared other features with the hippies: an interest – in John Coltrane's case an obsession – with oriental mysticism and non-Christian religion, particularly the contemplative and occult features; an emphasis on non-rational and non-verbal communication which produce heightened states of empathy; an antagonism towards formal and articulated criteria of judgement emphasising technical training and skill, and an emphasis on individual freedom for expression or for 'doing one's thing' unhindered by formal discipline.

It seems quite clear that the ghetto riots and general social turmoil of the 1960s politicised and moulded the self-consciousness of the black jazz musician. Yet the ambiguities and paradoxes of the jazz musician's status in America which had begun to emerge in the 1930s were reproduced in new forms. While bebop innovations had at first caused a great deal of controversy among jazz musicians and critics, these had rapidly waned as bop itself moderated and many swing era musicians found themselves able to work with the new genre and its practitioners. The New Thing likewise ushered in a period of bitter disputes which cut deeply into the ranks of jazz musicians. Not only white critics but black and white musicians as diverse as Ray Bryant and Charles Mingus came to condemn much of the New Thing as fraudulent cover for inept and undisciplined individuals searching for a quick route to economic success. Much of the New Music was also criticised for its abstractness and lack of emotional accessibility. Essentially these criticisms display a contradiction already embodied in the jazz tradition's ambivalence towards solo instrumental virtuosity as against the need for greater overt audience response and involvement than classical concert music.[17]

The concern for the audience expressed in some jazz musicians' response to the New Thing also must be related to the massive popularity of rock which occurred at the same time as Coleman, Shepp, Coltrane, Ayler and others became prominent in jazz. Although the evolution of post-bop jazz permitted a great deal of mutual collaboration between swing era and modern stylists, with some mutual modifications of style into a broad 'mainstream', few established swing musicians made a full transition and became accomplished bop players. Consequently many musicians in their prime years were performing stylistically dated music and found their performing opportunities constricted as a result. In the 1960s the established musicians in hard bop found themselves besieged on two fronts; the New Thing stylists appeared to be capturing critical attention while a new, revitalised rock music was capturing the white college audience which had formed a significant proportion of the jazz audience. The combination of these processes created a pervasive anomie, a sense of loss of boundaries and standards. In rock it appeared that indifferent musicians could make fortunes while in the New Thing a new cohort of jazz musicians with questionable technical capacities – in established terms – were launched on their musical careers without having to 'pay the dues'.[18] Ultimately the boundaries of jazz themselves seemed to disappear altogether as rock groups experimented with elements of jazz, Miles Davis and others experimented with electronic orchestration characteristic of rock, and New Thing musical styles were assimilated into the experiments of post-classical musicians. As had happened before, a major stylistic revolution originating primarily in the playing of a cohort of black jazz musicians came to be a vital influence on a variety of musical endeavours often associated with white musicians and audiences.

Jazz and modernism

The three works which I have drawn on to develop the foregoing account of the development of modern jazz in its socio-political context all bear the marks of the high expectations produced by the social polarisations of the 1960s. All three authors stress the parallels, congruences and convergences between growing political militancy in the black community and innovations in jazz since the 1940s. However, reading changes in jazz styles as artistic expressions of a growing black nationalism overlooks the real complexity of the social location of jazz in American society and fails to account for some key factors contributing to the evolution of jazz.

Jazz, like rock 'n' roll, is a music which has evolved entirely within the era of the mass production and mass consumption of culture within advanced capitalist societies. Consequently the development of jazz is very much moulded by twentieth-century conditions of cultural expression and transmission. Jazz also shares with rock 'n' roll the experience of becoming rapidly diffused as a popular music throughout the advanced industrial countries. This latter phenomenon suggests that these musical forms resonate with the emotional and perceptual experiences generated by modern living. Jazz, then, is embedded in a broader configuration of social processes which are likely to be expressed in its evolution as much as is the particular cultural experience of its primary creators who, of course, share in the experience of modernism. I want to explore, then, the location of jazz in the culture of modernism not as an exclusive alternative to the socio-political interpretations of Jones *et al.*, but as an equally important dimension which is underemphasised in their works. I shall develop this analysis first by looking at the evolution of jazz as a musical tradition, and second by comparing that evolution with the development of the arts in the western world.

The classical music critic Henry Pleasants has argued that the evolution of jazz has paralleled that of western classical music in an accelerated manner.[19] Until the 1930s, when the emergence of harmonically advanced players like Coleman Hawkins and Roy Eldridge laid the foundations for the bop revolution, jazz improvisation focused on the elaboration of melodic lines which approximated eighteenth-century classical melodies in their complexity. The bebop revolution moved jazz to harmonically focused improvisation resembling the expansion of permissible notes and harmonies which arose with chromaticism in nineteenth-century European classical music. In the process of its development, bop divorced jazz from its earlier associations with the popular song and with the function of social dancing, and became an art form which, like the other arts in western society, is isolated from other social functions. The rise of avant-garde jazz from the late 1950s on intensified the art music character of jazz. The New Thing was a broad scale onslaught on the received forms of the bop tradition and attempted to demolish the inherited compositional forms of the blues and popular song, to break from constant tempo, and to improvise without melodic or harmonic restraints. These characteristics of the New Thing had many parallels with avant-garde post-classical European art music which explored sounds, textures, and moods without recognisable melodies and harmonies, and adopted accidental constructions and electronically mediated forms of composition and performance.

Associated with these trends in jazz were fundamental changes in the self-conception of the musician and in the relationships between the musician and his audience. Prior to the 1940s the jazz musician's status was unambiguously that of an entertainer or creator of popular music in close and sympathetic relationship with popular song and dance fashions. Only outside America did a few European critics and composers see jazz as an art – a folk art – which was the spontaneous expression of unschooled musicians of natural genius whose rich creativity was untrammelled by formal, aesthetic self-consciousness. In their revolt against the restrictions of a commercially stereotyped big band dance music, the bop musicians also sought to change the stereotyped images of jazz musicians as entertainers or exotic primitives. In their stage demanour the bop players were aloof and distant where earlier musicians had been expansively open in their cultivation of audience involvement.[20] The core of the modern jazz performance, improvisation over a series of chord changes, became an esoteric enterprise hidden from all but the most committed listener. Like modern literature at the turn of the century, which dropped the notion of the 'common reader', the jazz musician came to despise the 'square'. Jazz performance became a mystery, involving an 'unperformed *cantus firmus*' – the popular tune with its chord changes so modified as to be unrecognisable to the casual listener. The titles of these compositions were themselves invested with cultic significance, full of *double entendres*, puns and in-jokes known only to the initiated.[21]

Lacking the easier identification with the musician's practice through the link of memorable melody or social dancing, the technical virtuosity required by the bebop innovations in harmony and rhythm became the only general link with the audience.

> Trumpets were played higher than they had ever before been played . . .. Saxophones were made to yield a thousand or so notes a measure, along with uncouth grunts and squeals at the extremes of the range. Double-bass players developed a dexterity beyond the wildest imaginings of any symphony orchestra bassist, and drummers opened up an entirely new world of rhythmic and percussive variety. Pianists adopted a driving velocity modeled on the symptoms of Bud Powell's infatuations with Parker . . . vibraharp and guitar virtuosity added to the fun.[22]

Such virtuosity, however, tended to feed stylistic fragmentation as subsequent generations of musicians chose from the innovations and discoveries of the boppers only those devices which appealed to them and which might be useful in generating a following as an 'original' player. This stylistic fragmentation was intensified, of course, by the greater efficacy of electronic mass media which communicated changes in musical fashion through recordings at an ever-increasing pace.

Rhetorically the bop musicians asserted that their music was serious art. They were not unlettered primitives but musically sophisticated *virtuosi* who were fully cognisant of the nature and significance of Bartok, Stravinsky and other modern classical composers. As practitioners of a serious music they demanded the consideration accorded to artists in other fields. Like avant-garde artists elsewhere the bop musician

> 'formed an elite of his own – a model of any exclusive grouping in any society anywhere, idealistic, self-satisfied and disdainful of the outside world, protecting itself against intrusion by constantly changing modes of expression and behaviour. In this pattern the modern jazz musician has adopted the attitudes of the serious music establishment. The artist stands alone, and must be independent of the public. Only artists are qualified to pass judgement on fellow artists. The public is obliged to listen,

> to be respectful and to pay; the artist is not to please the public, for entertinment is beneath the true artist's calling. These romantic into modernist visions have been supported by jazz critics and have produced in jazz an accelerated history of the development of classical music.'[23]

Although modern jazz musicians' claims to be treated as artists have been only partially successful, there has been an increasing legitimation of jazz involving its separation from other varieties of popular music, and a decline in sweeping condemnations of it as being simply part of mass culture. Associated with this rise in status has been the institutionalisation of the role of the critic who mediates between the artist and his audience. In this development, as well as those outlined above, jazz's evolution has followed that of the arts as a whole since the nineteenth century. Thus, in characterising the literary avant-garde of the early twentieth century, Irving Howe could easily be describing the status of the jazz musician since 1940 when he writes about the literary avant-garde.

> Forming a kind of permanent if unacknowledged and disorganized opposition, the modernist writers and artists constitute a special caste within or at the margin of society, an *avant garde* marked by aggressive defensiveness, extreme self-consciousness, prophetic inclination and the stigmata of alienation.[24]

This avant-garde, Howe notes, has its own community, Bohemia, which is both 'an enclave of protection within a hostile society' and 'a place from which to launch guerilla raids upon the bourgeois establishment, frequently upsetting but never quite threatening its security'.[25] Again the modern jazz musician's conception of his artistic practices is well captured by Howe's description of modern literary artists.

> The *avant garde* abandons the useful fiction of 'the common reader', it demands instead the devotions of a cult. The *avant garde* abandons the usual pieties toward received aesthetic assumptions; 'no good poetry', writes Ezra Pound in what is almost a caricature of modernist dogma, 'is ever written in a manner twenty years old.' The *avant garde* scorns notions of 'responsibility' toward the audience; it raises the question of

> whether the audience exists – of whether it should exist. The *avant garde* proclaims its faith in the self-sufficiency, the necessary irresponsibility, and thereby the ultimate salvation of art.[26]

It is no accident perhaps that Leroi Jones, a modernistic literary practitioner himself, clearly perceived the common grounds between modern jazz musicians and other modern artists. Jones argued that the

> artist and his fellow-traveller, the Bohemian, are usually regarded in this society as useless con-men and as such, are treated as enemies. The complete domination of American society by what Brooks Adams called the economic sensibility, discouraging completely any significant participation of the imaginative sensibility in the social, political, and economic affairs of the society, is what has permitted this hatred of the artist by the 'average American'. This phenomenon has also caused the estrangement of the American artist from American society, and made the formal culture of the society (the diluted formalism of the academy) anemic and fraught with incompetence and unreality. It has also caused the high art of America to be called 'the art of alienation'. The analogy to the life of the Negro in America and his subsequent production of a high art which took its shape directly from the nature and meaning of his own alienation should be obvious. This consideration (dealt with consciously or instinctively) certainly reshaped certain crucial elements of the American art of the last two decades, and gave a deeply native reference to the direction of American Bohemianism, or the artist's life of the fifties.[27]

That jazz becomes a terrain of avant-gardism before it is half a century old is scarcely surprising. The role of the individual in the development of jazz, as John Storm Roberts points out, has been of overriding importance.

> Virtually all the major changes in jazz have been associated with a few individuals (though clearly they could not have wrought the changes single-handedly): Buddy Bolden, who appears to have provided a bridge between band marches and ragtime and band jazz; Jelly Roll Morton, in somewhat the same position; Armstrong, who introduced the era of jazz as a

> music for soloists; Coleman Hawkins and Lester Young, who helped turn jazz from a trumpeter's to a saxist's music; Charlie Parker and Dizzy Gillespie; Ornette Coleman and Cecil Taylor; and perhaps Archie Shepp.

Moreover, jazz musicians 'speak for a people whose major group experience has been a denial not so much of humanity as of individuality.'[28] By the mid-1920s jazz had emerged as an improvisational idiom whose key agent was the individual soloist. Hereafter compositions and arrangements were predominantly platforms or settings for the display of individual instrumental (and in the 1930s and 1940s, at least, vocal) virtuosity. At the heart of jazz, then, were two characteristics fundamental to artistic modernism: the emphasis on the unique creative potential of the individual artist – the cult of genius; and an emphasis on the *process* of creation – improvisation – rather than an emphasis on its formal end-product.

The general characteristics of modernism in the arts became significant in bop and all-pervasive in the New Thing music of the late 1950s onward. In the twentieth century the arts have lost the coherence which comes from a unifying set of principles focused on a particular *form* of artistic creation. In painting and the plastic arts the conventions of realism which attempted to centre everything in the natural abilities of human sight have been abandoned. In literature the conventional narrative based upon the fixed sequence of a social career or the natural life cycle is outmoded. In modern jazz, particularly since the 1960s, the Afro-American song (the blues) and the Tin Pan Alley song are no longer the basic framework for arrangement, composition and improvisation. In each of these instances the aim of the art prior to modernism was the production of aesthetic objects which were accessible to and expressive of essential and universal features of all humanity.

> The convention of perspective, which is unique to European art and which was first established in the early Renaissance, centres everything on the eye of the beholder, on the specifically human eye. Pre-modern literature operated to sustain empathy and emotional involvement by appealing to the experiences of the 'common reader'.[29]

Pre-modern music, both popular and classical, is melodically based, their composers seeking memorable melodies and repeating them to ensure the listener's memory of them. Even in elaboration of the melodies, and in subjecting them to juxtaposition and development in a composition, repetition and regular return to the initial melody made sure that the remembered strain was not easily lost. The Renaissance humanism which celebrated the active powers and senses of the human individual is, of course, the foundation of these artistic conventions. Each artistic domain, in the Renaissance perspective, was designed to cultivate, enhance, celebrate, and organise the active faculties of human reason, emotion, and imaginative perception.

Modernism developed in the arts as a reaction to both the exhaustion of humanistic conventions as guides to further creativity, and in response to the increasing sense of dislocation between humanism and the experience of modern world living. Instead of basing its artistic conventions on some presumed set of naturally given universal human faculties, artistic modernism takes artistic conventions themselves as the terrain for creative exploration. For example, painting becomes preoccupied with texture, structure, and medium – breaking away from the problem of painting recognisable objects in a recognisable manner – exploring techniques for representing the intangible qualities of lights and ultimately breaking away from the easel, using paint itself as a subject for art, and involving the artist's own person in the painting. In classical music there occurs a gradual 'emancipation of dissonance' as the harmonic vocabulary is enlarged to admit previously unacceptable discords. The resulting level of chromaticism in European classical harmony at the turn of the century required new formal principles as its basis. These organising principles were partially provided by serialism but, ultimately, the very shift away from earlier conventions opened up a broad range of possibilities to be played with – atonality, *musique concrète*, neo-classicism, electronic music – all of which remould musical conventions without replacing them with a dominant organising tradition.

Parallel processes, amounting to what Ortega has called 'inversion',[30] occur throughout the arts where the conventions of the arts themselves become the essential object of manipulation and exploration rather than being the means to the representation of human realities. These processes bring with them obsession with techniques, abstraction from general human experience and stylistic fragmentation. With the loss of a unifying set of principles of organisation the modern artist questions 'the right of the ordinary world to be considered more real than the fabricated world of play'.[31] The artist's feelings and imagination become established as the ultimate foundation of aesthetic practice. In the process both art and life come to be treated as fiction, the arbitrary imposition of meaning on otherwise meaningless experiences. In contrast to the Renaissance vision of art as presenting coherent and generally recognised truths, art becomes the field of pure intuition and imagination in a world which is seen as a shadowplay without substance. In modern art human *experience* rather than human *perception* is the foundation and focus of aesthetic practice.

In jazz, of course, the experience which is fundamental is the black experience. Herein lies a major difference between jazz and the other modern arts; the bulk of jazz musicians have been members of an oppressed and disprivileged group and not inhabitants of a deracinated footloose Bohemia. However, the black population of America has been subject to extremely rapid urbanisation and its associated social changes, including incorporation into a peculiarly homogenised society where cultural differences are diminished by the power of the mass media and a very narrow political-ideological spectrum. Further, class and ethnic identity in America has always been evanescent and marginal in the face of the hegemonic ideology of liberal pluralism.[32] Black collective identity, rooted largely in the black middle classes – caught between wanting the acceptance and rewards of white society and dominating and leading the black community – has shared this fragility in the extreme. Cultural nationalism could not be easily generated in a society characterised by a high degree of anti-intellectualism, an emphasis on and institutionalisation of technical professionalism, and a consequent lack of an intelligentsia. All of this contrasts with the conditions producing the black intellectuals of the French African colonies who were to articulate visions of Negritude and African socialism.[33] American political and cultural conditions by contrast have provided very little in the way of symbolic resources for the American black community to articulate a communal identity. Jazz musicians have shared this weakness, adopting the Romantic tradition's conception of art and the artist in the 1940s and the 'do your own thing' ethic of the hippies in the 1960s. Both aesthetic visions are variants of the general tendencies of modernism in the arts.

To summarise the argument, then, we have attempted to identify some of the ways in which jazz shares the evolution of modern art: the disassociation of its aesthetic, organising conventions from the human centre of song and dance; the exploration of new techniques and instruments at an increasingly rapid pace; and an intensification of stylistic fragmentation which, at this point in time, threatens to dissolve jazz as a musical idiom. Jazz also shares with modernism in the arts an intense individualism which is embodied in the cult of artistic genius and, increasingly, in the subjectivism which exalts the artist's experience as the object-discipline whose expression subordinates all artistic conventions. While Jones, Kofsky and Sidran correctly indicate some of the links between black collective consciousness and jazz, they overestimate the strength and autonomy of these connections. Consequently they overlook the parallels between the evolution of jazz and the other arts and the way these developments are related to a large cultural and social configuration.

Notes

1 I am indebted to Frank Nutch and Deborah van Wyck for their criticisms and stimulation in the course of writing this paper.
2 Leroi Jones, *Blues People*, William Morrow, New York, 1963.
3 Frank Kofsky, *Black Nationalism and the Revolution in Music*, Pathfinder Press, New York, 1969.
4 Ben Sidran, *Black Talk*, Holt Rinehart, New York, 1971.
5 Jones, op. cit., pp. 177–80.
6 A detailed investigation of the pre-Second World War reception of jazz by white society in America is found in Morroe Berger, 'Jazz: resistance to the diffusion of a culture-pattern', *Journal of Negro History*, 32 (1947), pp. 461–4.
7 Paul Oliver, 'Jazz is where you find it: the European experience of jazz', in C.W.E. Bigsby (ed.), *Superculture: American Popular Culture in Europe*, Bowling Green University Popular Press, Bowling Green, Ohio, 1975.
8 Jazz musicians associated with bebop are emphatic on the importance of other musicians' appreciation of their music. For characteristic statements see Nat Shapiro and Nat Hentoff, *Hear Me Talkin' To Ya*, Dover Publictions, Toronto, 1966, pp. 335–70.
9 Martin Williams, *The Jazz Tradition*, New American Library, New York, 1973, p. 106.
10 James Lincoln Collier, *The Making of Jazz*, Delta, New York, 1978, pp. 360–1.
11 James A. Geschwender, *Racial Stratification in America*, William C. Brown, Dubuque, 1978, pp. 201–18.
12 Kofsky, op. cit., Introduction, Chapter 1; Ron Wellburn, 'The black aesthetic imperative', in Gayle Addison (ed.), *The Black Aesthetic*, Doubleday, New York, 1971, pp. 132–49.
13 Geschwender, op. cit., pp. 222–38; Robert L. Allen, *Black Awakening in Capitalist America*, Doubleday, New York, 1970.
14 Leroi Jones, *Black Music*, William Morrow, New York, 1967; A.B. Spellman, *Four Lives in the Bebop Business*, MacGibbon & Kee, London, 1967.
15 See Shepp's statements in 'Point of contact' and 'A view from the inside', in *Music '66, Down Beat 11th Yearbook*, Down Beat Publications, New York, 1966.

16 Collier, op. cit., p. 475.
17 A compact survey of established jazz musicians' reactions to Ornette Coleman's first New York appearance in1960 is found in Nat Hentoff, *The Jazz Life*, Peter Davies, London, 1962, pp. 227–32, 239–40. More broadly *Down Beat*'s 'Blindfold test' column is a useful source of information on jazz musicians' opinions on each other's work.
18 Sidran, op. cit., pp. 154–5.
19 Henry Pleasants, *Serious Music and All That Jazz*, Simon & Schuster, New York, 1969.
20 Leslie B. Rout, Jr, 'Reflections on the evolution of post-war jazz', in Gayle Addison (ed.), op. cit., pp. 155–6.
21 Frank Tirro, 'The silent tradition in jazz', *The Musican Quarterly* (July 1967), cited in Pleasants, op. cit., p. 142.
22 Pleasants, op. cit., p. 144.
23 Ibid., p. 140.
24 Irving Howe, 'Introduction: the idea of the modern', in *The Idea of the Modern in Literature and the Arts*, Irving Howe (ed.), Horizon Press, New York, 1967, p. 23.
25 Ibid.
26 Ibid., pp. 23–4.
27 Leroi Jones, *Blues People*, pp. 230–1.
28 John Storm Roberts, *Black Music of Two Worlds*, William Morrow, New York, 1974, p. 216.
29 John Berger, *Ways of Seeing*, London, British Broadcasting Corporation and Penguin Press, 1972, p. 16.
30 Jose Ortega Y Gasset, *The Dehumanisation of Art*, Princeton University Press, Princeton, New Jersey, 1948.
31 Christopher Lasch, *The Culture of Narcissism*, W.W. Norton, New York, 1979, p. 161.
32 Robert L. Allen, *Black Awakening in Capitalist America*, Doubleday, New York, 1970; Gareth Stedman Jones, 'The history of US imperialism', in Robin Blackburn (ed.), *Ideology in Social Science*, Fontana, London, 1972, pp. 207–37.
33 Mercer Cook and Stephen Henderson, *The Militant Black Writer in Africa and the United States*, University of Wisconsin Press, Madison, 1969.

Towards a sociology of musical styles

John Shepherd

The idea that different groups and societies create and appreciate their own stylistically distinguishable kinds of music is not one that would be likely to invite dissension from musicians or sociologists. Neither, on the face of it, is the assumption that the stylistic characteristics of these different kinds of music might have some connection with what may be loosely termed the 'cultural background' of their creation. As Lévi-Strauss has argued with respect to language:

> between culture and language there cannot be *no* relations at all . . . . If there were no relations at all that woud lead us to assume that the human mind is a kind of jumble – that there is no connection at all between what the mind is doing on one level, and what the mind is doing on another level.' (1968, p. 79)

That there are connections between 'what the mind is doing on one level, and what the mind is doing on another level' is not difficult to illustrate on a *prima facie* basis where music is concerned. Is it a complete coincidence, for example, that functional tonality arose from the fervour of an intellectual and artistic movement (the Renaissance) which arguably laid the foundations for modern capitalist society? Is it a complete coincidence that alternatives to that musical 'language' began to be offered at a time when the 'reality' of three-dimensional perspective in painting was under attack, and when classical physics was facing a very considerable crisis? Is it completely without foundation that many people have seen in the rise of Afro-American-influenced popular musics social implications of great significance?

It is, of course, possible to argue that the cultural and social implications of different musical styles are completely associative in nature. That is, that although there are connections between what the mind is doing on different levels, a particular musical style carries the cultural and social implications it does only because the group or society in question externally imposes a set of meanings or significances on the music in a manner completely arbitrary to the music's basic structure. The argument is that any kind of music will serve a group or society provided the music is stylistically distinguishable from all others. There is nothing internal to the basic structure of the music, in other words, which predisposes it to impart any one kind of significance above all others.

In contrast, it is also possible to argue that the internal structure of a musical style is of itself significant. This is not necessarily to assume that the significance of music is located in some form of a-social, ultimate reality, however. It can be asserted that because *people* create music, they reproduce in the basic structure of their music the basic structure of their own thought processes. If it is accepted that people's thought processes are socially mediated, then it could be said that the basic structures of different styles of music are likewise socially mediated and so socially significant.

It is in the light of this second possibility that a sociology of musical styles becomes a viable proposition, at least in theory. If musical styles have an inherent social significance, then it should be possible to demonstrate that significance by carrying out musical analysis in terms of the social reality which gave birth to and is articulated by a particular musical style.

Such analyses are notably absent from both the musicological and sociological worlds. Surface reasons for the scant attention given to the sociology of *music* (as opposed to the sociology of musical life) are not difficult to find. Few sociologists feel themselves to be competent in a discipline which requires a significant degree of technical knowledge as well as, preferably, some first-hand experience as a practitioner. Musicologists, on the other hand, repelled by what they see as unending waves of pseudo-scientific jargon, have apparently decided that the area should be left well alone. The art of musical analysis is well established, and musicologists see in sociology no good reason for changing their methods or approaches where traditional analysis is concerned. But reasons for the neglect of a sociology of musical styles go deeper than sociologists' lack of musical knowledge, or musicologists' perhaps healthy scepticism for social 'science'. This paper seeks to outline the major difficulties which stand in the way of a sociology of musical styles, and to indicate the way in which those difficulties might be overcome.

The first block to a sociology of musical styles derives from the way in which the majority of musicologists subscribe, either implicitly or explicitly, to an elitist view of art. This view of art, it can be argued, forms an integral aspect of the structure of capitalist society.

Capitalist society is usually taken to be characterised by a highly developed division of labour which reinforces a markedly hierarchical class system. These characteristics are in turn taken to be symptomatic of extended centralised lines of social control which alienate many people from their essential natures and preclude them from participating in society to the fullest of their potential. Due to the highly developed division of labour, hierarchical class structure and centralism of capitalist society, the 'intellectual' in all spheres of society has remained very much in the position of producing and defining knowledge for other people.[1] For the centralised dissemination of knowledge to remain intact in the face of challenge, it is necessary that knowledge be conceived according to the canons of an absolute or objective idealism. It is necessary, in other words, that reality be thought of as 'given', rather than socially constructed.

It is precisely with this type of absolute and idealist concept that art has traditionally concerned itself since the time of the Ancient Greeks. As far as the modern world is concerned, we are told by Raymond Williams that the argument that 'an artist's precepts were . . . the "universals" (in Aristotle's terms) or permanent realities" is one which "had been completed in the writings of the Renaissance"' (1961, p. 52). And as the same author goes on to point out, it is also an argument which united the otherwise disparate creeds of Classicism and Romanticism:

> The tendency of Romanticism is towards a vehement rejection of dogmas of method in art, but it is also very clearly, towards a claim which all good classical theory would have recognised: the claim that the artist's business is to 'read the open secrets of the universe'. A 'romantic' critic like Ruskin, for example, bases his whole theory of art on just this 'classicist' doctrine. The artist perceives and represents Essential Reality, and he does so by virtue of his master faculty Imagination. In fact the doctrines of 'the genius' (the autonomous creative artist) and the 'superior reality of art' (penetration to a sphere of universal truth) were in Romantic thinking two sides of the same claim. Both Romanticism and Classicism are in this sense idealist theories of art. (1961, p. 56)

This concern with truth as the ultimate aim of art and culture has persisted into the twentieth century, albeit in rather less explicit forms. In his *Notes towards the Definition of Culture*, for example, T.S. Eliot argues that diversity of cultural activity is essential to the maintenance of a valid spiritual life. Dialectic is a necessary prerequisite for truth:

> As in the relation between the social classes, and as in the relation of the several regions of a country to each other and to the central power; it would seem that a constant struggle between the centripetal and centrifugal forces is desirable . . . there should be an endless conflict between ideas – for it is only by the struggle against constantly appearing false ideas that truth is enlarged and clarified, and in the conflict with heresy that orthodoxy is developed to meet the needs of the time. (1948, p. 82)

The complex of arguments associated with an elitist concept of art tends only to be explicitly stated when the concept is faced with a substantial challenge. It could be argued that the first notable challenge to the centralised definition and dissemination of knowledge in post-Renaissance society did not occur until the late eighteenth century, with the rise to power and influence of the middle classes. It is not entirely coincidental, therefore, that it was at this time that the notion of art as an approach to essential reality received, in the words of Raymond Williams, 'significant additional emphases' (1961, pp. 60-1). Faced with a deviant cultural reality, in other words, writers and artists were forced back on the notion that all culture attains to one, indivisible, essential truth.

But this is only the first step in the line of defence, because it is equally possible for the perpetrators of a deviant cultural reality to claim that they too have access to the essential nature of truth. Further, they may claim that their art-forms interpret this essential reality more successfully than the traditional art-forms with which they vie. Those who produce such traditional art-forms are therefore driven first to claim that it is *their* art-forms which best reveal the inner nature of essential reality, and then to maintain that it is only a limited number of highly tuned minds (such as themselves) who are capable of appreciating this reality in an unaided fashion. F.R. Leavis puts this view most explicitly:

> In any period it is upon a very small minority that the discerning appreciation of art and literature depends: it is (apart from

> cases of the simple and familiar) only a few who are capable of unprompted, first-hand judgement. They are still a minority, though a larger one, who are capable of endorsing such a first-hand judgement by geniune personal response. The accepted valuations are a kind of paper currency based upon a very small proportion of gold. (1948, p. 143)

The reverse side of the coin, of course, is a disdain for the critical abilities of the 'culturally untutored'. Although such disdain is necessarily implicit in the very notion of a centrally defined culture, it is again interesting to note that the attitude became more deeply entrenched at the beginning of the nineteenth century. As Raymond Williams says:

> Writers had . . . often expressed, before this time, a feeling of dissatisfaction with the 'public', but in the early nineteenth century this feeling became acute and general. One finds it in Keats: 'I have not the slightest feeling of humility towards the Public'; in Shelley: 'Accept no counsel from the simple-minded. Time reverses the judgement of the foolish crowd. Contemporary criticism is no more than the sum of the folly with which genius has to wrestle.' One finds it, most noticeably and extensively, in Wordsworth. (1961, p. 51)

Coupled with the belief that art reveals higher truths fathomable only by a minority of superior minds is the idea that these minds are responsible for preserving the cultural values of a society. This idea is as prevalent in the twentieth century as it was in the nineteenth. The early nineteenth-century writer, we are told by Williams, continued

> to insist, in fact, on an Idea, a standard of excellence, the 'embodied spirit' of a People's knowledge, as something superior to the actual run of the market. This insistence, it is worth emphasising, is one of the primary sources of the idea of Culture. Culture, the 'embodied spirit of a People', the true standard of excellence, became available, in the progress of the century, as the court of appeal in which real values were determined. (1961, p. 52)

Over a century later, F.R. Leavis states that

> Upon this minority depends our power of profiting by the finest human experience of the past; they keep alive the subtlest and most perishable parts of tradition. Upon them depend the implicit standards that order the finer living of an age, the sense that this is worth more than that, this rather than that is the direction in which to go, that the centre is here rather than there. (1948, pp. 144-5)

It is this last line of thought in the complex of arguments under discussion that is most obviously allied to the central dissemination of knowledge in capitalist society. Yet it is important to understand that this line of thought cannot be maintained without the presence of the other two. In other words, unless there are a set of objective values and standards against which all cultural activity can ultimately be judged, and unless it is the case that only a minority are capable of perceiving the essential truth underlying those values, then the legitimacy of the role played by that minority quickly comes into question.

It is further interesting to note that this elitist attitude towards culture is based on the questionable premise that society is divided between those who have inherently superior, and those who have inherently inferior intellects. This premise in turn gives birth to a circular or self-maintaining view of cultural apprehension: it is only those with superior minds who can fathom the ultimate realities of art, yet it is those who can fathom these realities who by definition have superior minds; equally, those with inferior minds cannot fathom the ultimate realities of art, yet it is precisely those who cannot fathom those realities who by definition have inferior minds. This circularity is implicitly acknowledged by T.S. Eliot when he says that 'it is an essential condition of the preservation of the quality of the culture of the minority that it should be a minority culture' (1948, p. 107), and through Arnold Schoenberg's famous aphorism that 'if it is art it is not for all, and if it is for all, it is not art'.

Not surprisingly, the attitudes so far described are to be found in the musical as well as in the literary worlds. The idea that the composer mediates between 'the open secrets of the universe' and the music he writes finds classical expression in the work of Victor Zuckerkandl. For Zuckerkandl, musical significance is located in laws which may only be discovered by the composer in objective reality:

> It is not that the mind of the creative artist expresses itself in tones, words, colours, and forms as its medium; on the contrary, *tone, word, colour, form express themselves through the medium of the creative mind.* The finer that medium the better tone, word, colour, form can express themselves. The greater the genius, the less it speaks *itself*, the more it lends its voice to the tones, the words, the colours, the forms. In this sense, then, music does write itself – neither more nor less, by the way, than physics does. The law of falling bodies is no invention of the genius of Galileo. The work of the genius consists in bringing the mind, through years of practice, so into harmony with things, that things can express their laws through him. (1956, pp. 222-3)

A similar view has more recently been expressed by Ruth Gipps. For her, music is a mystic experience founded on truth:

> I know that from one God comes music and all musical gifts. Some of us were composers from the beginning of our lives; we had no choice in the matter, only a life-long duty to make the most of a given talent. This talent may be large or small, but without it a person is not a composer . . .. My own conception of God is of a limitless contrapuntal mind; perhaps this concept lacks humanity, but that is my own business. From personal experience I know that mysticism is founded on truth. (1975, p. 13)

Consequently

> no human being has ever created anything. The most that a composer can do is to present to other people, in a comprehensible form, music that already existed. Bach wrote 'S.D.G.' at the end of works. None of his music was a product of the cleverness of J.S. Bach. (1975, p. 13)

The idea that a minority of people are imbued with a special gift of musicality which may subsequently be cultivated into genius is a commonplace in many people's thinking about music, and needs no further comment in the present context. But such belief in the other-worldly nature of musical inspiration, and the ability of only a minority to exploit it, in turn leads to the concept of an objective aesthetic. That is, it is assumed that there are a fixed set of musical criteria against which *all* music can ultimately be judged. Not surprisingly, these criteria tend to be rooted in the musical language of the ruling classes. Leonard B. Meyer, for example, has spent a large part of his working life attempting to extrapolate a universally applicable theory of music from albeit insightful analyses of functional tonality. Again not surprisingly, pre-literate music does not fair very well:

> The differentia between art music and primitive lies in speed of tendency gratification. The primitive seeks almost immediate gratification of his tendencies whether these be biological or musical. Nor can he tolerate uncertainty. And it is because distant departures from the certainty and repose of the tonic note and lengthy delays in gratification are insufferable to him that the tonal repertory of the primitive is limited, not because he cannot think of the other tones. It is not his mentality that is limited, it is his maturity. (1967, p. 32)

The tendency to judge all music in terms of functional tonality finds its clearest expression at the hands of Ruth Gipps:

> The corollary of the truth that all real music comes from inspiration is that all so-called music written without inspiration is not music at all, and the people who write it are not composers. Ranging from the super-intellectual to the wildest wooliest lunatic fringe, we have for years been given performances of worthless nonsense, while real composers have been labelled backward-looking, unenterprising, or unwilling to experiment. (1975, p. 14)

Opinions of this sort are not infrequently backed up with arguments of a technical or analytic nature. Marshall Stearns, for example, reports the following conversation with a friend about jazz:

> 'Jazz', he told me one evening, 'is unnatural, abnormal and just plain unhealthy.' I know of no effective way to answer this sort of pronouncement on any human activity. When pressed for reasons, however, he fell back on more rational assertions: 'the harmonies of jazz are childish, the melodies are a series of clichés, and the rhythms are monotonously simple.' Here is something technical and specific. What is more these criticisms

> are reasonably typical and comprehensive. Since my friend (and others like him) occupies an important position in the world of music on the strength of his unquestioned merits, his comments should be taken seriously. (1956, p. 183)

Since, as Henry Pleasants puts it, the musical 'establishment is concerned with the preservation of what it regards, sincerely, I think, as immutable cultural criteria' (1969, p. 118), its criticisms of music which does not conform to pre-ordained technical or analytic criteria also tends to carry an accompanying moralistic component. This tendency in the denunciation of various forms of jazz, rock and 'pop' music is so well known that it hardly requires substantiation. One need only refer, for example, to Merriam's cataloguing of the tirade launched against jazz in the United States between the 1920s and 1940s,[2] or, as far as 'pop' is concerned, to the unfailing Ruth Gipps:

> In fact, the pop craze has done much serious harm to thousands. Every time a misguided teacher uses commercial pop in school the kids concerned are being led from the good and spiritual in their natures towards the evil and hypocritical. (1976, p. 17)

It now becomes clear why aestheticians and music theorists are likely to refrain from assigning music (by which they almost without exception mean 'serious' music) an inherent social significance. For if the significance of music is taken to be socially located, then it must be understood to form an aspect of the socially constructed reality of the group or society responsible for producing the music in question. In other words, the music can only be legitimately understood in terms of the categories of analysis which themselves form an aspect of the reality of that particular group or society, and there can consequently be no question of recourse to the notion that musical significance is derived from the 'open secrets of the universe' or some other form of mystical, other-worldly truth.

Once the significance of music *is* taken to be socially located, the circle of argument predicated on the notion of inherently superior and inferior minds is broken. Difference in cultural values is due not so much to questions of inherent intelligence as to the existence of socially constructed and different cultural criteria which not infrequently display a mutual incompatibility.[3] With this central pillar of the elitist position removed, the right of the institutionalised musician or aesthetician in capitalist society to approach most music in terms of certain idealistically conceived categories thus comes into serious question. Consequently, the propensity for such musicians and aestheticians to attempt to impose a certain kind of musical knowledge on the rest of society would also come into question.

The fact that an acceptance of the social mediation of music might result in a weakening of role-security is significant, but is perhaps not the most telling point against such acceptance. Quite clearly, *any* assertion that the reality or knowledge of a society is socially constructed not only brings into question the notion of absolutely and objectively conceived knowledge, but thereby questions the right of one group in society to use that notion in order to attempt a centralised manipulation and control of knowledge and values for all other groups. Because centralised social structures ultimately depend for their survival on such modes of cognitive manipulation and control, questioning of the sort indicated would ultimately result in the scrutiny of the *entire* centralised structure of capitalism.

The connection may to some people seem a distant one, but it is more than possible that the lack of a disposition on the part of musicians and aestheticians to accept the significance of 'serious' music as socially located is due to the fact that such acceptance would implicitly require a questioning of the social and political structure within which we all live. Not only would it mean accepting that the various forms of jazz, rock and 'pop' music are equally as 'good' as serious forms, but it would also mean accepting the social and moral relativity of the deviant realities they have come to represent and articulate.

It may be the institutional restraint just outlined which has prevented Leonard B. Meyer, perhaps the most intellectually honest of musicologists, from seriously exploring the possibility that the significance of music is, indeed, inherently social. His quest for a universally applicable theory of music has always been partially circumscribed by adherence to approaches which are essentially psychologistic, a tendency which can be illustrated by reference to his book, *Explaining Music*.

Meyer in fact admits to this circumscription in a roundabout way. At the beginning of *Explaining Music* (p. ix), the author states, 'as I intend the term, criticism seeks to explain how the structure and process of a particular composition are related to the competent listener's comprehension of it.' The nature of this comprehension is expounded on towards the end of the book (p. 242):

> A competent listener perceives and responds to music with his total being . . . . Through such empathetic identification, music is quite literally *felt*, and it can be felt without the mediation of extramusical concepts of images. Such kinesthetic sensing of the ethos or character of a musical event is what the term ethetic refers to.

It is precisely this ethetic relationship, which stands at the heart of musical apprehension, that is problematic for Meyer: 'Ethetic relationships are unquestionably important . . . [but] are hard to analyse with rigor and precision . . . . [There is an] absence of an adequate theory of ethetic change and transformation' (pp. 245–6). Again, 'the analysis must end here . . . [because] the rigorous analysis of ethetic relationships is beyond my knowledge and skill' (p. 267).

The remedy, it would seem, is in Meyer's own hands. In his opening chapter, 'On the nature and limits of critical analysis', the author draws a basic distinction between critical analysis and style analysis. Whereas critical analysis is concerned with the singular and idiosyncratic, style analysis 'is concerned with discovering and describing those attributes of a composition which are common to a group of works' (p. 7). Theory, moreover, 'endeavours . . . to discover the principles governing the formation of the typical procedures and schemata described in style analysis' (pp. 7-8). To complete the relationship: 'Critical analysis uses the laws formulated by music theory . . . in order to explain how and why the particular events within a composition are related to one another' (p. 9).

It could be assumed from this last statement that the principles and laws of music theory would be of crucial importance to the development of a critical method. But apparently this is not so. In being required to explain why the melodies of Palestrina, for example, display a certain structural feature, Meyer suggests (p. 8) one answer 'with a general law of some sort'. This law might be 'the Gestalt law of completeness, which asserts that the human mind, searching for stable shapes, wants patterns to be as complete as possible'. Beyond this, however, Meyer does not think it necessary to go. There is thus no need to explore the processes inherent in the search for stable shapes: 'I doubt that the explanation of musical practice needs to be pushed back this far. As a rule we. are, I think, satisfied with the least inclusive law which will account for the events described.'

But satisfaction is surely the one thing Meyer does not attain. In one breath he tells us that 'the rigorous analysis of ethetic relationships is beyond my knowledge and skill' and in another he strongly implies that the psychological processes – which he clearly sees as important to those ethetic relationships – do not themselves require that same 'rigorous analysis'.

It is possible to trace this conundrum, not only to the institutional restraint already discussed, but to a central difficulty in understanding the functioning of music. Unlike words and pictures, the significance of music cannot, as Meyer has alredy said, be approached through 'the mediation of extra-musical concepts or images'. If, indeed, music can be said to have 'meaning' (given the usual referential significance of that term) then, in the minds of most musicians and musicologists, it is undoubtedly to be located within the internal structuring of the particular composition in question. And since music both originates in and is efficacious within the minds of men, it can be assumed: (a) that there must be a conformity between musical structures and the structure of the human mind, and consequently (b) that this structure can be ultimately revealed through the analysis of any musical idiom. Both these assumptions are implicit in Meyer's thought:

> In music, psychological constants such as the principles of pattern organisation, the syntax of particular styles, and typical schemata . . . constitute *the rules of the game* . . . . For any given musical repertory, the 'rules' determine the kinds of pattern that can be employed in a composition. (p. 14)

It follows, then, that music can be satisfactorily explained in terms of itself, and it is symptomatic that, in supporting his idea of the 'least inclusive law', Meyer incorporates Mario Bunge's view that 'every system and every event can be accounted for . . . primarily in terms of its own level and adjoining levels' (1969, p. 24).

Since, on the surface, there would appear to be nothing fallacious in this line of argument, Meyer looks elsewhere for the cause of his difficulties with ethetic relationships. He apparently concludes that the cause is to be found in the impossibility of distinguishing between psychological constants and the conventions of a particular musical idiom:

> In theory, it is possible to distinguish between archetypal patterns and schemata. The former would be those patterns which arise as a result of physiological and psychological constants presumed innate in human behaviour. The latter would be those norms which were the result of learning. But the distinction breaks down in practice. For most traditionally established norms have some basis in innate constants, and, on the other hand, patterns derived from innate constants become parts of tradition.

'This being the case,' concludes Meyer, 'the terms will be used more or less interchangeably' (p. 214).

It is not to be disputed that psychological or physiological constants are incorporated in all forms of musical expression. But since, on Meyer's own admission, the constants are assimilated in, and become indistinguishable from the norms of specific musical idioms, would it not be more fruitful to seek the basis of ethetic relationships in these different and *identifiable* norms? Here, however, the difficulty of musical 'meaning' comes into play again, because if it is assumed that musical significance is to be located in the structuring of particular norms, then it is not a very big step to further assume that this structuring is rooted in the extra-musical 'beliefs' and 'ideas' of the appropriate culture.

Even if a musicologist or aesthetician overcomes the institutional restraint already described, and seriously entertains the possibility that the significance of music is, indeed, inherently social, there remains, as just indicated, the difficulty of how music can have that significance. On the one hand, music would seem to have a significance which is located outside and beyond itself in society at large. On the other, most musicians and musicologists remain convinced that the significance of music has a great deal to do with its internal structure. That is why they do analysis.

A hint as to the cause of this difficulty is given by two sociologists. Terry Lovell, for example, has stated,

> content analysis – the categories of analysis being drawn from the categories of social life itself – is biased in favour of the representational arts. We have little in the way of sociology of music . . . . Sociology of 'pop' music is uniformly restricted to

> the analysis of the lyrics . . . . Where there are no lyrics we may get trivial results. (1972, p. 329)

Again, Hugh D. Duncan has said, in ironic mood, that 'communication . . . must be explained by everything but communication . . . it must have, as we read so often, a "referent" . . .' (1968, p. 31).

To translate these insights into everyday terms, a symbol has meaning for most people because it refers to something outside itself. Pictures have meaning because they refer to something in physical reality, and words have meaning because they refer to concepts and ideas. But the suggestion that a piece of music has meaning because of extra-musical references is, as already suggested, inadmissible to most musicians. The logical alternative on the part of musicologists and aestheticians is thus to look for the meaning of music within the structure of individual pieces, an alternative whose strictest formulation, as Meyer indicates (1956, p. 33) is to be found in the attitude of the absolutists:

> The absolutists have contended that the meaning of music lies specifically, and some would assert exclusively, in the musical processes themselves. For them musical meaning is non-designative. But in what sense these processes are meaningful . . . they have been unable to state with either clarity or precision . . . . This failure has led some critics to assert that musical meaning is a thing apart, different in some unexplained way from all other kinds of meaning. This is simply an evasion of the real issue.

The real issue can be stated in terms of the following comparison. Because their meaning is 'located outside them', words and pictures may be thought of as 'carrying' their meaning and 'giving' it to the recipient. The symbol, in other words, survives the divulgence of its message. If, on the other hand, musical meaning is acknowledged to lie within the musical process itself, then in 'giving away' that meaning, a piece seemingly compromises the very being or essence responsible for the meaning in the first place. As Susanne Langer has put it (1960, p. 236), the absolutists 'seem to feel that if musical structures should really be found to have significance, to relate to anything beyond themselves, those structures would forthwith cease to be musical.'

This difficulty results from confusing a symbol which has no *obvious* referent in the world of objects and ideas with one which is incapable of communicating outside itself. Music would seem to fall within the former but not, as the absolutists would imply, the latter category. It is this distinction which facilitates the psychologistic theories of musicologists such as Meyer and aestheticians such as Langer. As already indicated, psychologistic theories for the significance of music are broadly based on the premise that, since all music originates in the minds of individual people, and since all minds are assumed to possess similar psychological characteristics, there will be a conformity of patterning or structure between all music and all minds. Consequently, all minds are presumed to be suitably predisposed for the superimposition of the particular structure that constitutes a piece, and there is no longer any need to have recourse to the notion of symbols which divest themselves of externally referential meanings. Significance is imparted by another method.

The emphasis put by psychologistic theories on the conformity of structuring between minds and music might, on the face of it, seem to overcome the difficulty highlighted in the absolutists' position. The conformity guarantees a degree of 'outerness' for music, because the music is efficacious within minds which are essentially external to its structure. However, as Meyer himself has implied, purely psychologistic theories are not without their problems. They do not seem to explain musical significance convincingly.

The reason for the ultimate inadequacy of psychologistic theories is to be located, in Terry Lovell's words, in 'the categories of analysis . . . drawn from the categories of social life itself'. It can be argued (and this has been done in some detail elsewhere)[4] that the categories of analysis fundamental to the ways of thinking of many people in capitalist society are simply unsuited to a full and adequate understanding of the musical process. The absolutists' position, for example, is based on the assumption that because music does not obviously refer 'outside' itself to the material and concrete world, its 'content' must be contained 'inside' itself. The absolutist, in other words, must contradictorily assert that since the 'content' of music is not located in the 'outside', physical world, it must be found 'inside' in the 'form' of the music.

Psychologistic theories get over the difficulty of asserting that the 'content' of music is its 'form' by invoking another category, that of the psychological or 'mental'. Psychologistic theories state, in short, that the 'content' of music is to be found 'outside' the 'form' in the 'mental' processes common to all individuals. The only problem with this approach is that 'mental' processes are usually taken to belong very much to the 'inner' world which stands in stark opposition to the 'outer', 'material' and 'physical' world that the absolutist is at such pains to eschew. Formulated in these terms, psychologistic theories do not guarantee music an 'outerness' *where significance is concerned.* They only guarantee it *in the sense that music communicates beyond itself to people.* The theories might point to the way in which music imparts its significance, in other words, but they say nothing about the substance of that significance. As with absolutist theories, significance is restricted to the 'inner' world of 'form' or structure *alone*.

It should be emphasised that this argument is not based simply on a play on words. By examining their origins (and this examination has been carried out elsewhere[5]) it can be demonstrated that the categories of 'form' and 'content', 'inner' and 'outer', 'mental' and 'physical' are dialectic, and therefore structural correlates of one another. Indeed, there would seem to be in modern capitalist society a bivalent cognitive system which can be interpreted in any number of different ways at the level of concrete concepts and words. The system can quite easily be extended to include categories such as 'emotional' and 'intellectual', for example, 'subjective' and 'objective' or even 'female' and 'male'. When psychologistic theories assert that the 'content' of music is to be found 'outside' the 'form' in 'mental' processes, therefore, they would seem to be restricting the whole question of significance in music to one side of the cognitive system mentioned, and thereby emasculating music as a genuine and potent phenomenon in the world. They are, if the phrase can be excused, committing a structural tautology.

The view that the meaning or significance of music is inherently social overcomes the inadequacy of psychologistic theories by acknowledging that music does, indeed, have a significance of substance to impart. The significance of a piece of music lies in the way its internal structure both reflects and creatively articulates the structure of the group or society in which it was conceived. It is because the minds of individual people also reflect and creatively articulate the structure of those people's group or society that they are suitably predisposed to receive the significance a piece of music has to impart. Society, in other words, is creatively articulated 'in' and 'through' the dialectic interaction of people and symbols. Music is but one mode of symbolic communication.

It is possible to indicate a vital connection between the institutional restraint referred to in the first half of this paper and the aesthetic difficulty with the significance of music which has just been discussed. Because the notion that music forms an integral aspect of socially constructed reality is, as we have seen, totally incompatible with the idea that musical significance is derived from the 'open secrets of the universe', there can be no question, as it were, of a reverse information flow by which society informs the composer. Rather, the mass of people are informed, edified and improved through the composer's insights into truth. Now neither Langer nor Meyer makes any explicit reference to essential truth or a higher reality. But they maintain a unidirectional information flow from a revised form of idealist truth to society at large by locating the significance of music in the 'psychological constants' (Meyer, 1973, p. 14) or 'psychological "laws of rightness"' (Langer, 1960, p. 240) which are common to all men, but which only the composer is able to interpret with any degree of insight. To this extent Langer's and Meyer's theories remain implicitly elitist. While, therefore, they are able to distinguish between a symbol which has no obvious referent in the world of objects and ideas on the one hand, and one which is nevertheless 'informationally open' on the other, *they are constrained to severely restrict the degree of that openness*. Although it is admitted that music may refer 'outside' itself to the mental world, it is implicitly denied that it can refer 'outside' to the *external* symbolic interaction which is arguably responsible for a large measure of that world.

A belief in the inherent social significance of music not only removes the central pillar of the elitist's position, therefore, but transcends the strict psychologistic delimitation of mental processes responsible for the aesthetic difficulty discussed in the second half of this paper. Inherent in that delimitation is the implication that social phenomena result from the collective interaction of physiologically pre-determined consciousnesses, rather than from the interaction of consciousnesses which are socially mediated. It is in this way that the psychologistic delimitation of mental processes becomes essential to an elitist view of musical processes.

It would seem that, if musicologists can overcome the institutional and aesthetic difficulties outlined in this paper, they should be able to proceed towards a sociology of musical styles, and therefore give musical analysis added significance. It is not difficult, for example, to suggest structural parallels between capitalist society and functional tonality. Functional tonality has one note, the key-note, which is more important than all others. These others, in their turn, have an order of importance. This hierarchy of fundamental notes (or 'fundamentals') can be said to parallel the hierarchical nature of our own society. Again, all the other notes in functional tonality tend magnetically towards the key-note. In any particular piece, the desire to end in a satisfying manner on the key-note seems to make that note the controlling factor in pre-determining the placement of all other notes. It is as if the other notes are pre-existing atoms, to be placed at will in a piece in the same way that workers in capitalist society are sometimes seen as individual sources of labour to be placed at will in a pre-determined economic system.

Although a theoretical case has been made out for such parallels, their satisfactory substantiation on closer inspection becomes more difficult.[6] It is perhaps because both musical and social processes are so highly fluid that socio-musical analysis seems to slip all too easily between the fingers. Again, the establishing of such parallels pre-empts many questions of social theory. Is music epiphenomenal to the social process in the sense of forming part of a 'symbolic superstructure' that is determined by a 'political-economic infrastructure', for example? Or is music an equal partner in the social process, capable of contributing creatively to the social reality of which it forms a part?

Given an adequate airing of such problems, it should be possible to move towards a sociology of functional tonality as a musical style or 'language' that includes more detailed analyses of individual periods, composers and pieces than has hitherto been possible. However, once an attempt is made to examine the musics of other groups and societies, additional problems arise. We all still live within a society that is overwhelmingly capitalist in its organisation. To conduct a sociological analysis of the music of those who have political and economic power in that society in a hermeneutically satisfactory manner should not, essentially, be problematic. But once attention is shifted even as close as the 'popular' musics of our own society, the potential for ethnocentric analysis becomes considerable. Marshall Stearns's friend saw in jazz only 'childish harmonies', 'clichéd melodies' and 'monotonously simple rhythms', for example. He was seemingly deaf to the rich and complex melodic, harmonic and rhythmic inflections which characterises so much Afro-American music, and is responsible for a large part of its significance.

Even assuming that it is possible to reconstitute the socio-musical realities of other groups and societies in a hermeneutically satisfactory manner, there still remains the related problem of whether those realities can be legitimately expressed in the highly explicit and literate terms required by the academic world. Mary Douglas has indicated the dangers of explicit analysis for ethnology in general:

> The anthropologist who draws out the whole scheme of the cosmos . . . does the primitive culture great violence if he seems to present the cosmology as a systematic philosophy subscribed to consciously by individuals. We can study our own cosmology – in a specialised department of astronomy. But primitive cosmologies cannot be rightly pinned out for display like exotic lepidoptera, without distortion to the nature of a primitive culture. (1970, pp. 110-11)

It is easy to imagine distortions of this sort occurring in the analyses of other people's musics. Even if it were possible to identify explicitly the structural significance of the various melodic, harmonic and rhythmic inflections to be found in performances of the rural blues, for example, it is questionable whether that significance should be spelt out with quite the perspicacity which normally underlies an analysis of the complex melodic, harmonic and rhythmic structures to be found in a Bach fugue or a Beethoven symphony.

The gradual growth and increasing respectability of ethnomusicology as a discipline would seem to point to a growing awareness by musicologists of culturally relative values and criteria, and so of the problems likely to be encountered in undertaking a sociology of different musical styles. Yet perhaps it is because they are so far removed from home, and thus unlikely to challenge the *status quo*, that musicologists are more disposed to recognise the relative musical and cultural values of pre-literate musics. For these same musicologists still feel unable to extend a similar courtesy to different musical traditions within our own society. François-Bernard Mâche achieves the most explicit of contradictions in the same article, for example. In one breath we are told that 'sound recording . . . brought to ears which . . . were willing to hear . . . the voices of other musical civilisations, thus calling to mind the relativity of aesthetic dogma' (1973, p. 108), and in another that the output of 'serious' music 'is almost insignificant . . . as compared with the vast mass of sonorous banality liberated by the advent of the music industries' (1973, p. 101).

Such attitudes are implicit in the curricula of university and school music departments. Some ethnomusicology is to be found in the undergraduate programmes of university music departments, most notably in North America. But apart from that, curricula are formed almost exclusively around music of the western concert tradition.

It is not until musicologists face squarely the elitism inherent in such attitudes and policies that a sociology of musical styles will become a serious possibility. Perhaps for this reason, a good starting point for a sociology of musical styles would be not only functional tonality, but the various forms of Afro-American music which have become such a vital force in modern-day society. These Afro-American forms would raise all the difficulties referred to in this paper, yet their comparative accessibility, as well as the comparative accessibility of the people who create and appreciate them, would make for easier assessment of solutions offered to those difficulties.

It is clear that if the sociological analysis of musical styles is to become an identifiable area of research, there needs to be co-operation on the part of musicologists and sociologists. No one person can be expected to grasp the fundamentals of both disciplines with adequate depth. Musicologists need the help of sociologists both in confronting the methodological issues referred to earlier, and in undertaking the analysis of social structures. Sociologists need the help of musicologists in understanding the genuine complexities of musical analysis. Barriers between the two disciplines need to be broken down. Sad to say, it is musicologists who have shown the greatest reticence in this area.

Notes

1 To make this statement is not to indicate a belief in a consensual society. The intellectual (by which is meant any person in a position to legitimate any form of knowledge) still centrally defines knowledge for his group, even if that knowledge conflicts with the knowledge of other groups, whether at the same or a lower or higher level in the overall hierarchic structure.

2 See Merriam (1964), pp. 241-2.

3 Although, of course, it should not be forgotten that the different realities exist because of the growth of a cultural elite traditionally associated with those who hold political and economic power in society. It is, therefore, rather hypocritical of this elite to criticise the cultural values of dispossessed groups, because it is ultimately through the growth of this elite that those values came into existence

in the first place. In short, an elite of necessity implies the existence of dispossessed groups.

4 See Shepherd *et al.* (1977), pp. 7-34.

5 See Shepherd *et al.* (1977), pp. 18-24.

6 An attempt at such substantiation has been made in Shepherd *et al.* (1977), pp. 71-111.

Bibliography

Douglas, Mary, *Purity and Danger* (Penguin Books, 1970).

Duncan, Hugh D., *Symbols in Society* (Oxford University Press, 1968).

Eliot, T.S., *Notes Towards the Definition of Culture* (Faber & Faber, 1948).

Gipps, Ruth, 'A personal credo', *Composer*, no. 54 (1975).

Gipps, Ruth, 'The use of trendy "amplified pop" in school music classes', *Journal of the Incorporated Society of Musicians* (1976).

Langer, Susanne, *Philosophy in a New Key* (Harvard University Press, 1960).

Leavis, F.R., *Education and the University* (Chatto & Windus, 1948).

Lévi-Strauss, C., *Structural Anthropology* (Penguin Books, 1968).

Lovell, Terry, 'Sociology of aesthetic structures and contextualism', *Sociology of Mass Communication* (Penguin Books, 1972).

Mâche, François-Bernard, 'Musical composition today', *Cultures*, I (1973).

Merriam, Alan P., *The Anthropology of Music* (Evanston, 1964).

Meyer, Leonard B., *Emotion and Meaning in Music* (University of Chicago Press, 1956).

Meyer, Leonard B., *Music, the Arts and Ideas* (University of Chicago Press, 1967).

Meyer, Leonard B., *Explaining Music*(University of California Press, 1973).

Pleasants, Henry, *Serious Music and All That Jazz* (Victor Gollancz, 1969).

Shepherd, John, Virden, Phil, Vulliamy, Graham and Wishart, Trevor, *Whose Music? A Sociology of Musical Languages* (Latimer New Dimensions, 1977).

Stearns, Marshall, *The Story of Jazz* (Oxford University Press, 1956).

Williams, Raymond, *Culture and Society 1780-1950* (Penguin Books, 1961).

Zuckerkandl, Victor, *Sound and Symbol: Music and the External World* (Routledge & Kegan Paul, 1956).

WORDS AND MUSIC

Why do songs have words?

Simon Frith

In 1918 the chairman of Chappell & Co., Britain's largest music publishing company, wrote a letter to the novelist Radclyffe Hall. She had complained of receiving no royalties after a song for which she had been the lyricist, 'The Blind Ploughman', 'swept the country.' William Davey replied,

> Dear Miss Radclyffe Hall,
>
> I yield to no one in my admiration of your words for 'The Blind Ploughman'. They are a big contributing factor to the success of the song. Unfortunately, we cannot afford to pay royalties to lyric writers. One or two other publishers may but if we were to once introduce the principle, there would be no end to it. Many lyrics are merely a repetition of the same words in a different order and almost always with the same ideas. Hardly any of them, frankly, are worth a royalty, although once in a way they may be. It is difficult to differentiate, however. What I do feel is that you are quite entitled to have an extra payment for these particular words, and I have much pleasure in enclosing you, from Messrs Chappell, a cheque for twenty guineas.[1]

Davey had commercial reasons for treating lyrics as formula writing, but his argument is common among academics too. In the 1950s and 1960s, for example, the tiny field of the sociology of popular music was dominated by analyses of song words. Sociologists concentrated on songs (rather than singers or audiences) because they could be studied with a familiar cultural research method, content analysis, and as they mostly lacked the ability to distinguish songs in musical terms, sociologists, by default, had to measure trends by reference to lyrics. It was through their words that hit records were taken to make their social mark.

The focus on lyrics didn't just reflect musical ignorance. Until the mid-1960s British and American popular music was dominated by Tin Pan Alley. Tin Pan Alley's values derived from its origins as a publishing centre and the 'bland, universal, well-made song' (Whitcomb's description) remained central to its organisation even after rock 'n' roll.[2] In concentrating on pop's lyrical themes in this period, sociologists were reflecting the way in which the songs were themselves packaged and sold. Most of these songs did, musically, sound the same; most lyrics did seem to follow measurable rules; most songwriters did operate as 'small businessmen engaged in composing, writing or publishing music' rather than as 'creative composers'.[3] Etzkorn, one of the few sociologists to research lyricists not lyrics, discovered in 1963 that

> The composing activity of songwriters would seem to be constrained by their orientation towards the expectations of significant 'judges' in executive positions in the music business whose critical standards are based on traditional musical clichés. In their endeavour to emulate the norms of successful reference groups, songwriters (even with a variety of backgrounds) will produce compositions virtually homogeneous in form and structure, thereby strengthening the formal rigidity of popular music.[4]

And this simply confirmed what analysts anyway took for granted – that it was possible to read back from lyrics to the social forces that produced them.

Content analysis

The first systematic analyst of pop song words, J.G. Peatman, was influenced by Adorno's strictures on 'radio music' and so stressed pop's lyrical standardisation: all successful pop songs were about romantic love; all could be classified under one of three headings – the 'happy in love' song, the 'frustrated in love' song, and the 'novelty song with sex interest'.[5]

For Peatman, this narrow range reflected the culture industry's success in keeping people buying the same thing, but most subsequent content analysts, writing with a Cold War concern to defend American commercial culture, have taken pop market choices seriously. Thus in 1954 Mooney accepted Peatman's starting point – pop as happy/sad love songs – but argued that they 'reflected, as love songs always do, the deepest currents of thought; for as values change, so change the ideas and practice of love'.[6]

Mooney's argument was that pop song lyrics reflect the emotional needs of their time. The history of the American 'mood' can thus be traced through the shifting themes of popular songs: from 1895 to 1925 song lyrics were 'abandoned and unorthodox' and reflected the patriotism, proletarianism and hedonism of the rising American empire; from the 1920s to the 1940s songs were 'negativistic and rather morbid' and reflected the disillusion, the quiet despair of the Depression; in the 1950s pop reflected a new zeal, as 'the mass mood' invested the post-war consumer boom with Cold War fervour; and, in a later article, Mooney continued his readings into the 1960s, putting stress on songs' importance as a record of new sexual mores.[7]

Mooney related changing images of sex to changes in the class origins of pop – in the 1930s songs expressed the middle-class attitudes of their middle-class authors, by the 1960s they expressed the freer mores of their working-class performers – but his general point is that songs can be read as examples of popular ideology. Tin Pan Alley, he suggested in 1954,

> has responded to and revealed the emotional shifts of its public: sheet music and phonograph records are among the few artefacts which afford insight into the inarticulate Americans of the twentieth century.[8]

'The people' in a mass society may no longer make their own music, but choosing which songs and records to buy is still a means of cultural expression. Hits meet a popular need and so pop lyrics have changed over the century, despite corporate control of their production.

Mooney's survey of American cultural history is unsystematic, and he seems to choose his songs to support his thesis rather than vice versa, but his 'reflection theory' of pop lyrics has been shared by most of the more scientific content analysts who followed up his work. American sociologists have used song words, in particular, to chart the rise of a youth culture, with new attitudes to love and sex and fun, and to document the differences between 1950s and 1960s romance. In both eras the love drama passed through four acts – search, happiness, break-up, isolation – but 1960s pop stressed hedonism, movement, freedom (not dependence), choice (not fate). Courtship no longer led to marriage (relationships had a natural history, died a natural death); happiness meant sexual happiness; love was no longer an 'elusive quarry' but a passing, to-be-seized opportunity.[9]

The theoretical assumption here is that the words of pop songs express general social attitudes, but such song readings depend, in practice, on prior accounts of youth and sexuality. Content analysts are not innocent readers, and there are obvious flaws in their method. For a start, they treat lyrics too simply. The words of all songs are given equal value; their meaning is taken to be transparent; no account is given of their actual performance or their musical setting. This enables us to code lyrics statistically, but it involves a questionable theoretical judgment: content codes refer to what the words describe – situations and states of mind – but not to how they describe, to their significance as language.

Even more problematically, these analysts tend to equate a song's popularity with public agreement with its message – the argument is that songs reflect the beliefs and values of their listeners. This is to ignore songs' ideological work, the way they play back to people situations or ideas they recognise but which are inflected now with particular moral lessons. The most sophisticated content analysts have, therefore, used lyrics as evidence not of popular culture as such, but of popular cultural confusion.[10] Songs, from this perspective, articulate the problems caused by social change, so that Di Maggio, Peterson and Esco, for example, analyse post-war Southern history by looking at the tensions revealed by country music lyrics since the 1950s: country love songs continued to take the ideal of romantic love for granted, but increasingly explored the argument that 'a battle between the sexes is inevitable'; country drink songs described alcohol as both a solution to and a cause of emotional problems; country work songs celebrated 'the strong self-reliant worker', while despairing at the effects of the factory routine – 'by day I make the cars/and by night I make the bars.' Country lyrics, in short, reflected contradictions, as old communal values were used to measure the quality of the lives of the urban working class. The authors conclude that songs 'reflect' their listeners' concerns at the level of fantasy – such reflection means, in fact, giving people *new* shapes, new symbolic forms for their hopes and anxieties.[11]

Mike Haralambos has treated the history of black American song in this period similarly. Blues lyrics, he suggests, were essentially passive, bitter, sorrowful and fatalistic; soul words concern activity, pride, optimism and change:

> Whereas blues concentrates almost entirely on experience, usually the experience of failure, soul songs state the ideal. Moral principles are laid down, rules of conduct advocated, right and wrong involved. Blues merely states this is the way it is, and this is how I am suffering. By comparison, soul music implies life is not to be accepted as it comes, hardship is not to be borne, but life is to be made worth living.[12]

Haralambos argues that soul represented a lyrical as well as a musical merging of blues and gospel, as the free-flowing language and imagery of the church were applied to the socially realistic narratives of the blues. The resulting songs both drew on and gave shape to the new mood and vocabulary of 1960s ghetto streets. In the words of disc jockey Job Cobb:

> 'We're Rolling On' and songs like that gave a lot of people, and even a lot of civil rights organisations, hope and great strength, and made people believe in it, because actually within the record itself, it was telling you like what to expect, and what happened thus far, so like hold your head up high and keep on going, your day will come.[13]

This interpretation of lyrics as a form of ideological expression – asserting ideas in order to shape them, describing situations in order to reach them – complicates the concept of 'reflection' (these songs reflect ideals as well as realities) but retains the assumption that popular songs are significant because they have a 'real closeness' with their consumers.[14] The implication, in short, is that such readings only make sense of 'folk' forms; only in country music, blues, soul, the right strands of rock, can we take lyrics to be the authentic expression of popular experiences and need. In the mainstream of mass music something else is going on.

Mass culture

Most mass cultural critiques of pop songs words derive from 1930s Leavisite arguments. Pop songs are criticised for their banality, their feebleness with words, imagery and emotion; the problem is not just that lyrics picture an unreal world, but also that pop ideals are trite: 'One and all these refer to the world where June rhymes with moon, where there is no such thing as struggle for existence, where love does not have to be striven for through understanding.'[15]

In *The Uses of Literacy*, Richard Hoggart argues, similarly, that real needs to dream are being satisfied by debilitatingly thin fantasies, concepts of well-being defined in terms of conformity. Mass culture has turned visions of the extraordinary into clichés of the ordinary, and pop song lyrics have been subordinated to the performing conventions of 'forced intimacy' – 'the singer is reaching millions but pretends he is reaching only "you".' Love, the dominant topic of pop songs is represented now as a solution to all problems, 'a warm burrow, a remover of worry; borne on an ingratiating treacle of melody, a vague sense of uplift-going-on'.[16]

For Leavisites, the evil of mass culture is that it corrupts real feelings. Wilfrid Mellers (*Scrutiny*'s original commentator on popular music) notes that pop songs 'do insidiously correspond with feelings we have all had in adolescence'.

> Though these songs do not deny that love will hurt, they seek a vicarious pleasure from the hurt itself. So they create an illusion that we can live on the surface of our emotions. Sincere, and true, and touching though they may be, their truth is partial.[17]

The critical task is, therefore, to discover 'the amount of "felt life" in specific words and music', and Mellers and Hoggart agree that pop songs should not be dismissed without a proper hearing. Other Leavisites have been less generous. Edward Lee, for example, denounces the romantic banality of pop lyrics in terms of its social effects (citing the divorce rate in his disdain for silly love songs) and this argument about the corrupting consequences of the hit parade has been taken up by Marxist critics in their accounts of pop's 'class function'.[18] Dave Harker, for instance, reads Tin Pan Alley lyrics as straightforward statements of bourgeois ideology. Take 'Winter Wonderland': 'In the meadow we can build a snowman/Then pretend he is Parson Brown/He'll say "Are you married?" We'll say "No man/But you can do the job when you're in town."' This song, writes Harker, 'articulates the key fantasies not only about the Christmas period but, crucially, about the pattern of sexual relations felt to be most appropriate for a particular social order.'[19]

Love and romance, the central pop themes, are the 'sentimental ideology' of capitalist society. Like Lee, Harker stresses the importance of pop romance for marriage – it is thus that songs work for the reproduction of social relations. Love lyrics do express 'popular' sexual attitudes, but these attitudes are mediated through the processes of cultural control. Harker makes this Leavisite comment on Elvis Presley's 'It's Now Or Never':

> Of course, the song was popular in a commercial context precisely because it did articulate certain key strands in the dominant ideology. The denial of female sexuality, the reduction of love to ejaculation, the inability to come out with emotion honestly, the habit of implying intercourse is a 'dirty little secret', the acceptability of emotional blackmail on the part of man, and so on, tell us a good deal about the paradigms of femininity in the late 1950s, *and* about the paradigms of masculinity, for all those men who had to try, presumably, to imitate Elvis Presley.[20]

Songs are, in this account, a form of propaganda. As Goddard, Pollock and Fudger put it, from a feminist perspective, 'lyrics constantly reflect and reinforce whatever ethos society currently considers desirable.'[21] They express dominant sexual ideologies through their recurrently exploitative images of women, their stereotypes of sexual subjugation, their treatment of femininity as at once 'mysterious' and 'dependent', and, above all, through their systematic denial of the material reality of sexual exploitation. As Germaine Greer once wrote,

> The supreme irony must be when the bored housewife whiles away her duller tasks, half-consciously intoning the otherwise very forgettable words of some pulp lovesong. How many of them stop to assess the real consequences of the fact that 'all who love are blind' or just how much they have to blame that 'something here inside' for? What songs do you sing, one wonders, when your heart is no longer on fire and smoke no longer mercifully blinds you to the banal realities of your situation? (But of course there are no songs for that.)[22]

Most critics of mass music assume that there are, nonetheless, alternatives to commercial pop. Hoggart, for example, praises pre-war pop songs by reference to their *genuineness*:

> They are vulgar, it is true, but not usually tinselly. They deal only with large emotional situations; they tend to be open-hearted and big-bosomed. The moral attitudes behind them are not mean or calculated or 'wide'; they still just touch hands with an older and more handsome culture. They are not cynical or neurotic; they often indulge their emotions, but are not ashamed of showing emotion, and do not seek to be sophisticatedly smart.[23]

Harker praises the 'muscular compactness' of Bob Dylan's language, and makes a telling comparison of the Beatles' 'She Loves You' and Dylan's thematically similar 'It Ain't Me Babe':

> The Beatles' song drips with adolescent sentiment. It is structured around the person of a go-between, and cheerfully reinforces the preferred mode of courtship in a capitalist society, using guilt-invoking mindlessness ('you know you should be glad', 'you know that can't be bad'), and generally relying on emotional blackmail at the shallowest of levels. To their inane 'Yeh, yeh, yeh' Dylan counterposed a full-throated 'No, no, no'. Instead of their emotional tinkering and patching up, Dylan insists on breaking the conventions of bourgeois courtship, refusing to accept anything less than full-hearted love. Instead of their magic 'solution', he reminded us that it's sometimes better to call it a day. While they denied individuality he celebrated it – even in those forms with which he could not agree. While they underwrote the surface chatter of socially acceptable but emotionally stifling forms of interpersonal behaviour, Dylan raises a wry pair of fingers at the conventions, *not* at the woman.[24]

For Harker, 'authentic' lyrics express 'authentic' relationships, and expose bourgeois conventions with an honest vital language – a language which reflects experience directly and is not ideologically mediated. A similarly argument underpinned Hayakawa's classic 1955 critique of American pop songs. He analysed lyrics in terms of

> the IFD disease – the triple-threat semantic disorder of Idealisation (the making of impossible and ideal demands upon life), which leads to Frustration (as the result of the demands

> not being met), which in turn leads to Demoralisation (or Disorganisation or Despair).[25]

Hayakawa compared pop lyrics with blues lyrics, in which there was no 'chasing rainbows', no search for the ideal partner, no belief in love as magic, but an exploration of all the problems of sex and romance, 'a considerable tough-mindedness', and 'a willingness to acknowledge the facts of life'. Francis Newton wrote in parallel terms about the corruption of blues lyrics by pop publishers in what he called the 'mincing process'.

> Essentially it consists of a rigid restriction of themes which excludes the controversial, the uncomfortable, or unfamiliar, and above all the exclusion of reality. For the main industrial innovation of the pop-music business is the discovery that the day dream, or the sentimental memory (which is the day dream reversed) is the single most saleable commodity.[26]

In the 1960s this process was reversed as young musicians and audiences rejected Tin Pan Alley for rhythm 'n' blues – pop's vapidity was replaced by blues 'realism'. The function of rock lyrics became the exposure of false ideology so that, for Harker, Bob Dylan's lyrics ceased to matter (and Dylan himself 'sold out') when they ceased to be true, when (with the release of *John Wesley Harding*) they began to 'sentimentalise the family, legalised sex and the home, in ways wholly supportive of the dominant ideology'. The implication here – an implication embedded deep in rock criticism – is that all songs have to be measured against the principles of lyrical realism. The problem for Dylan and the other 1960s rock stars arose when they began to make music according to the logic of commercial entertainment, for, as Eisler had put it, entertainment music

> expresses a mendacious optimism that is absolutely unjustified, a flat pseudo-humanity, something like 'Aren't we all?' a stuffy petit-bourgeois eroticism to put you off. Feeling is replaced by sentimentality, strength by bombast, humour by what I would call silliness. It is stupid to the highest degree.[27]

Realism

At its simplest, the theory of lyrical realism means asserting a direct relationship between a lyric and the social or emotional condition it describes and represents. Folk song studies, for example, work with a historical version of reflection theory: they assume that folk songs are a historical record of popular consciousness. Thus Roy Palmer describes orally transmitted folk songs as 'the real voice of the people who lived in the past', and folk ballads as 'a means of self-expression; this was an art form truly in the idiom of the people'. With the development of industrial capitalism, according to A.L. Lloyd, 'the song-proper becomes the most characteristic lyrical form through which the common people express their fantasies, their codes, their aspirations', and folk realism was not just a matter of accurate description and convincing narrative. Songs were about hopes as well as facts.

> Generally the folk song makers chose to express their longing by transposing the world on to an imaginative plane, not trying to escape from it, but colouring it with fantasy, turning bitter, even brutal facts of life into something beautiful, tragic, honourable, so that when singer and listeners return to reality at the end of the song, the environment is not changed but they are better fitted to grapple with it.[28]

The question is: how does folk 'consolation' differ from pop 'escapism'? The answer lies in the modes of production involved: folk songs were authentic fantasies because they sprang from the people themselves; they weren't commodities. If certain folk images and phrases recur ('lyrical floaters', Lloyd calls them) these are not clichés (like the equivalent floaters in pop songs) but mark, rather, the anonymous, spontaneous, communal process in which folk songs are made. Lloyd continually contrasts the 'reality and truth' of folk lyrics with the 'banal stereotype of lower-class life and limited range of sickly bourgeois fantasies that the by-now powerful entertainment industry offers its audiences to suck on like a sugared rubber teat', but such comparisons rest almost exclusively on an argument about production.[29]

The problem of this 'sentimental socialist-realist' argument is its circularity: folk 'authenticity' is rooted in folk songs' 'real' origins, but we recognise these origins by the songs' authenticity and, in practice, the assessment of a song's realism is an assessment of its use of assumed *conventions* of realism. Folk song collections are folk song selections, and, to be chosen as authentic, songs have to meet literary or political criteria – authenticity lies in a particular use of language, a particular treatment of narrative and imagery a particular ideological position. The problem, then, is not whether folk songs *did* reflect real social conditions, but why some such reflections are taken by collectors to be authentic, some not. Whose ideology is reflected in such definitions of folk 'realism'?[30]

Authenticity is a political problem, and the history of folk music is a history of the struggle among folk collectors to claim folk meanings for themselves, as folk songs are examined for their 'true working-class views', for their expressions of 'organic community', for their signs of nationalism. For a Marxist like Dave Harker, some 'folk' songs are inauthentic because they obviously (from their use of language) weren't written or transmitted by working-class people themselves; others are judged inauthentic because of their ideological content, their use not of bourgeois language but of bourgeois ideas. Left-wing intellectuals can write authentic working-class songs (though not working-class themselves) as long as they represent the *real* reality of the working class – Alex Glasgow, for example, penetrates 'the elements of bourgeois ideology which have penetrated working-class culture'.[31]

This argument challenges the usual measure of folk realism, its relationship to common sense, and raises a crucial question: is lyrical realism a matter of accurate surface description or does it mean getting behind appearances, challenging given cultural forms? Taylor and Laing argue that 'cultural production occurs always in relation to ideology and not to the "real world"', and I want to examine the implications of this by looking at the blues.[32]

The original blues analysts assumed, like folk theorists generally, that the blues could be read as the direct account of their singers' and listeners' lives. Paul Oliver, for example, treated blues lyrics as a form of social history. The blues reflected American social conditions and personal responses to those conditions. They gave 'a glimpse of what it must mean to be one among the many rejected; homeless migrants – to be one single unit in the impersonal statistics that represent millions of rootless men and women.'[33]

Charles Keil read post-war urban blues lyrics similarly, as the direct expression of their singers' attempts to handle conditions in the new urban ghettos. He suggested that

> a more detailed analysis of blues lyrics might make it possible to describe with greater insight the changes in male roles within

> the Negro community as defined by Negroes at various levels of socio-economic status and mobility within the lower class. Certainly, the lyric content of city, urban and soul blues also reflects varying sorts of adjustment to urban conditions generally. A thorough analysis of a large body of blues lyrics from the various genres would help to clarify these patterns of adjustment and the attitudinal sets that accompany those patterns.[34]

The blues, according to Oliver, was 'a genuine form of expression revealing America's gaunt structure without a decorative facade'. In its treatment of love and sex the blues was 'forthright and uncompromising. There is no concealment and no use of oblique references.' Blues were expressed in realistic words, uninhibited words, words which were 'a natural transposition of the everyday language of both users and hearers'. Even blues' fancy terms, its rich store of imagery, were derived from everyday life – the blues was a 'tough poetry', a 'rough poetry'. In the words of Francis Newton, blues songs are not poetic 'because the singer wants to express himself or herself in a poetic manner', but because 'he or she wants to say what has to be said as best it can'. The poetic effects 'arise naturally out of the repetitive pattern of ordinary popular speech.'[35]

Linton Kwesi Johnson makes similar points about Jamaican lyrics. Jamaican music, he writes,

> is the *spiritual expression* of the *historical experience* of the Afro-Jamaican. In making the music, the musicians themselves enter a common stream of consciousness, and what they create is an invitation to the listeners to be entered into that consciousness – which is also the consciousness of their people. The feel of the music is the feel of their common history, the burden of their history; their suffering and their woe; their endurance and their strength, their poverty and their pain.[36]

Johnson stresses the spiritual aspects of this process – 'through music, dreams are unveiled, souls exorcised, tensions canalized, strength realised', and notes the way in which shared religious metaphors of hope and damnation enable Jamaican lyricists to intensify their political comment. (Rastafarian songs draw on the store of religio-political imagery accumulated by black American spirituals – 'Babylon' as a symbol of slavery and white oppression, for example.)[37]

Black songs don't just describe an experience, but symbolise and thus politicise it. For Newton, the lyrical world of the blues was 'tragic and helpless' – 'its fundamental assumption is that men and women live life as it comes; or if they cannot stand that they must die.' Johnson, by contrast, argues that in Jamaican music, 'Consciously setting out to transform the consciousness of the sufferer, to politicise him culturally through music, song and poetry, the lyricist contributes to the continuing struggle of the oppressed.'[38]

We're back to the original question in a new form: does 'realism' mean an acceptance of one's lot or a struggle against it, the imagination of alternatives? And there is a new question too. If blues lyrics express the suffering of an oppressed people, express them realistically, why do we enjoy them? In the words of Paul Garon, 'how is it that we gain definite pleasure by identifying with the singers' *sadness*?'[39]

Garon suggests that the blues, like all poetry, gives pleasure 'through its use of images, convulsive images, images of the fantastic and the marvellous, images of *desire*'. Blues power comes from its 'fantastic' not its 'realistic' elements. What makes a blues song poetic is not its description 'without facade', but the game it plays with language itself. Take a simple erotic blues like 'You Can't Sleep In My Bed':

> You're too big to be cute, and I don't think you're clean,
> You're the damnest looking thing that I have ever seen.
>
> What you got in mind ain't gonna happen today
> Get off my bed, how in the world did you get that way?
>
> (Mary Dixon, 'You Can't Sleep In My Bed')

The point of this song is not its acceptance of the 'non-ideal' sexuality of real life, but its humour – the humour of its tone of voice, its descriptive terms – and humour involves not just the acceptance of reality, but also its mockery. Humour is a form of *refusal*. The blues singer, in short, 'functions as a poet through his or her refusal to accept the degradation of daily life.' In Bessie Smith's 'Empty Bed Blues', to give another example, her emotional plight is described 'realistically', but this description is invigorated, made pleasurable, by the fanciful pursuit of a sexual language:

> Bought me a coffee grinder,
> The best one I could find.
> Bought me a coffee grinder,
> The best one I could find.
> Oh, he could grind my coffee,
> 'Cause he had a brand-new grind.
>
> He's a deep, deep diver,
> With a stroke that can't go wrong.
> He's a deep, deep diver,
> With a stroke that can't go wrong.
> Oh, he can touch the bottom,
> And his wind holds out so long.
>
> He boiled first my cabbage,
> And he made it awful hot.
> He boiled first my cabbage,
> And he made it awful hot.
> When he put in the bacon,
> It overflowed the pot.
>
> (Bessie Smith, 'Empty Bed Blues')

Refusal doesn't have to be expressed in political, ideological or even collective terms and, indeed, for Garon, individualism is the essence of blues poetry: 'the essence of the blues is not to be found in the daily life with which it deals, but in the way such life is critically focused on and imaginatively transformed.' Blues lyrics work not as spontaneous expression and natural language but through individual imaginations. Garon attacks the argument that 'it is only through "realism" ("socialist" or otherwise) that human desires find their most exalted expression'. The blues is poetry, rather, in so far as it is *not* simply documentary, 'for it is poetry that seeks to illuminate and realise the desires of all men and women.'[40]

Ames had earlier argued that

> regardless of the attitudes of any individual singer, the objective social necessity of American Negro songs over a period of time was to create forms, patterns, habits and styles which would conceal the singer. Perhaps the commonest technique of

> concealment has been to disguise meaning in some kind of fantastic, symbolical or nonsensical clothing.[41]

Irony, rather than direct description, is the essence of blues realism, and Garon suggests that the techniques involved give blues lyricists their poetic potential, their ability to 'eroticise everyday life', to use language itself to shock and shake the dominant discourse:

> New modes of poetic action, new networks of analogy, new possibilities of expression all help formulate the nature of the supersession of reality, the transformation of everyday life as it encumbers us today, the unfolding and eventual triumph of the marvellous.[42]

Ian Hoare makes a related point about soul songs. The soul singer, like the blues singer, expresses 'personal feelings in a very public manner, stating the problems and drawing the audience together in a recognition that these problems are in many ways shared', and soul is, again, a form of realism – 'the grassroots strength of soul love lyrics lies partly in the fact that the most indulgent pledges of devotion are characteristically accompanied by a resilient sexual and economic realism.' But Hoare goes on to suggest that soul lyricists' 'realism' is simply a frame for their use of pop's romantic conventions – 'the containment of the other-worldly in the worldly is close to the essence of the soul tradition.' Soul songs are not simple statements – life is like *this* – but involve a commentary on the terms of pop romanticism itself.[43] A song like the Temptations' 'Papa Was A Rollin' Stone' gets its punch (and its pleasure) from its punning use of language rather than from its descriptive truth:

> Papa was a rollin' stone,
> Wherever he lay his hat was his home,
> And when he died,
> All he left us was
> Alone.
>
> (The Temptations, 'Papa Was A Rollin' Stone')

One of Britain's first jazz critics, Iain Lang, threw away the remark in 1943 that 'there is much material in the blues for a Cambridge connoisseur of poetic ambiguity', and his point was that it was precisely blues realism, its use of everyday black talk, that made it so poetically interesting – the blues is popular music's most literary form, contains the most sophisticated explorations of the rhythmic, metaphoric and playful possibilities of language itself. And blues singers' use of the vernacular doesn't make them simply vehicles for some sort of spontaneous collective composition – if the blues are a form of poetry, then blues writers are poets, self-conscious, individual, more or less gifted in their uses of words.[44]

There's a tension in jazz criticism, then, between theorists who root blues power in the general, diffuse social realism of black popular culture, and critics who search out individual writers for particular praise or blame. It is a tension which has re-emerged, more recently, in white critical commentaries on 'rap', the contemporary Afro-American use of the rhythms of street-corner gossip, threat and argument. Rap is rooted in a long history of jousting talk, formalised in a variety of names – 'signification', the Dozens, the Toast, the Jones.[45] These are rituals of name calling, boasting and insult, in which rhyme, beat and vocal inflection carry as much meaning as the words themselves, and the irony is that while the participants are clearly engaged in individual competition – some people are simply better at the Dozens than others – white fans admire rap as a spontaneous, 'natural' black youth form. Unless acts claim specifically to *be* poets (like some Jamaican dub performers or a relatively arty New York act like the Last Poets) they are not heard to write poetry, and rock fans have always gone along with the idea that 'naturally' realistic forms (folk, blues, soul, rap) have to be distinguished from 'art' forms, which are 'original', elaborate, and rooted in personal vision and control.[46]

From the start, rock's claim to a superior pop status rested on the argument that rock songwriters (unlike the Brill Building hacks and folk and blues circuit 'primitives') were, indeed, poets. Beginning with Richard Goldstein's *The Poetry of Rock* in 1969, there has been a slew of pompous rock anthologies, and while Goldstein had the grace to include rock 'n' roll writers like Chuck Berry and Leiber/Stoller, subsequent anthologists have been quite clear that 1960s rock lyrics represented something qualitatively remarkable in pop history:

> Despite the fertile sources on which rock music of the 1950s drew, it was musically innovative and vibrant but lyrically almost unrelievedly banal and trivial. If it contained any poetry at all, that poetry was pedestrian doggerel full of unrefined

> slang and trite neoromantic convention. But in the early 1960s there burst upon the scene a number of exceptionally talented artists, perhaps even poets, who managed to bring together in various degrees all the many elements of what we now call rock and to make something of quality.[47]

What is most striking about anthologies of rock poetry, though, is their consensus – no black songs, no country music, no Lou Reed even. Rock 'poets' are recognised by a particular sort of self-consciousness; their status rests not on their approach to words but on the types of word they use; rock poetry is a matter of planting poetic clues. Ian Hoare compares the Four Tops' 'Reach Out I'll Be There' and Bob Dylan's 'Queen Jane Approximately'. The Four Tops sang:

> When you feel hurt and about to give up
> 'Cause your best just ain't good enough . . .
> . . . Reach out, I'll be there.
> (The Four Tops, 'Reach Out I'll Be There')

Dylan sang:

> When all of your advisers heave their plastic
> At your feet to convince you of your pain . . .
> . . . Won't you come see me, Queen Jane?
> (Bob Dylan, 'Queen Jane Approximately')

Dylan is the poet because his images are personal and obscure rather than direct or commonplace – his words are not plain, and the rock singer/songwriters who emerged from folk clubs in the 1960s followed his seminal example, drawing words from classic balladry, from the beat poets, from 150 years of Bohemian romantic verse.[48]

Rock 'poetry' opened up possibilities of lyrical banality of which Tin Pan Alley had never even dreamt, but for observing academics it seemed to suggest a new pop seriousness – 'the jingles and vapid love lyrics' had evolved into a genuinely 'mystical vision'.[49] This was to suggest a new criterion of lyrical realism – truth-to-personal-experience or truth-to-feeling, a truth measured by the private use of words, the self-conscious use of language. And truth-to-feeling became a measure of the listener too. 'True songs', wrote *Rolling Stone* record editor Paul Nelson, are 'songs that hit me straight in the heart'. Nelson quotes the opening stanza of Jackson Browne's 'Farther On':

> In my early years I hid my tears
> And passed my days alone,
> Adrift on an ocean of loneliness
> My dreams like nets were thrown,
> To catch the love that I'd heard of
> In books and films and songs,
> Now there's a world of illusion and fantasy
> In the place where the real world belongs.
>
> (Jackson Browne, 'Farther On')

This song of illusion and disillusion illustrates numerous singer/songwriter techniques – Browne uses 'poetic' terms like 'adrift', an extended self-consciously literary metaphor, the 'ocean of loneliness', and an intimate mode of address – but for Nelson the point of the song is not its technique but its effect. Alan Lomax had once written that the 'authentic' folk singer had to 'experience the feelings that lie behind his art'. For Nelson the good rock singer made the listener experience those feelings too. He treasured the Jackson Browne song because 'when I first heard it I was absolutely unable to put any space between myself and someone else's childhood'.[50]

Making meaning

All comparisons of lyrical realism and lyrical banality assume that songs differ in their effects – effects which can be read off good and bad words. For mass culture critics, as we've seen, the problem of pop is that fans treat *all* songs as if they were real and have a false view of life accordingly. Pop lyricists themselves have always found this suggestion bemusing. Ira Gershwin, for example, made his own mocking reply to his critics:

> 'Every night I dream a little dream,/And of course Prince Charming is the theme . . . .' One is warned that this sort of romantic whimwham builds up 'an enormous amount of unrealistic idealisation – the creation in one's mind, as the object of love's search, of a dream girl (or dream boy) the fleshly counterpart of which never existed on earth'. Sooner or later, unhappily, the girl chances on a Mr Right who, in turn, is

> certain she is Miss Inevitable; and, both being under the influence of 'My Heart Stood Still' (which even advocates love at first sight) they are quickly in each other's arms, taxiing to City Hall for a marriage license. On the way he sings 'Blue Room' to her – she 'My Blue Heaven' to him. But, alas, this enchanted twosome is wholly unaware of the costs of rent, furniture, food, dentist, doctor, diaper service, and other necessities. There is no indication in the vocalising 'that, having found the dream-girl or dream-man, one's problems are just beginning'. It naturally follows that soon the marriage won't work out, when 'disenchantment, frustration' and 'self-pity' set in. Shortly after, they buy paper dolls, not for each other, but ones they can call their own. This comfort is, however, temporary. Subsequently, he, helpless, is in the gutters of Skid Row; she, hopeless, in a mental institution.[51]

Back in 1950 David Riesman had argued that 'the same or virtually the same popular culture materials are used by audiences in radically different ways and for radically different purposes'. Riesman accepted the critics' description of pop's lyrical message ('a picture of adolescence in America as a happy-go-lucky time of haphazard behaviour, jitterbug parlance, coke-bar sprees, and "blues" that are not really blue') but distinguished between the majority of pop fans, who took the message for granted but didn't listen to it, and a minority of 'rebels', who heard the message but rejected it.[52]

Subsequent empirical research has confirmed Riesman's scepticism about the importance of song words, and by the end of the 1960s Norman Denzin was arguing that pop audiences only listened to the beat and melody, the *sound* of a record, anyway – the 'meaning of pop' was the sense listeners made of songs for themselves; it could not be read off lyrics as an objective 'social fact'.[53]

This argument was the norm for the sociology of pop and rock in the 1970s. Frith, for example, ignored lyrical analysis altogether and simply assumed that the meaning of music could be deduced from its users' characteristics. In the USA empirical audience studies measured pop fans' responses to the words of their favourite songs quantitatively. Robinson and Hirsch concluded from a survey of Michigan high school students that 'the vast majority of teenage listeners are unaware of what the lyrics of hit protest songs are about', and a follow-up survey of college students suggested that the 'effectiveness' of song messages was limited: the majority of listeners had neither noticed nor understood the words of 'Eve of Destruction' or 'The Universal Soldier', and the minority who did follow the words weren't convinced by them.[54]

The implication of this sort of research (which continues to fill the pages of *Popular Music and Society*) is that changes in lyrical content cannot be explained by reference to consumer 'moods', and American sociologists have turned for explanations instead to changing modes of lyrical production, to what's happening in the record industry, the source of the songs. Paul Hirsch, for example, argues that during the period 1940 to 1970 song performers gained control of their material while the music industry's censors lost it, and Peterson and Berger extend this analysis (looking at 'the manufacture of lyrics' since 1750!), concluding that 'the outspoken rock lyric of the 1960s (and the counter-culture it animated) were largely unintended byproducts of earlier mundane changes in technology, industry structure and marketing'. In the rock era airwaves and studios had been opened to competition, and

> the proliferation of companies competing for audience attention together with the broadening range of radio programming formats of the 1950s reversed the process which had created the Tin Pan Alley formula tune in the previous era of oligopoly. With competition, there was a search for lyrics that would be ever more daring in exposing the old taboo topics of sex, race, drugs, social class, political commentary, and alternatives to middle-class standards generally.[55]

The changing music did change the audience too ('by gradually creating a self-conscious teen generation') but the general point is that 'the amount of diversity of sentiments in popular music lyrics correlates directly with the number of independent units producing songs', and more recent research has shown how a tightening of corporate control (in the country music industry) leads to a narrowing range of song forms.[56]

In this account of pop the banality of Tin Pan Alley words is taken for granted and explained in terms of the organisation of their production, but pop is defended from charges of corruption on the grounds that nobody listens to the words anyway. This became one way in which 'authentic' rock was distinguished from its commercial, degenerate versions – real rock lyrics matter because they can be treated as poetry or politics, involve social commentary or truth-to-feeling; bad rock words are just drivel. What most interests me about this position, though, are the questions it begs. Mainstream, commercial pop lyrics – silly love songs – may not 'matter' to their listeners like the best rock words do, but they're not therefore insignificant. Popular music is a song form; words are a reason why people buy records; instrumental hits remain unusual – to paraphrase Marilyn Monroe in *Seven Year Itch*, you can always tell classical music: 'it's got no vocals!' People may not listen to most pop songs as 'messages' (the way they're presented in all that American empirical research) and the average pop lyric may have none of the qualities of rock realism or poetry, but the biggest-selling music magazine in Britain by far is still *Smash Hits*, a picture paper organised around the words of the latest chart entries, and so the question remains: why and how do song words (banal words, unreal words, routine words) work?

The poetry of pop

In songs, words are the sign of a voice. A song is always a performance and song words are always spoken out, heard in someone's accent. Songs are more like plays than poems; song words work as speech and speech acts, bearing meaning not just semantically, but also as structures of sound that are direct signs of emotion and marks of character. Singers use non-verbal as well as verbal devices to make their points – emphases, sighs, hesitations, changes of tone; lyrics involve pleas, sneers and commands as well as statements and messages and stories (which is why singers like the Beatles and Bob Dylan in Europe in the 1960s would have profound significance for listeners who didn't understand a word they were singing).[57]

I don't have the space here to describe how these techniques work in particular songs but from the work that has been done it is possible to draw some general conclusions.[58] First, *in analysing song words we must refer to performing conventions which are used to construct our sense of both their singers and ourselves, as listeners.* It's not just what they sing, but the way they sing it that determines what a singer means to us and how we are placed, as an audience, in relationship to them. Take, as an example, the way sexual identities are defined in pop songs. All pop singers, male and female, have to express emotion. Their task is to make public performance a private revelation. Singers can do this because the voice is an apparently transparent reflection of feeling: it is the sound of the voice, not the words sung, which suggests what a singer *really* means. In fact, there's nothing natural about the singing voice at all (compare the popular vocal sounds of Britain and Italy, say, or the USA and Iran), and so the conventions of male and female pop singing are different, reflect general assumptions about the differences between women and men.

The female voice in Anglo-American pop has usually stood for intimacy and artlessness – this is the link which has given women access to pop (they have been excluded from most other productive roles). We hear women as better able than men to articulate emotion because femininity is defined in emotional terms. The public world is masculine and there is no agreement about how public, unemotional women should sound (which is why the tone of Margaret Thatcher's voice keeps changing). By the same token, the intimate male voice is unmasculine, unnatural. In pop this is registered by the recurrent use of the falsetto, by the high-pitched, strained vocal that has been a feature of mainstream rock singing from Yes to the Police.

The conventions of female pop singing have both reflected and shaped the idea of femininity as something decorative and wistful secret and available, addressed, by its very nature, at men. The voice is so intimately connected with the person that sound and image cannot be separated in this respect. As a man, I've always taken it for granted that rock performances address male desires, reflect male fantasies in their connections of music and dance and sexuality. The first time I saw a women's band perform for women I was made physically uneasy by the sense of exclusion, became suddenly aware how popular music works as a social event. Its cultural (and commercial) purpose is to put together an audience, to construct a sense of 'us' and 'them'. Such pop consciousness depends primarily on the use of voices to express the identity at issue.

In raising questions of identity and audience I am, implicitly, raising questions of genre – different people use different musics to experience (or fantasise) different sorts of community; different pop forms (disco, punk, country, rock, etc.) engage their listeners in different narratives of desire – compare, for example, the different uses of male/female duets in soul and country music: the former use the voices to intensify feeling, the latter to flatten it. In soul music realism is marked by singers' inarticulacy – they are overcome by their feelings – and so duets, the interplay of male and female sounds, add a further erotic charge to a love song. In country music realism is marked by singers' small talk – the recognition of everyday life – and so duets, domestic conversations, are used to add further credibility to the idea that we're eavesdropping on real life (an effect heightened when, as is often the case, the couples *are* lovers/married/divorced).

The immediate critical task for the sociology of popular music is systematic genre analysis[59] – how do words and voices work differently for different types of pop and audience? – but there is a second general point to make about all pop songs: *they work on ordinary language*. What interests me here is not what's meant by 'ordinary' (as different genres draw on different communal terms and images and codes) but what's meant by 'work'. Songs aren't just any old speech act – by putting words to music, songwriters give them a new sort of resonance and power. Lyrics, as Langdon Winner once put it, can 'set words and the world spinning in a perpetual dance'.[60]

'In the best of songs,' according to Christopher Ricks, 'there is something which is partly about what it is to write a song, without in any way doing away with the fact that it is about things other than the song.' Sociologists of pop have been so concerned with these 'other things' – lyrical content, truth and realism – that they have neglected to analyse the ways in which songs are about themselves, about language. Tin Pan Alley songs are customarily dismissed as art (in those anthologies of rock poetry, for example), but they have their own literary importance. Bernard Bergonzi describes the resonance that pop lyrics had for writers in the 1930s, for example. W.H. Auden, Louis McNeice and Graham Greene all wrote and used such songs for their own purposes. Brecht was similarly concerned to draw on 'the directness of popular songs', and for him the appeal of pop lyrics lay in their ability to open up language – Brecht used the rhymes and rhythms of popular clichés to say significant things *and* to expose the commonsense phrases in which such things are usually said. As David Lodge writes of slang generally,

> Slang is the poetry of ordinary speech in a precise linguistic sense; it draws attention to itself *qua* language, by deviating from accepted linguistic norms, substituting figurative expressions for literal ones, and thus 'defamiliarises' the concept it signifies.[61]

'What could a popular song be which scorned or snubbed cliché?' asks Ricks, and Clive James, another literary pop critic, answers that the best lyricists are bound to celebrate common speech. The Beatles' genius, for example, was that they 'could take a well-worn phrase and make it new again'. They could spot the 'pressure points' of language, 'the syllables that locked a phrase up and were begging to be prodded'.

> The sudden shift of weight to an unexpected place continually brought the listener's attention to the language itself, engendering a startled awareness of the essentially poetic nature of flat phrases he'd been living with for years.[62]

The songwriter's art, suggests James, is to hear 'the spoken language as a poem', to cherish words 'not for their sense alone but for their poise and balance', and this is a matter of rhythm too – the rhythm of speech. If, in many pop songs, the regularity of the beat seems to reduce the lyrics to doggerel, on the other hand, as Roy Fuller puts it, music can 'discover subtleties in the most commonplace of words'. Fuller gives the example of George Gershwin's setting of the line, 'how long has this been going on?'

> When he has to set that, a line of regular iambic tetrameter, surely he sees how banal it would be to emphasise the word 'this' as the underlying stress pattern of the words requires:
> 'Hŏw lóng hăs thís bĕen góiňg ón?'
> What he does is to give the line three beats only – on 'long', the first syllable of 'going' and on 'on'. The three middle words, including the word 'this', are unaccented, giving the effect of a little skip in the middle of the line –
> 'Hŏw lonǵ hăs thĭs beĕn góiňg ón?'
> It is the action itself and the action's duration that Gershwin brings out, and how right it seems when he does it.[63]

Last words

In his study of Buddy Holly, Dave Laing suggests that pop and rock critics need a musical equivalent of the film critics' distinction between *auteurs* and *metteurs en scene*:

> The musical equivalent of the *metteur en scene* is the performer who regards a song as an actor does his part – as something to

> be expressed, something to get across. His aim is to render the lyric faithfully. The vocal style of the singer is determined almost entirely by the emotional connotations of the words. The approach of the rock *auteur* however, is determined not by the unique features of the song but by his personal style, the ensemble of vocal effects that characterise the whole body of his work.[64]

Ever since rock distinguished itself from pop in the late 1960s, *auteurs* have been regarded as superior to *metteurs* and lyrics have been analysed in terms of *auteur* theory. But Laing's point is that the appeal of rock *auteurs* is that their meaning is *not* organised around their words. The appeal of Buddy Holly's music, for example, 'does not lie in what he says, in the situations his songs portray, but in the exceptional nature of his singing style and its instrumental accompaniment.' My conclusion from this is that song words matter most, as words, when they are *not* part of an *auteur*-ial unity, when they are still open to interpretation – not just by their singers, but by their listeners too. Billie Holiday, the greatest *metteur* Tin Pan Alley pop had, wrote:

> Young kids always ask me what my style derived from and how it evolved and all that. What can I tell them? If you find a tune and it's got something to do with you, you don't have to evolve anything. You just feel it, and when you sing it other people feel something too.[65]

The pleasure of pop is that we can 'feel' tunes, perform them, in imagination, for ourselves. In a culture in which few people make music but everyone makes conversation, access to songs is primarily through their words. If music gives lyrics their linguistic vitality, lyrics give songs their social *use*.

This was, indeed, the conclusion that Donald Horton reached from his original content analysis of the lyrical drama of courtship. 'The popular song,' he wrote, 'provides a conventional language for use in dating.' The 'dialectic' of love involved in pop songs – the conversational tone, the appeal from one partner to another – was precisely what made them useful for couples negotiating their own path through the stages of a relationship. Most people lacked skill in 'the verbal expression of profound feelings' and so a public, impersonal love poetry was 'a useful – indeed a necessary alternative'. The singer became a 'mutual messenger' for young lovers, and pop songs were about emotional possibilities. The singer functioned 'in dramatising these songs to show the appropriate gestures, tone of voice, emotional expression – in short the stage directions for transforming mere verse into personal expression'.[66]

Pop love songs don't 'reflect' emotions, then, but give people the romantic terms in which to articulate and so experience their emotions. Elvis Costello once suggested that

> Most people are confused regarding their identities, or how they feel, particularly about love. They're confused because they're not given a voice, they don't have many songs written for or about them. On the one hand there's 'I love you, the sky is blue,' or total desolation, and in between there's a lack of anything. And it's never that clear-cut. There's a dishonesty in so much pop – written, possibly with an honest intent – all that starry stuff. I believe I fulfill the role of writing songs that aren't starry eyed all the time.[67]

Pop song lyrics have been criticised in these terms since the 1920s; they've been condemned for their romantic fictions, their 'exclusion of reality'. But that doesn't mean that we must, like the mass culture critics, listen to pop songs as if they were sociology. Costello's point is that what is at issue is fantasy – the problem of romantic ideology is not that it is false to life, but that it is the truth against which most people measure their desires. We need still to heed, therefore, the words of Marcel Proust:

> Pour out your curses on bad music, but not your contempt! The more bad music is played or sung, the more it is filled with tears, with human tears. It has a place low down in the history of art, but high up in the history of the emotions of the human community. Respect for ill music is not in itself a form of charity, it is much more the awareness of the social role of music. The people always have the same messengers and bearers of bad tidings in times of calamity and radiant happiness – bad musicians . . . . A book of poor melodies, dog-eared from much use, should touch us like a town or a tomb. What does it matter that the houses have no style, or that the gravestones disappear beneath stupid inscriptions?[68]

Notes

1 Lovat Dickson: *Radclyffe Hall at the Well of Loneliness*, Collins, London, 1975, pp. 45–6.
2 See Ian Whitcomb: *After the Ball*, Penguin, Harmondsworth, 1972, and Charlie Gillett: *The Sound of the City*, Souvenir Press, London, 1971.
3 Terms used by an American congressional Committee on song publishing, cited in K. Peter Etzkorn: 'On esthetic standards and reference groups of popular songwriters', *Sociological Inquiry*, vol. 36, no. 1, 1966, pp. 39–47.
4 K. Peter Etzkorn: 'Social context of songwriters in the United States', *Ethnomusicology*, vol. VII, no. 2, 1963, pp. 103–4.
5 J.G. Peatman: 'Radio and popular music', in P.F. Lazersfeld and F. Stanton (eds): *Radio Research*, Duell, Sloan & Pearce, New York, 1942–3.
6 H.F. Mooney: 'Song, singers and society, 1890–1954', *American Quarterly*, vol. 6, 1954, p. 226.
7 H.F. Mooney: 'Popular music since the 1920s', *American Quarterly*, vol. 20, 1968.
8 Mooney, op. cit., 1954, p. 232.
9 See D. Horton: 'The dialogue of courtship in popular song', *American Journal of Sociology*, vol. 62, 1957; J.T. Carey: 'Changing courtship patterns in the popular song', *American Journal of Sociology*, vol. 74, 1969; R.R. Cole: 'Top songs in the sixties: a content analysis', *American Behavioural Scientist*, vol. 14, 1971. In recent years the most prolific content analyst, B. Lee Cooper, has traced a variety of ideological issues through pop and rock songs, though he seems less concerned to chart changing values than to point to the recurring problems of American ideology. For a summary account of his work see his *A Resource Guide to Themes in Contemporary American Song Lyrics*, Greenwood, London, 1986. Very little similar work seems to have been done in Britain but for the 1950s/1960s contrast see Antony Bicat: 'Fifties children: sixties people', in V. Bogdanor and R. Skidelski (eds): *The Age of Affluence 1957–64*, Macmillan, London, 1970, and for the rock/punk contrast in the 1970s see Dave Laing: *One Chord Wonders*, Open University Press, Milton Keynes, 1985, pp. 63–73.
10 For an interesting use of music hall material this way see G. Stedman Jones: 'Working-class culture and working-class politics in London 1870–1900', *Journal of Social History*, vol. 7, no. 4, 1974.
11 P. Di Maggio, R.A. Peterson and J. Esco: 'Country music: ballad of the silent majority', in R.S. Denisoff and R.A. Peterson (eds): *The Sounds of Social Change*, Rand McNally, Chicago, 1972.
12 M. Haralambos: *Right On: From Blues to Soul in Black America*, Eddison, London, 1974, p. 117.
13 Ibid., p. 125.
14 'Real closeness' is a term used by Richard Hoggart to distinguish authentic from commercial working-class ballads – see *The Uses of Literacy*, Penguin, Harmondsworth, 1958, pp. 223–4.
15 D. Hughes: 'Recorded music', in D. Thompson (ed.): *Discrimination and Popular Culture*, Penguin, Harmondsworth, 1964, p. 165.
16 Hoggart, op. cit., p. 229.
17 W. Mellers: *Music in a New Found Land*, Faber & Faber, London, 1964, p. 384.
18 E. Lee: *Music of the People*, Barrie & Jenkins, London, 1970, p. 250. For a Marxist reading of the 'genteely romantic' bourgeois ideology of British pop music until rock 'n' roll began to use blues and folk idioms that expressed 'bottom dog consciousness' and to 'speak for the excluded and rebellious', see

Eric Hobsbawm: *Industry and Empire*, Penguin, 'Harmondsworth, 1968, p. 284.
19 Dave Harker:*One for the Money*, Hutchinson, London, 1980, p. 48.
20 Ibid., p. 61.
21 T. Goddard, J. Pollock and M. Fudger: 'Popular music', in J. King and M. Stott (eds): *Is This Your Life?*, Virago, London, 1977, p. 143.
22 Germaine Greer: *The Female Eunuch*, Paladin, London, 1971, p. 164.
23 Hoggart, op.cit., p. 163.
24 Harker, op.cit., p. 129.
25 S.I. Hayakawa: 'Popular songs vs. the facts of life', *Etc.*, vol. 12, 1955, p. 84.
26 Francis Newton: *The Jazz Scene*, Penguin, Harmondworth, 1961, p. 162.
27 Hans Eisler: *A Rebel in Music*, International Publishers, New York, 1978, p. 191.
28 R. Palmer: *A Touch of the Times*, Penguin, Harmondsworth, 1974, pp. 8, 18, and A.L. Lloyd: *Folk Song in England*, Baladin, London, 1975, pp. 158, 170.
29 Lloyd, op.cit., p. 369.
30 For full discussion of these issues see Dave Harker: *Fake Song*, Open University Press, Milton Keynes, 1985, and Vic Gammon: 'Folk song collecting in Sussex and Surrey, 1843–1914', *History Workshop*, no. 10, 1980.
31 See Harker, op.cit., p. 189.
32 J. Taylor and D. Laing: 'Disco-pleasure-discourse', *Screen Education*, no. 31, 1979, p. 46.
33 Paul Oliver: *Meaning of the Blues*, Collier, New York, 1963, p. 68. And see Iain Lang: *Background of the Blues*, Workers' Music Association, London, 1943, and Samuel Charters: *The Poetry of the Blues*, Oak, New York, 1963.
34 Charles Keil: *Urban Blues*, University of Chicago Press, Chicago, 1966, p 74.
35 Oliver, op.cit., pp. 133–4, 140 and Newton, op.cit., pp. 145–6.
36 Linton Kwesi Johnson: 'Jamaican rebel music', *Race and Class*, no. 17, 1976, p. 398.
37 See R. Ames: 'Protest and irony in Negro folk song', *Science and Society*, vol. 14, 1949.
38 Newton, op.cit., p. 150 and Johnson, op.cit., p. 411.
39 Paul Garon: *Blues and the Poetic Spirit*, Eddison, London, 1975.
40 Ibid., pp. 21, 26, 76, 64.
41 Ames, op.cit., p. 197.
42 Garon, op.cit., p. 167.
43 Ian Hoare: 'Mighty Mighty Spade and Whitey: black lyrics and soul's interaction with white culture', in I. Hoare (ed.): *The Soul Book*, New York, 1975, pp. 157, 162.
44 Lang, op.cit., p. 39. For a suggestive general study of 'oral poetry' see Ruth Finnegan: *Oral Poetry*, Cambridge University Press, Cambridge, 1977.
45 See Claude Brown: 'The language of soul', in R. Resh (ed.): *Black America*, D.C. Heath, Lexington, 1969; Ulf Hannerz: *Soulside*, Columbia University Press, New York, 1969; Geneva Smitherman: *Talkin' and Testifyin', The Language of Black America*, Houghton Mifflin, Boston, 1977; David Toop: *The Rap Attack*, Pluto, London, 1984.
46 For an unusually intelligent version of this argument see Peter Guaralnick: *Feel Like Going Home*, Vintage, New York, 1971, pp. 22–3.
47 David Pichaske: *Beowulf to the Beatles and Beyond*, Macmillan, New York, 1981, p. xiii (quoting the 1972 edition). And see Richard Goldstein: *The Poetry of Rock*, Bantam, New York, 1969; B.F. Groves and D.J. McBain: *Lyric Voices: Approaches to the Poetry of Contemporary Song*, John Wiley, New York, 1972; Bob Sarlin: *Turn It Up* (*I Can't Hear the Words*), Simon & Schuster, New York, 1973; Matt Damsker (ed.): *Rock Voices! The Best Lyrics of an Era*, St Martins Press, New York, 1980.

48 For a brilliantly detailed discussion of Dylan's poetic sources see Michael Gray: *Song and Dance Man: The Art of Bob Dylan*, Hamlyn, London, 1981.

49 R.R. Rosenstone: '"The Times they are A-Changing": the music of protest', *Annals of the American Academy of Political and Social Science*, no. 382, 1969.
The English poet Thom Gunn, writing in 1967, suggested that the Beatles represented a completely new pop sensibility, and had at last seen off Tin Pan Alley, 'the fag-end of the Petrarchan tradition'. The change had come with the line 'I've been working like a dog'. 'As soon as that line had been written immense possibilities became apparent. For what lover in a Sinatra song ever *works at a job?*' (*The Listener*, 3 August 1967)

50 Paul Nelson: 'The pretender' in G. Marcus (ed.): *Stranded*, Knopf, New York, 1979, p. 120.

51 Ira Gershwin: *Lyrics on Several Occasions*, Elm Tree Books, London, 1977, pp. 112–13.

52 David Riesman: 'Listening to popular music', *American Quarterly*, vol. 2, 1950, pp. 360–1.

53 Norman Denzin: 'Problems in analysing elements of mass culture: notes on the popular song and other artistic productions', *American Journal of Sociology*, vol. 75, 1969. And see J. Johnstone and E. Katz: 'Youth and popular music: a study of taste', *American Journal of Sociology*, vol. 62, 1957.

54 J.P. Robinson and P.M. Hirsch: 'Teenage responses to rock and roll protest songs', in Denisoff and Peterson, op.cit., p. 231; R.S. Denisoff and M. Levine: 'Brainwashing or background noise? The popular protest song', in the same colection; S. Frith: *The Sociology of Rock*, Constable, London, 1978.

55 Paul Hirsch: 'Sociological approaches to the pop music phenomenon', *American Behavioural Scientist*, vol. 14, 1971, and R.A. Peterson and D.G. Berger: 'Three eras in the manufacture of popular music lyrics', in Denisoff and Peterson, op.cit., pp. 283, 296.

56 Ibid., p. 298, and see J. Ryan and R.A. Peterson: 'The product image: the fate of creativity in country music songwriting', *Sage Annual Review of Communication Research*, vol. 10, 1982.

57 For a very interesting discussion of Bob Dylan's 'meaning' in Germany see Dennis Anderson: *The Hollow Horn: Bob Dylan's Reception in the US and Germany*, Hobo Press, Munich, 1981, chs 9, 20.

58 For detailed readings of lyrics in performance see, for example, the comparison of Kate Bush's 'The Kick Inside' and Millie Jackson's 'He Wants to Hear the Words', in S. Frith and A. McRobbie: 'Rock and sexuality', *Screen Education*, no. 29, 1978, and the psychoanalytic account of Buddy Holly's 'Peggy Sue' in B. Bradby and B. Torode: 'Pity Peggy Sue', *Popular Music*, vol. 4, 1984. For general discussions see S. Frith: *Sound Effects*, Pantheon, New York, 1981, pp. 34–38; Alan Durant: *Conditions of Music*, Macmillan, London, 1984, pp. 186–95, 201–11; and the introduction to Mark Booth: *The Experience of Song*, Yale University Press, New Haven, 1981.

59 This approach has been developed most interestingly in the Italian work of Franco Fabbri and Umberto Fiori. See, for example, Fabbri's 'A theory of musical genres: two applicatons', in D. Horn and P. Tagg (eds): *Popular Music Perspectives*, IASPM, Gothenburg and Exeter, 1982.
From a continental European perspective one of the more intriguing aspects of contemporary pop lyrics is their use of a 'foreign' language, English. One of the defining features of the punk music that swept Europe in the late 1970s was its use of the different performers' 'native' tongues – the question rose as to what, in pop and rock, is a native tongue. Dave Laing suggests that even in Britain it meant bands determinedly *not* singing in 'American' – see Laing, op.cit., pp. 54–9.

60 See L. Winner: 'Trout mask replica', in Marcus (ed.), op.cit.

61 D. Lodge: 'Where it's at: California language', in L. Michaels and C. Ricks (eds): *The State of the Language*, University of California Press, Berkeley, 1980, p. 506; and see C. Ricks: 'Clichés' in the same collection; B. Bergonzi: *Reading the Thirties*, Macmillan, London, 1978, ch. 6; and C. Ricks: 'Can this really be the end?', in E.M. Thompson (ed.): *Conclusions on the Wall: New Essays on Bob Dylan*, Thin Man, Manchester, 1980.

62 Clive James: 'The Beatles', *Cream*, October 1972.

63 Roy Fuller: *Professors and Gods*, André Deutsch, London, 1973, p. 86. Compare Ace's solution to the same problem in their hit song, 'How Long'. Their more maudlin emphasis is on the initial syllable: 'Hów lŏng, hăs tȟis beĕn góiňg ŏn.'

Stephen Sondheim suggests another example of the precise attention to words necessary in good lyric writing:

> The opening line of *Porgy and Bess* by Dubose Heyward is 'Summertime and the livin' is easy' – and that 'and' is worth a great deal of attention. I would write 'Summertime when' but that 'and' sets up a tone, a whole poetic tone, not to mention a whole kind of diction that is going to be used in the play; an informal, uneducated diction and a stream of consciousness . . . . The choices of 'and's and 'but's become almost traumatic as you are writing a lyric – or should anyway – because each one weighs so much. (S. Sondheim: 'Theatre Lyrics', in G. Martin (ed.): *Making Music*, Muller, London, 1983, p. 75)

64 D. Laing: *Buddy Holly*, Studio Vista, London, 1971, pp. 58–9.

65 Quoted in Mellers, op.cit., p. 379.

66 Horton, op.cit., p. 577.

67 Elvis Costello interview in *New Musical Express*, 21 August 1982, p. 10. And see Steve Coombes: 'In the mood', *Times Educational Supplement*, 12 February 1982, p. 23. He writes:

> Writing for shows, thirties lyric writers were in both the best and worst senses of the word in the business of creating fictions. The moods of their lyrics do not reflect emotions they had actually felt nor that they expected anyone to think that they had felt nor even that they expected anyone else to feel for that matter. Nothing would have distuirbed the cosmopolitan Cole Porter more than the idea that people might think that he actually did sit and moon over lost love – that emphatically was not his style. The moods of thirties lyrics are about what you ought to have felt or more accurately what you might like to have felt given the chance to think about it. Paradoxically, then, the tone is at the same time extremely sophisticated yet highly idealised.

68 Quoted in Eisler, op.cit., pp. 189–90.

The price you pay: an introduction to the life and songs of Laurence Price

Dave Harker

Introduction

In spite of rock journalists, punk authors, folk academics and sociologists of 'popular culture', it is *not* the case that the history of popular song in Britain began in 1956. Neither was *Rock around the Clock* the biggest 'hit' to cross the Atlantic, in either direction. In fact, Bill Haley's record may have entered the British singles charts four times between 1955 and 1968, and it may have reached no. 1 for a few weeks, but the thirty or so weeks the song lasted in the Top Twenty are as nothing compared to other songs.[1] In fact, the thirty years in which Haley's recording has remained at some level of cultural significance – even if it has only an antiquarian aura to it today – is hardly a blip on the history of popular song. I want to speak of a song which was *really* popular, one which has lasted some 330 years, crossed the Atlantic and then crossed back again, and is still sung in Britain, the United States and Eire, and probably elsewhere too. That song is known today as *The Banks of the Sweet Vilidee*, sometimes as *The Distressed Ship's Carpenter* or *The House Carpenter*, and probably most often as *James Harris* or *The Daemon Lover*, the titles by which it was known to Francis James Child, editor of the monumental 1882–1898 edition of what he termed *The English and Scottish Popular Ballads*.[2]

I want to say at the outset that the idea of studying this song was not my own. In fact, left to my own devices, I am certain I would never have considered it; and all I knew of it when Professor Charles Hamm of Dartmouth College suggested a collaborative research project was that Child had put it in his canon. However, my reservations were temporarily overcome, and I began work on the earliest known broadside texts of what was called *A Warning for Married Women*, dating from seventeenth-century London. This chapter is by way of a provisional report, and is entirely my own work, except for the incorporation of suggestions from friends and colleagues, which are acknowledged in their proper place. Two acknowledgments, however, need to be made here: without the support of my colleagues in the Department of English and History, and that of Manchester Polytechnic's Librarian, Ian Rogerson, this work would have remained undone.

From '*James Harris*' to '*A Warning for Married Women*'

Child refers to six broadside versions of the song he calls *James Harris* (*The Daemon Lover*), all of which bear another title, *A Warning for Married Women*. His 'A' text is said to be taken from the Pepys Collection exemplar in Magdalene College Cambridge – 'Pepys Ballads, IV, 101' –

> The Pepys copy was printed for Thackeray and Passenger. Others are: Crawford, No 1114, Printed for A. M[ilbourne], W. O[nley], and T. Thackeray; Ewing, 377, for Coles, Vere, and Gilbertson; the same, 378, by and for W. O[nley]. No 71 in Thackeray's List, printed 1685. A later copy in the Douce ballads, II, fol. 249 b, Bodleian Library, printed by Thomas Norris at the Looking-Glass on London Bridge. Another without publisher's name, in the Roxburghe collection, I, 502; Ballad Society, III, 200.

Child then goes on to note the (to him) more interesting publications of texts said to be taken from singing in the late eighteenth or early nineteenth century – by Walter Scott, William Motherwell, Peter Buchan, and George Kinloch – and, later in the century, a text cited in a Philadelphia magazine in 1858, and another (with music) given by William Christie in an Edinburgh publication of 1876. However, his head-note to his 'B' text cites *The Rambler's Garland* of (?) 1785, held by the British Museum, and his 'Additions and Corrections' note another British Museum edition of this garland, which Child thought was 'perhaps slightly earlier'.[3]

According to Child, it did not 'seem necessary to posit a tradition' behind his 'A' text; and he was content to rely on a 'copy in Percy's papers' for his 'A' text, rather than going back to the Magdalene collection. Had he examined the Euing texts (or even had them checked for him), he would have found that the initials 'L.P.' were appended to no. 377; and had he gone to the trouble of going through the registers of the Stationers' Company of London, he would have discovered that *A Warning for Married Women* was entered under the name of Fran[cis] Grove on 21 February 1657.[4] (Such routine scholarly labour on the 'veritable dunghills' of broadsides was, for Child, not only tedious but unnecessary. And as for authors, they should be heard but not seen.) However, in following up Child's spare references, it became clear that though no copy of the text advertised as *Jane Reynolds* in William Thackeray's list (published solely by him)[5] has yet been traced, and neither has a broadside published (as opposed to printed) by Francis Coles, there seems to have been an interesting sequence of publishing of *A Warning for Married Women* from perhaps so early as 1658 until some point in the 1710s, after which the text *appears* to have gone out of print until it resurfaced on a pair of broadsides and in two editions of *The Rambler's Garland* possibly in the mid-1780s, not long after which it was 'collected' from singers in Scotland.

Dating broadsides is a difficult business, and future scholars will owe a great deal to the work of Cyprian Blagden.[6] Since then, Robert S. Thomson has added several conjectural dates for the period 1690–1720; and both these works have thrown the guesses of William Chappell and J.W. Ebsworth and of the Earl of Crawford into sharp relief.[7] Neither the editors of the *Roxburghe Ballads* nor the owner of the Crawford Collection had a firm grasp of publishers' dates. Similarly, the presence of another exemplar of our text in the Houghton Library, Harvard indicates that perhaps not even Child had a full listing of the contents of the various collections; while the failure of the original editor of Wing to note the 'L.P.' on the Euing text meant that *A Warning for Married Women* is listed separately from others known to be so subscribed, under its title.[8] However, a search of the contents of many collections (and many published selections) has revealed yet another exemplar of 'L.P.'s' text in the British Museum; and so we can suggest the following chronology for its publication up to c. 1720:[9]

[1657	Stationers' Company Register	Fran[cis] Grove]
1658–1664	Euing Collection, no. 377	Printed for F. Coles, T. Vere and W. Gilbertson
1686–1688	Pepys Collection, vol. IV, no. 101	Printed for W. Thackeray, and T. Passinger
[1688–1689*	Thackeray's List	William Thackeray]
?1689**	Roxburghe Collection, vol. I, no. 502	No Imprint

1689–1709	Euing Collection, no. 378	London: Printed by and for W[illiam] O[nley] and are to be sold by the Booksellers
1693–1694	Crawford Collection, no. 1114 *and* British Museum C 22 f 6 *and* Houghton pE BB 65	London: Printed for A[lexander] M[ilbourn] W[illiam] O[nley] and T[homas] Thackeray, in Duck-Lane
1710–1720	Douce Collection, vol. II, fol. 249 v	Printed by Tho[mas] Norris and the Looking-glass on London-bridge

* Child dated this list as 1685.

** This dating is based (with reservations) on William Chappell's belief that the Roxburghe exemplar was later than both Euing exemplars and that in Pepys.

At this point, several sets of questions present themselves, in relation to the identity, life and writing of 'L.P.', the practices of broadside printers and publishers in the period 1650–1720, and the relationship between *A Warning for Married Women* and the society in which it was produced and republished (especially between the mid-1680s and the mid-1690s). Was it possible to explain how and why this text resurfaced as *The Distressed Ship Carpenter*[10] and then on the lips of lowland Scots singers in the early nineteenth century?[11] And what of the song's travel to Ireland and to North America? At this point, I had to discipline myself to what seemed to be the first tasks: to find out everything I could about 'L.P.', to try to reconstitute any repertoire she or he may have had; and to try to understand more about the broadside publishing trade up to c. 1720.

Laurence Price

An extremely speculative dip into the *Dictionary of National Biography* came up trumps. The entry for Laurence Price (fl. 1628–1680?) revealed him to be a

> writer of ballads and political squibs, who was a native of London, and who compiled between 1625 and 1680 numberless ballads, pamphlets, and broadsides in verse on political and social subjects. During the civil war he seems to have occasionally been a hanger-on of the parliamentary army, and published his observations . . . . He adapted his views to the times, and the godly puritan strain which he affected during the Commonwealth gave place to the utmost indecency after the

A warning for married Women.

By the Example of Mrs. *Jane Renalds*, a West-Country Woman, born near unto *Plymouth*; who having plighted her troth to a Seaman, was afterwards Married to a Carpenter, and at last carried away by a Spirit: the manner how shall be presently recited,

To a gallant West-country tune, cal'd, *The fair maid of Bristol*, Or, *Bateman*, or, *John True*

THere dwelt a fair Maid in the West,
of worthy birth and Fame,
Near unto Plimouth stately Town,
Jane Renalds was her name.

This Damsel dearly was beloved
by many a proper Youth,
And what of her is to be said,
is known for very truth.

Amongst the rest a Sea-man brave
unto her a wooing came;
A comely proper Youth was he,
Iame Harris was his name.

This Maid and Youngman were well (agreed
as time did them allow:
And to each other secretly,
they made a solemn vow.

That they would ever faithful be,
whilst Heaven afforded life:
He was to be her Husband kind,
and she his loving Wife.

A day appointed was also,
when they were to be married: (pass
But before these things were brought to
matters were strangely carried.

All you that fatal Lovers be,
give ear and hearken well;
And what of them became at last,
I will directly tell.

The Young-man he was Prest to Sea,
and forc'd he was to go:
His Sweet-heart she must stay behind,
whether she would or no.

And after she was from him gone,
she three long years for him stayed,
Expecting of his coming home again,
and kept her self a Maid.

At last came news that he was dead,
within a Forraign Land,
And how that he was buried,
she well did understand.

For whose sweet sake the Maiden she,
lamented many a day,
And never was she known at all
the wanton for to play.

A Carpenter that lived hard by,
when he heard of the same,
Like as the other had done before,
to her a Wooing came.

But when that he had gain'd her love,
they married were with speed;
And four years space being man & wife
they lovingly agreed.

Three pretty Children in that time,
this loving Couple had;
Which made their Father heart rejoyce
and Mother wondrous glad.

BUt as occasion serv'd one time,
the Good-man took his way,
Some three days journy from his home
intending for to stay.

But whilst that he was gone away,
a Spirit in the night,
Came to the window of the house,
and did her sorely fright.

Which Spirit spake like to a man,
and unto her did say,
My dear and only love (quoth he)
prepare and come away.

Iame Harris is my name (quoth he)
whom thou didst love so dear,
And I have travelled for thy sake,
at least this long seven year.

And now I am returned again,
to take thee to my wife;
And thou with me shall go to Sea,
to end all further strife.

O tempt me not sweet James (she said)
with thee away to go;
If I should leave my Children small
alas what should they do?

My Husband is a Carpenter,
and a Carpenter of great fame,
I would not for five hundred pounds,
that he should know the same.

I might have had a Kings Daughter,
and she would have married with me,
But I forsook her golden crown,
and all for love of thee.

Therefore if thou wilt thy husband for(sake,
and thy children three also,
I will forgive all that is past,
if thou with me wilt go.

If I forsake my Husband, and
my little Children three,
What means hast thou to bring me to,
if I should go with thee.

I have seven Ships upon the Sea,
when they are come to Land,
Both Marriners and Merchandize
shall be at thy command.

The Ship wherein my Love shall sail,
so glorious to behold:
The Sails shall be of finest Silk,
and the Masts of shining Gold.

When he had told her these fair tales,
to love him she began:
Because he was in humane shape,
she thought he had bin a man,

And so together away they went,
from off the English shore,
And since that time the woman kind,
was never heard of more.

But when her Husband he came home,
and found his wife was gone,
And left her sweet pretty Babes
within the house alone.

He beat his brest, he tore his hair,
the tears fell from his eyes,
And in the open streets he run,
with heavy doleful cryes.

And in this sad distracted case
he hang'd himself for woe,
Upon a tree near to that place,
the truth of all is so.

The Children now are fatherless,
and left without a guide;
But yet no doubt but heavenly powers,
will for them well provide. Finis. L.P.

Printed for F. Coles, T. Vere, and W. Gilbertson.

A Warning for Married Women.

Being an Example of Mrs. Jane Reynolds (a west-country-Woman) born neer Plimouth who having plighted her troth to a Seaman, was afterwards married to a Carpenter, and at last carried away by a Spirit, the manner how shall presently be recited.
To a west-country Tune, called, *The fair Maid of Bristol: Bateman, or, John True.*

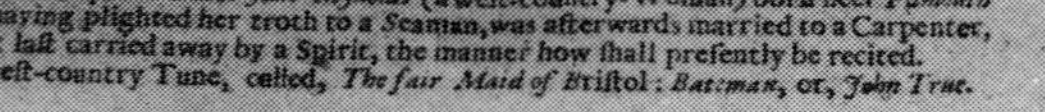

There dwelt a fair Maid in the West,
of worthy Birth and Fame,
Neer unto Plimouth stately Town
Jane Reynolds was her name.

This Damsel dearly was belov'd,
by many a proper youth:
And what of her is to be said,
is known for very truth:

Among the rest a Seaman brave,
unto her a wooing came,
A comely proper youth he was,
James Harris call'd by Name.

The Maid and Young-man was agreed
as time did them allow,
And to each other secretly,
they made a solemn vow.

That they would ever faithful be,
whilst Heaven afforded life,
He was to be her Husband kind,
and she his faithful Wife.

A day appointed was also,
when they were to be married,
But before these things were brought to pass
matters were strangely carried.

All you that faithful Lovers be,
give ear and hearken well,
And what of them became at last,
I will directly tell.

The Young man he was prest to Sea,
and forced was to go,
His Sweet-heart she must stay behind
whether she would or no.

And after he was from her gone,
she three years for him staid,
Expecting of his coming home,
and kept her self a Maid.

At last news came that he was dead,
within a Forraign Land,
And how that he was buried,
she well did understand.

For whose sweet sake the maiden she,
lamented many a day:
And never was she known at all,
the wanton for to play.

A Carpenter that liv'd hard by,
when he heard of the same,
Like as the other had done before,
to her a wooing came.

But when that he had gain'd her love,
they married were with speed,
And four years space (being man & wife)
they lovingly agreed.

Three pritty Children in this time,
this lovely couple had,
Which made their Fathers heart rejoyce
and Mother wondrous glad.

But as occasion serv'd one time,
the good man took his way,
Some three days journey from his home
intending not to stay.

But whilst that he was gone away,
a spirit in the night,
Came to the window of his Wife,
and did her sorely fright.

Which Spirit spake like to a man,
and unto her did say,
My dear and onely love (quoth he)
prepare and come away.

James Harris is my name (quoth he)
whom thou didst love so dear,
And I have travel'd for thy sake,
at least this seven year.

And now I am return'd again,
to take thee to my wife,
And thou with me shalt go to Sea,
to end all further strife.

O tempt me not sweet *James* (quoth she)
with thee away to go,
If I should leave my children small,
alas what would they do?

My Husband is a Carpenter,
a Carpenter of great fame,
I would not for five hundred pounds,
that he should know the same.

I might have had a Kings Daughter,
and she would have married me,
But I forsook her Golden Crown
and for the love of thee.

Therefore if thou'lt thy Husband forsake
and thy children three also
I will forgive thee what is past
if thou wilt with me go.

If I forsake my husband, and
my little Children three,
What means hast thou to bring me to,
if I should go with thee.

I have seaven Ships upon the Sea,
when they are come to Land,
Both Marriners and Merchandize,
shall be at thy command.

The Ship wherein my love shall sail,
is glorious to behold,
The sails shall be of finest silk,
and the mast of shining gold.

When he had told her these fair tales,
to love him she began,
Because he was in humane shape,
much like unto a man.

And so together away they went,
from off the English shore,
And since that time the Woman-kind,
was never seen no more.

But when her Husband he came home,
and found his Wife was gone,
And left her three sweet pretty babes,
within the house alone.

He beat his breast, he tore his hair,
the tears fell from his eyes,
And in the open streets he run,
with heavy doleful cries.

And in this sad distracted case,
he hang'd himself for Woe,
Upon a tree, near to the place,
the truth of all is so.

The children now are fatherless,
and left without a guide,
But yet no doubt the heavenly powers,
will for them well provide.

Printed for *W. Thackeray*, and *T. Passinger*.

Pepys Collection. By permission of the Master and Fellows, Magdalene College, Cambridge

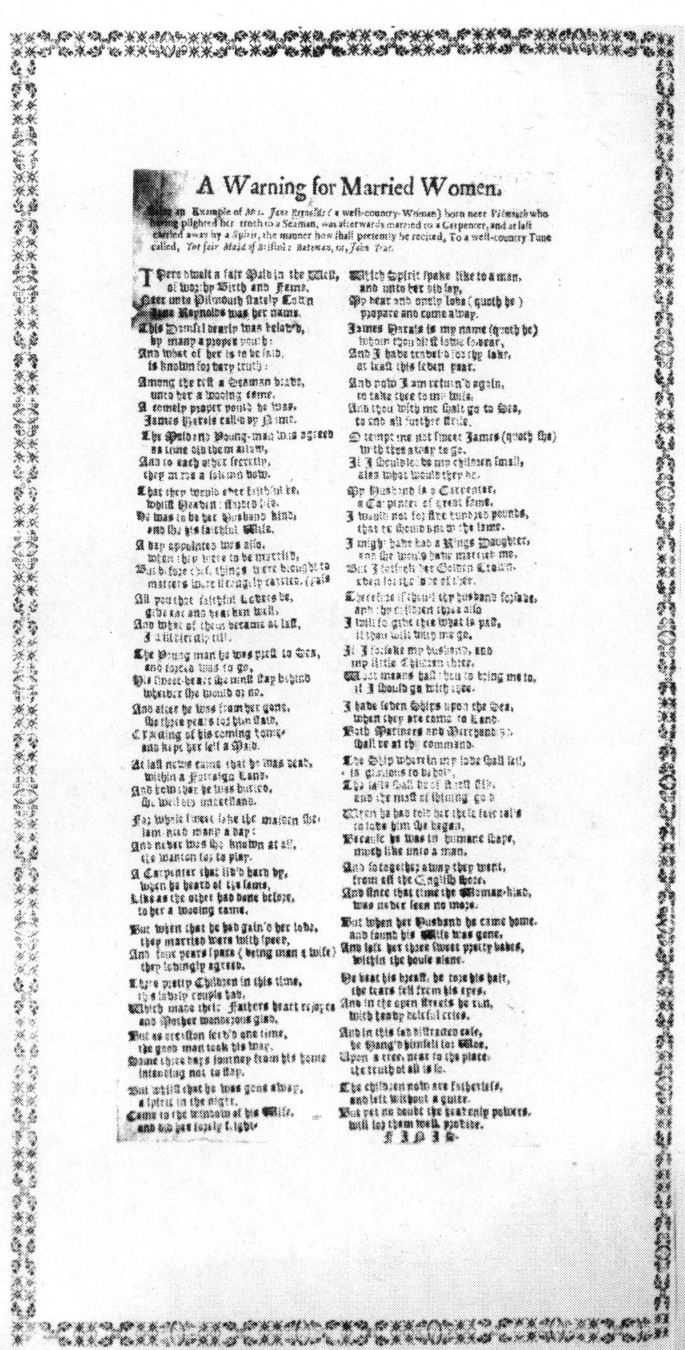

A Warning for Married Women.

Being an Example of *Mrs. Jane Reynolds* (a west-country-Woman) born neer *Plimouth* who having plighted her troth to a Seaman, was afterwards married to a Carpenter, and at last carried away by a *Spirit*, the manner how shall presently be recited, To a west-country Tune called, *The fair Maid of Bristol; Bateman*, or, *John True*.

There dwelt a fair Maid in the West,
of worthy Birth and Fame,
Neer unto Plimouth stately Town
Jane Reynolds was her name.

This Damsel dearly was belov'd,
by many a proper youth:
And what of her is to be said,
is known for very truth:

Among the rest a Seaman brave,
unto her a wooing came,
A comely proper youth he was,
James Harris call'd by Name.

The Maid and Young-man was agreed
as time did them allow,
And to each other secretly,
they made a solemn vow.

That they would ever faithful be,
whilst Heaven afforded life:
He was to be her Husband kind,
and she his faithful Wife.

A day appointed was also,
when they were to be married,
But before these things were brought to pass
matters were strangely carried.

All you that faithful Lovers be,
give ear and hearken well,
And what of them became at last,
I will directly tell.

The Young man he was prest to Sea,
and forced was to go,
His sweet-heart she must stay behind
whether she would or no.

And after he was from her gone,
she three years for him staid,
Expecting of his coming home,
and kept her self a Maid.

At last news came that he was dead,
within a Forraign Land,
And how that he was buried,
she well did understand.

For whose sweet sake the maiden she
lamented many a day:
And never was she known at all,
the wanton for to play.

A Carpenter that liv'd hard by,
when he heard of the same,
Like as the other had done before,
to her a wooing came.

But when that he had gain'd her love,
they married were with speed,
And four years space (being man & wife)
they lovingly agreed.

Three pretty Children in this time,
this loving couple had,
Which made their Fathers heart rejoyce
and Mother wonderous glad.

But as occasion serv'd one time,
the good man took his way,
Some three days journey from his home
intending not to stay.

But whilst that he was gone away,
a spirit in the night,
Came to the window of his Wife,
and did her sorely fright.

Which Spirit spake like to a man,
and unto her did say,
My dear and onely love (quoth he)
prepare and come away.

James Harris is my name (quoth he)
whom thou didst love so dear,
And I have travel'd for thy sake,
at least this seven year.

And now I am return'd again,
to take thee to my wife,
And thou with me shalt go to Sea,
to end all further strife.

O tempt me not sweet James (quoth she)
with thee away to go,
If I should leave my children small,
alas what would they do.

My Husband is a Carpenter,
a Carpenter of great fame,
I would not for five hundred pounds,
that he should know the same.

I might have had a Kings Daughter,
and she would have married me,
But I forsook her Golden Crown,
even for the love of thee.

Therefore if thou'lt thy husband forsake,
and thy children three also,
I will forgive thee what is past,
if thou wilt with me go.

If I forsake my husband, and
my little Children three,
What means hast thou to bring me to,
if I should go with thee.

I have seven Ships upon the Sea,
when they are come to Land,
Both Mariners and Merchandize,
shall be at thy command.

The Ship wherein my love shall sail,
is glorious to behold,
The sails shall be of finest silk,
and the mast of shining gold.

When he had told her these fair tales
to love him she began,
Because he was in humane shape,
much like unto a man.

And so together away they went,
from off the English shore,
And since that time the Woman-kind,
was never seen no more.

But when her Husband he came home,
and found his Wife was gone,
And left her three sweet pretty babes,
within the house alone.

He beat his breast, he tore his hair,
the tears fell from his eyes,
And in the open streets he run,
with heavy doleful cries.

And in this sad distracted case,
he hang'd himself for woe,
Upon a tree, near to the place;
the truth of all is so.

The children now are fatherless,
and left without a guide,
But yet no doubt the heavenly powers,
will for them well provide.

FINIS.

A WARNING for Married WOMEN:

Being an Example of Mrs. JANE REYNOLDS, (a West-country Woman) born near Plymouth, who having plighted her Troth to a Seaman, was afterwards married to a Carpenter, and at last carried away by a Spirit, the manner how shall be recited. To a West-country Tune, called, The fair Maid of Bristol; or, John True, &c.

Evinc Collection. Acknowledgements to the Librarian of Glasgow University Library.

A WARNING for Married Women.

Being an Example of Mrs. *Jane Reynolds* (a West-country Woman) born near *Plimouth*, who having plighted her Troth to a Seaman, was afterwards married to a Carpenter, and at last carried away by a Spirit, the manner how shall presently be recited.
To a West-country Tune, call'd, *The fair Maid of Bristol*: or, John True.

There dwelt a fair Maid in the West,
of worthy birth and fame,
Near unto Plimouth stately town,
Jane Reynolds was her name.

This damsel dearly was belov'd,
by many a proper youth;
And what of her is to be said,
is known for very truth:

Among the rest a Seaman brave
unto her a wooing came,
A comely proper youth he was,
James Harris call'd by name.

The maid and young man was agreed,
as time did them allow,
And to each other secretly
they made a solemn vow.

That they would ever faithful be,
whilst Heaven afforded life,
He was to be her Husband kind,
and she his faithful Wife.

A day appointed was also,
when they were to be married,
But before these things were brought to pass,
matters were strangely carried.

All you that faithful Lovers be,
give ear and hearken well,
And what of them became at last
I will directly tell:

The young man he was prest to Sea,
and forced was to go,
His sweet-heart she must stay behind
whether she would or no.

And after he was from her gone,
she three years for him staid,
Expecting of his coming home,
and kept her self a maid.

At last news came that he was dead
within a Foraign Land,
And how that he was buried,
she well did understand.

For whose sweet sake the maiden she
lamented many a day:
And never was she known at all
the wanton for to play.

A Carpenter that liv'd hard by,
when he heard of the same,
Like as the other had done before,
to her a wooing came.

But when that he had gain'd her love,
they married were with speed,
And four years space (being man and wife)
they lovingly agreed.

Three pritty children in this time,
this lovely couple had,
Which made their father's heart rejoyce,
and mother wondrous glad.

But as occasion serv'd one time,
the good man took his way
Some three days journey from his Home,
intending not to stay.

But whilst that he was gone away,
a Spirit in the night,
Came to the window to his wife,
and did her sorely fright.

Which Spirit spake like to a man,
and unto her did say:
My dear and only love, quoth he,
prepare and come away.

James Harris is my name, quoth he,
whom thou didst love so dear,
And I have travell'd for thy sake,
at least this seven year.

And now I am return'd again,
to take thee to my wife,
And thou with me shalt go to Sea,
to end all further strife.

O tempt me not, sweet James (quoth she)
with thee away to go,
If I should leave my children small,
alas, what would they do?

My husband is a Carpenter,
a Carpenter of great fame,
I would not for five hundred pounds
that he should know the same.

I might have had a King's Daughter,
and she would have married me,
But I forsook her golden crown,
and for the love of thee.

'Therefore if thou'lt thy husband forsake,
and thy children three also,
'I will forgive thee what is past,
'if thou wilt with me go.

If I forsake my husband and
my little children three,
What means hast thou to bring me to,
if I should go with thee?

'I have seven ships upon the sea,
'when they are come to Land,
'Both Marriners and Merchandize
'shall be at thy command.

The ship wherein my love shall sail,
is glorious to behold,
The sails shall be of finest silk,
and the mast of shining gold.

When he had told her these fair tails,
to love him she began,
Because he was in humane shape,
much like unto a man.

And so together away they went,
from off the English shore,
And since that time the woman kind,
was never seen no more.

But when her Husband he came home,
and found his Wife was gone,
And left her three sweet pretty Babes
within the house alone.

He beat his breast, he tore his hair,
the tears fell from his eyes,
And in the open Streets he run,
with heavy doleful cries.

And in this sad distracted case,
he hang'd himself for woe,
Upon a Tree, near to the place,
the truth of all is so.

The children now are fatherless,
and left without a Guide,
But yet no doubt the heavenly Powers
will for them well provide.

London: Printed for A. M. W. O. and T. Thackeray, in Duck Lane.

(1696)

A Warning for Married Women.

Being an Example of Mrs. *Jane Reynolds* (a West-Country-Woman) born near *Plymouth*, who having plighted her Troth to a Seaman, was afterwards married to a Carpenter, and at last carried away by a Spirit, the manner how shall presently be recited. *Tune of, Fair Maid of Bristol*; or, *John True*.

There dwelt a fair Maid in the *West*,
of worthy Birth and Fame,
Near unto *Plymouth* stately Town,
Jane Reynolds was her Name:
This Damsel dearly was beloved
by many a proper Youth;
And what of her is to be said,
is known of very Truth:

Among the rest a Seaman brave,
unto her a wooing came,
A comly proper Youth he was
James Harris call'd by name.
The Maid and young Man was agreed,
as Time did them allow;
And to each other secretly
they made a solemn Vow;

That they would ever faithful be,
whilst Heaven afforded Life;
He was to be her Husband kind,
and she his wedded wife,
A Day appointed was also,
when they were to be married,
But before things was brought to pass,
matters were strangely carry'd.

All you that faithful Lovers be,
give ear and hearken well,
And what of them became at last,
I will directly tell:
The young Man he was prest to Sea
and forced was to go,
His Sweet-heart she must stay behind
whether she would or no.

And after he from her was gone,
she three Years for him staid
Expecting of his coming home,
and kept herself a Maid.
At last News came that he was dead,
within a foreign Land:
And how that he was buried,
she well did understand.

For whose sweet sake the Maiden she
lamented many a Day
And never was she known at all
the wanton for to play.
A Carpenter that liv'd hard by,
when he heard of the same,
Like as the other had done before
to her a wooing came.

But when that he had gained her love,
they married were with speed,
And four year's space (being Man and Wife
they lovingly agreed.
Three pretty Children in this time
this loving couple had,
Which made their Father's heart rejoyce,
and Mother wondrous glad.

But as occasion served one time,
the good Man took his way,
Some three days Journey from his home,
intending not to stay.
But whilst that he was gone away,
a Spirit in the night
Came to the window to his wife
and did her sorely fright.

Which Spirit spake like to a Man,
and unto her did say
My Dear and only Love, quoth he,
prepare and come away:
James Harris *is my name* quoth he
whom thou didst love so dear
And I have travell'd for thy sake
at least this seven Year;

And now I am return'd again
to take thee to my Wife
And thou with me shalt go to Sea
to end all further Strife.
O tempt me not, sweet *James* (quoth she)
with thee away to go:
If I should leave my Children small,
Alas, what would they do!

My Husband is a Carpenter,
a Carpenter of Fame,
I should not for five hundred pounds
that he should know the same.
I might have had a Kings Daughter,
and she would have married me,
But I forsook her golden Crown,
and for the love of thee.

Therefore if thou'lt thy Husband forsake,
and thy Children three also,
I will forgive thee what is past,
if thou wilt with me go.
If I forsake my Husband, and
my little Children three,
What means hast thou to bring me to,
if I should go along with thee?

I have seven Ships upon the Sea,
when they are come to land
Both Mariners and Merchandize
shall be at thy Command.
The Ship wherein my Love shall sail
is glorious to behold,
The Sails shall be of finest Silk
and the Mast of finest Gold.

When he had told her these fair tales,
to love him she began,
Because he was in human Shape
much like unto a Man.
And so together away they went
from off the English shore;
And since that time the woman-kind
was never seen no more.

But when her Husband he came home,
and found his wife was gone,
And left her three sweet pretty Babes
within the house alone,
He beat his breast, he tore his hair,
the tears fell from his Eyes,
And in the open streets he ran
with heavy doleful cries.

And in this sad distracted case,
he hang'd himself for woe,
Upon a tree near to the place,
the truth of all is so.
The Children now are Fatherless,
and left without a Guide,
But yet no doubt the heavenly powers
will for them well provide.

Printed by *Tho. Norris* at the Looking-glass on *London-bridge*.

Reproduced with permission. Acknowledgements to the Librarian, Bodleian Library, Oxford.

> Restoration. The fact that he published much anonymously, under the initials 'L.P.', renders it difficult to identify his work.[12]

Though the *DNB* did not mention *A Warning for Married Women*, it was fairly clear that we now had a name to those initials; and it proved possible to glean a few more details from other works, notably Rollins's, who discovered remarkably little in spite of his massive reading.[13] Evidently, a broadside of 1652 sneers at Price for producing astrological pamphlets. The anonymous writer of *Mercurius Democritus*, in April 1653, breaks off in the middle of a scurrilous tale to tell readers that they will have 'more of this the next week; because you shall then have the true relation in a *Ballad*, to the Tune of the *7 Champions* of the *Pens* in *Smithfield*, written by *Lawrenc[e] Price*'. And in a comic elegy of 1656, Price is classed as one of the 'glorious three of poetry', alongside Samuel Smithson and Humphrey Crowch:

> Ye glorious three
> Who grasp the Poles of Star-crown'd Poesie;
> Has some[e] Cask-piercing Youth poison'd your wine
> With wicked Laethe? Did you ever dine
> On Turnep-tops, without or Salt, or Butter,
> That amongst all your Canzonets, or clutter
> You fail'd to mention this deceased *Robbin*,
> It seems you ne'r-quaft *Nectar* in his Noggin,
> As I have done.

After 'covering the period with some care', these were the only direct contemporary references that Rollins could find; but he knew enough of Price's repertoire to claim him as 'almost the last of the distinguished line of ballad-writers that began in 1559 with William Elderton (or in 1512 with John Skelton)'. Like his contemporary, Martin Parker the songwriter and alehouse-keeper, Price was a butt for would-be polite poets; and though Parker and Price were rivals (and were politically opposed), Price could refer to Parker's *Robin Conscience* with approval, contribute to Parker's pamphlet, *Harry White's Humour*, and mention him by name in his own *Map of Merry Conceits*. By way of return, Parker wrote 'answers' to some of Price's songs, and adopted tunes used by Price before him; but both men could write to order – one of Price's songs appeared only four days after the pamphlet on which it was based

– and they sometimes wrote in competition with each other, and with other versifiers.

So much for 'factual' evidence. Rollins goes on to speculate that the Bishop's War of 1639–1640 forced writers like Parker and Price to take sides in print, and especially in prose; but what was unusual about Price, Rollins believes, was his evolution towards the Parliamentary cause at a time when most other songwriters were ardent royalists. In 1642, Price wrote what Rollins calls an 'abusive' pamphlet against the 'two Lordly Bishops, Yorke and Canterbury'; and by the later 1640s Price had become what Rollins chooses to term a 'renegade':

> certainly he affected a peculiar moralizing and sanctimonious tone, as in his prose pamphlet on *England's Unhappy Changes* (1648), that was greatly at variance not only with the spirit of the Royalists but also with the licentiousness of his work during the last days of the Protectorate.[15]

Rollins agrees with Chappell and Ebsworth that the Restoration marked a watershed in Price's writing, and speculates that he 'wrote for only a brief time after the Restoration'. Yet the *DNB*'s latest-dated *song* was of 1660![16] Once again, even through the prejudiced assertion and obvious lack of sympathy, we can discern another battery of unanswered questions. Was Price a native Londoner or, like many others, a migrant? How did he earn his living – could he have existed by writing and singing songs? Who bought his songs, and why? What was his relationship with the ballad trade, and did it change during and after the Civil War? What can we glean from his songs about his attitudes, assumptions, loyalties and ideas? Why did he choose the more hazardous path, as a songwriter and pamphleteer, of being a 'hanger-on' of the Parliamentary cause, and did he really become a turncoat in 1660 or soon after? Was he *alive* after 1660, and, if he was, did he keep on writing? Obviously, before we can begin to answer any of these questions – since Laurence Price does not figure in the standard history books about the period – we need to try to reconstitute his repertoire of songs, and to think about doing the same for his prose writings.

Price's repertoire of songs

The entry in the *DNB* for Laurence Price does mention his writings, but claims that many of them were 'lost'. All the same, the writer knew of sixty-eight:

> Specimens of them may be found in the Thomason collection of tracts at the British Museum, in the Pepysian collection at Magdalene College, Cambridge, or in the Roxburghe and Bagford collections of ballads at the British Museum. Most of the latter have been reprinted by the Ballad Society.[17]

There then follow examples of Price's titles in verse and prose, with firm or attributed dates, plus references to published selections and to W. Carew Hazlitt's *Hand-book*,[18] where, sure enough, were twenty-nine titles (including prose pamphlets) known to be by Price. Yet more song titles turned up in Chappell and Ebsworth's edition of the *Roxburghe Ballads*, and in Ebsworth's editions of the *Bagford Ballads* and of the *Amanda* group of ballads.[19] Further references from these sources (and from Wing, the British Museum Catalogue)[20], and from the National Union Catalogue, *Eighteenth Century Bristish Books*, and other library catalogues, from published collections – notably those by Rollins, Ashton and Collier[21] – plus the published index to the Crawford Collection and Simpson's work on broadside tunes,[22] and a range of esoteric publications listed in the Bibliography, helped me to compile a useful handlist of Price's prose and verse works, together with sources for the various exemplars of each. The list is currently being checked against the various holdings of major libraries in Britain and the USA. This, of course, is a laborious and not wholly scientific procedure, in the absence of thorough listings (and especially after 1700 and before 1641, the dates within which Wing's catalogue operates); and no doubt further examplars and perhaps even further titles will crop up. But at least it has been possible to reconstitute a working checklist of Price's song repertoire and to begin to identify a substantial number of prose works.

Here follows my current listing of Price's known songs, in what I hope is a reasonably accurate chronological order, either by date of entry in the *Stationers' Company Registers*, or by internal or other evidence, together with the location of a signed (usually, initialled) exemplar, the person or persons to whom the piece was entered, the name of the (currently) earliest known *publisher* (printer's names rarely appear on the earlier texts), and the dates between which that publisher (or group of publishers) is known to have been active.

The second list is the same except that the titles have been attributed to Price by one authority or another, with varying degrees of confidence and likelihood. Almost all of the *DNB*'s list has been found, so there is little reason to doubt that *The young man's feast* existed (if it does not still exist); and Chappell and Ebsworth's guesses have proved accurate with other titles, so we should not despair of these attributions either, even when the texts are claimed for some other writer. For example, *The Constant Lover* is attributed by Crawford (who is not at all reliable on dates) to Peter Lowberry, but Chappell and Ebsworth follow Payne Collier in believing that Price inverted his initials with this text (a not uncommon practice, when anonymity was preferred).[23] On *The Coy Shepherdess* they seem to have changed their minds, but I have retained the attribution just in case they were right first time.[24] *Deplorable News from Southwark* reads like a Price text, and uses the tune of his *The Merry Man's Resolution*; but its inclusion here remains problematical, and I would not go to the stake on the issue of its being definitely his, particularly since writers often pinched each other's tunes and themes. However, when all exemplars have been traced and studied, it is possible that some of these attributions will be shown to be accurate: meanwhile, we can note that Price published at least forty-nine songs, and perhaps as many as sixty-two.

There are those who would find the most significant thing about this reconstituted repertoire to be the fact that Laurence Price wrote not one but *three* 'Child ballads' – not only *A Warning for Married Women*, entered to Francis Grove in February 1657, but also *Robin Hood's goulden pryse* (also entered to Grove) and *The famous flower of Serving-Men* (entered to John Andrews), in June and July 1656. As it happens, Child knew from Ebsworth that *The famous flower of Serving-Men* was signed by 'L.P.', and did not doubt that the initials were those of Laurence Price. Similarly, he noted that what he called *Robin Hood's Golden Prize* was also by Price (again relying on Ebsworth); but in neither case did he take the matter any further in print.[25]

What is more important is the fact that, even though reconstitution is not yet complete, these three texts are all of them among the most frequently found in broadside and other collections: indeed, of the texts known to be by Price, they are all in the top four of what we may call his 'greatest hits'. *A Warning for Married Women* appears on broadsides and in garlands at least a dozen times up to the end of the eighteenth century: *Robin Hood's goulden pryse* is found no fewer than fifteen times from the 1650s up to the early nineteenth century, on broadsides, in garlands and

Title	*Signed exemplar*	*Stationers' Company entry*	*Entry date*	*Date*	*Earliest known colophon*	*Active*
Oh Grammercy Penny	Pepys, I, 218-19	–	–	1628?	Printed for M[argaret] Trundle, widdow	1626-1629
Rocke the Cradle, John	Roxburghe, III, 176	Ed. Blackmore	4.11.1631		Printed at London for E[dward] B[lackmore]	1618-1658
Newes from Hollands Leager	Pepys, I, 98-99	Henry Gosson, Fran Coles	24.5.1632		London, printed for I[ohn] W[right]	1605-1658
The Honest Age	Pepys, I, 156	Henry Gosson, Fran Coles	24.5.1632		London, printed for H[enry] G[osson]	1603-1640
The two fervent Lovers	Roxburghe, I,416-17	Henry Gosson, Fran Coles	24.5.1632		London, printed for Fr[ancis] Coules	1626-1681
Friendly Counsaile	Roxburghe, I, 16	Rich Harper	22.5.1633		London: printed for Richard Harper	1633-1652
A Compleate Gentle-woman	Roxburghe, I, 62-3	Jno. Wright & partners	8.7.1633		No Imprint	
A Warning for all Lewd Livers	Roxburghe, I, 442-3	Tho Lambert	14.7.1633		printed at London for Thomas Lambert	1633-1643
A wonderfull wonder	Roxburghe, I, 482-3	–	–	1635?	Printed at London for Iohn Wright, junior . . .	1634-1667
The Bachelor's feast	Roxburghe, I, 12/17	Jno. Wright, Jr	28.6.1636		Printed at London for I[ohn] W[right] the younger . . .	1634-1667
Bee Patient in Trouble	Roxburghe, I, 496-7	Jno. Wright, Jr	28.6.1636		Printed at London for John Wright junior . . .	1634-1667
Round boyes indeed	Pepys, I, 442	Jn Wright Jr	24.6.1637		Printed at London for I[ohn] Wright	1634-1667
The Young-man's Wish	Roxburghe, I, 440-1	Fran Grove	25.1.1638		Imprinted at London for Iohn Wright, the younger	1634-1667

Title	*Signed exemplar*	*Stationers' Company entry*	*Entry date*	*Date*	*Earliest known colophon*	*Active*
A new Spanish Tragedy	Wood, 401, 137-8	Jno. Stafford	15.10.1639		London, printed for Samuel Rand	–?1642–
Cupid's Wanton Wiles	Roxburghe, III, 172	–	–	1640?	Printed at London for John Wright the Younger . . .	1634-1667
The merry-conceited Lasse	Roxburghe, I, 240-1	–	–	1640?	Printed at London for Thomas Lambert . . .	1633-1643
A Monstrous Shape	Wood, 401, 135-6	–	–	1640?	Printed by M[iles] F[lesher] for Tho[mas] Lambert . . .	1633-1643
The true manner of the Life and Death of Sir Thomas Wentworth	BM C 20 f 2 (8)	–	–	1641	London, printed for Richard Burton . . .	1641-1674
The poore Musitioner's Song	BM E 1113 (2)	–	–	1642?	London, printed by E[lizabeth?] P[urslowe?] for J[ohn] Wright	1634-1667
Good Ale for my money	Roxburghe, I, 138-9	–	–	1645?	Printed at London	
The dainty Damsel's Dream	Roxburghe, III, 226	–	–	1654?	London, printed for John Andrews	1654-1661
Strange and wonderfull news	BM, C 20 f 14 (2)	–	–	1655?	London, printed for Fran[cis] Grove	1623-1661
A Warning for all wicked Livers	Manchester, I, 32	–	–	1655?	[L]ondon printed for F[rancis] Grove . . .	1623-1661
The famous Woman Drummer	Roxburghe, III, 234	–	–	1655?	London printed for F[rancis] Coles, J[ohn] Wright, T[homas] Vere, and W[illiam] Gilbertson	1655-1658

The Countrey peoples Felicity	Euing, 49	Fran Grove	12.3.1656	London, printed for Francis Grove . . .	1623-1661
Dead and Alive	Roxburghe, III, 210	Fran Grove	12.3.1656	London, printed for F[rancis] G[rove] . . .	1623-1661
flora's farewel	Euing, 121	Fran Grove	12.3.1656	London, printed for F[rancis] G[rove] . . .	1623-1661
The Maydens of London's brave Adventures	Roxburghe, III, 224	Fran Grove	12.3.1656	London, printed for Fran[cis] Grove . . .	1623-1661
The Maid's Revenge upon Cupid and Venus	Roxburghe, III, 222	Fran Grove	12.3.1656	London, printed for Fra[ncis] Grove . . .	1623-1661
The Merry Man's Resolution	Manchester, I, 27	Fran Grove	12.3.1656	London, printed for F[rancis] Grove . . .	1623-1661
Joy after Sorrow	Wood E25, fol 60	Tho Vere	25.3.1656	Printed for Tho[mas] Vere . . .	1646-1680
Loves fierce desire	Euing, 175	Tho Vere	25.3.1656	London, printed for Tho[mas] Vere . . .	1646-1680
A Wonderful Prophecy	Euing, 400	Jno. Wright	26.3.1656	London, printed for J[ohn] Wright . . .	1667-1677
Give me the Willow Garland	Crawford, 105	Fran Grove	23.4.1656	Printed for F[rancis] Coles, T[homas] Vere, J[ohn] Wright, and I[ohn] Clarke	1674-1679
The Quaker's feare	Wood 401, 165-6	FC, JW, TV, WG	25.4.1656	Printed for F[rancis] Coles, J[ohn] Wright, T[homas] Vere, and W[illiam] Gilbertson	1655-1658
A New merry Dialogue	BM, C 20 f 14 (6)	W. Gilbertson	15.5.1656	London, printed for William Gilbertson . . .	1640-1665

Title	*Signed exemplar*	*Stationers' Company entry*	*Entry date*	*Date*	*Earliest known colophon*	*Active*
The two Jeering Lovers	BM, C 20 f 14 (2)	W Gilbertson	15.5.1656		London, printed for William Gilbertson	1640-1665
The Matchless Shepheard	Rawlinson 566, fol 36	Fran Grove	30.5.1656		London, printed for F[rancis] Coles, T[homas] Vere, and J[ohn] Wright	1663-1674
Robin Hood's goulden pryse	Wood 401, 39-40	Fran Grove	2.6.1656		London, printed for F[rancis] Grove . . .	1623-1661
The famous flower of Serving-Men	Euing, 111	Jno. Andrews	14.7.1656		London, printed for John Andrews	1654-1663
The Maiden's Delight	Euing, 205	Fran Grove	24.9.1656		London, printed for Fran[cis] Grove . . .	1623-1661
A Warning for Married Women	Euing, 377	Fran Grove	21.2.1657		Printed for [Francis] Coles, T[homas] Vere, and W[illiam] Gilbertson	1658-1664
The Seaman's Compass	Euing, 325	Fran Grove	26.6.1657		London, printed for F[rancis] G[rove] . . .	1623-1661
The True-Lovers' Holidaies	Crawford, 857	–	–	1660?	Printed for F[rancis] Coles, T[homas] Vere, and J[ohn] Wright	1663-1674
Win at First, Lose at Last	Roxburghe, II, 522	–	–	1660	London, printed for Fra[ncis] Grove . . .	1623-1661
The faithful Maids Adventures	BM, C 20 f 14 (7)	–	–	1661?	London, printed for Francis Grove	1623-1661
Seldome cleanly	Euing, 330	–	–	1661?	London, printed for Iohn Wright	1634-1667
The young man's resolution to follow		–	–	1661?	London, printed for Fran[cis] Grove	1623-1661
Welcome Merry Christmas		–	–	1675?	London, 1675. Printed for	1644-1680

Title	*Attribution*	*Stationers' Company entry*	*Entry date*	*Date*	*Earliest known colophon*	*Active*
A new little Northern Song	Chappell & Ebsworth	Fran Coles & partners	13.6.1631		London, printed for H[enry] G[osson]	1603-1640
The young man's feast	DNB	–	–	1635?		
The Constant Lover	Chappell & Ebsworth	Henry Gosson	8.1.1638		London, printed for Henry Gosson	1603-1640
The honour of Bristol	Ebsworth, Crawford, Chappell & Ebsworth	–	–	1639?	Printed for T[homas] Vere	1644-1680
A New Game at Cards	Chappell & Ebsworth	Francis Coles, John Wright, Thomas Vere, William Gilbertson	(13.6.1656)	1646?	No Imprint	
The Gallant She-Souldier	Chappell & Ebsworth	–	–	1655?	London, printed for Richard Burton . . .	1641-1674
The Ship-Carpenter's Love	Chappell & Ebsworth	–	–	1656?	No Imprint	
The Coy Shepherdess	Chappell & Ebsworth	–	–	?	Printed for R[ichard] Burton . . .	1641–1674
Deplorable News from Southwark	Harker	–	–	?	Printed for Tho[mas] Vere	1644-1680
The Distressed Pilgrim	Chappell & Ebsworth	–	–	?	London, printed for W[illiam] Thackeray, T[homas] Passenger, and W[illiam] Whitwood	1666-1695
Cupid's Delight	Chappell & Ebsworth	–	–	?	Printed for J[ohn] Deacon . . .	1693-1695
A Pleasant Ditty of the King & the Souldier	Chappell & Ebsworth	–	–	?	No Imprint	
The Chamberlain's Tragedy	Chappell & Ebsworth	–	–	?	London, printed for J[ohn] Deacon	1693-1695

as part of compilations such as Evans's *Old Ballads* and Percy's *Reliques*;[26] while *The famous flower of Serving-Men* has so far been found in early print twenty-four times, not only in the 1723 *A Collection of Old Ballads* and in the *Reliques*, but also in Ritson's *Select Collection of English Songs*, [27] and on broadsides published well into the nineteenth century, and as far afield from London as Coventry, Worcester, Gloucester and Newcastle-upon-Tyne.

In all, I have so far been able to trace some 235 early exemplars of Price's known *and* attributed songs.[28] Thirty texts have been found in more than one exemplar – an average of over six apiece – while six texts, including the three canonised by Child, have eleven or more exemplars. Of those pieces known to be by Price, I have so far found 191 exemplars, twenty-three of which have more than one extant example – an average of some eight apiece – with five texts, again including the three 'Child ballads', having eleven or more exemplars. It is clear that we are dealing with a songwriter whose work was not only significantly popular over time and geographical/cultural space, but was also an important cultural commodity in the broadside trade, and then, later, in the market for 'antiquarian' poetry and song in book form. But before we go on to these matters we can glean some general information about Price from the chronology of his known song-texts.

As the *DNB* guesses, Price seems to have begun writing songs for publication in the later 1620s, when he may well have been not yet 20. A provisional birth date of around 1610 does not then seem unreasonable. Aside from *Welcome Merry Christmas*, which formed part of a pamphlet issued by Thomas Vere in 1675, there seems no reason to believe that Price wrote songs after 1660 or perhaps 1661. It is true that his initials linger on some broadside exemplars into the early eighteenth century – for example, on the Chetham Library copy of *A Wonderful Prophecy*, which was published by John White in Newcastle-upon-Tyne probably after 1708 (and possibly at any time up to 1760) – but the general tendency was for 'L.P.' to be missed off known Price texts much earlier than that. Of texts so far examined, the following can be definitely dated after 1661: *Flora's farewel* (Douce Collection, 1, 78v, dating from 1674-9), *Give me the Willow Garland* (BM C 22 f 6 (47), and Crawford no. 105, both dating from 1674-9), *Loves fierce desire* (BM C 22 f 6 (59) the Houghton Library exemplar, the Douce exemplars, 1, 114r and 132 and Crawford no. 909, all dating from 1678-80), *The Seaman's Compass* (Rawlinson Collection, 566, 64, dating from 1663-74, and Jersey Collection, dating from

1674-9), *The True-Lovers' holidaies* (Rawlinson Collection, 566, 195, and Crawford no. 857, dating from 1663-74), *A Warning for all Lewd Livers* (Crawford no. 828, dating from 1693-5), *Win at first, Lose at Last* (Roxburghe Collection, II, 522, dated on the text, 1680), and *A Wonderful Prophecy* (Roxburghe Collection, III, 664, Chetham Library, no. 226, dating from after 1708, Pepys Collection, II, 55, dating from 1681-4, Euing Collection, no. 400, dating from 1667-1677, and the Crawford no. 801 and BM C 22 f 6 (25) exemplars, perhaps dating from the 1690s).

Logically, this could suggest that Price did not die until 1708, or even 1760, if he kept his rights in his texts as long as he could![29] More likely, however, is that his initials were carried over by printers as part of the text. This certainly could be understood in relation to *A Wonderful Prophecy*, which ends with a lot of prose, amongst which 'Contrived into metre, by L.P.' could well have been missed by printer and publisher alike. As for *Win at First, Lose at Last*, Chappell and Ebsworth took it as read that the exemplars bearing the date 1680[30] were reprints of what they expected to have been an original publication of 1660. Of Price's prose works, only eight of the thirty-three so far identified were *not* first published before 1661, and chances are that a similarly thorough search of library holdings would turn up earlier editions of these. So the date of 1680 for his death seems less certain; and there is some reason to suppose that Price may well have died by 1661 or not long afterwards.[31]

In terms of his activity, however, there seems little question that he wrote most of his known songs in (or just before) the period 1655-1657, given that he would be unlikely to risk keeping manuscripts by him for fear of plagiarism, and that the people who entered the texts at the Stationers' Company were unlikely to delay publication for much the same reason. According to the current chronology, after his first-known text appeared in the late 1620s, he published barely one song a year for the entire 1630s, the same for the early 1640s, and nothing at all *in verse* for the years 1646-1654. 1655 marked his re-entry, perhaps, and on one day in March 1656 no fewer than nine of his songs were entered in the Register, to be followed by another eight in the next six months. Thereafter, only two more of his known songs were entered, one of them *A Warning for Married Women* in February 1657, and another piece in June of that year; and the remaining six songs may have been first published around the time of the Restoration. (Interestingly, of his prose works so far tracked down, the earliest dates from 1639, three more appear in 1641-2, another two in 1648, one in 1650 and another in 1652, then come four in 1653, one in 1654, four in 1655, three in 1656 and four in 1657, followed by a gap until one more appears in 1660, and then those eight other texts from after 1665.) One of the attributed texts, *A New Game at Cards* – which had its colophon 'cautiously omitted' around 1646,[32] but which was evidently the basis for Price's later *Win at first, lose at last* – reminds us that the date of entry in the Register did not *have* to be the same time as when a text was written, or bought by a printer or publisher. This text was also registered in 1656, by Francis Coles and three partners who had recently entered Price's *The Quaker's feare*, and it suggests that Price didn't necessarily have an attack of writing fever in 1656, but that his earlier pieces were being safeguarded now that it was appropriate so to do. Similarly, we find that some of Price's texts were re-entered in the Register in 1675[33] – as it happens, by three of these same four partners, Gilbertson having died in 1665 – including *Dead and Alive*, *flora's farewel*, *The Maiden's Delight*, and *A Warning to all Lewd Livers*; so questions of what we now call copyright were evidently by no means clear, thirty years before the first Copyright Act of 1709.

Obviously, we need to look at the relationship between Price and the broadside printing and publishing trade; and when we examine his known songs we can discern some evidence of sustained relationships. In terms of entries in the Registers, for example, we note that the names of Henry Gosson and Francis Cole appear in the year 1632, among what seem to be one-off purchases, and then John Wright and partners and John Wright junior figure largely in the mid-1630s. Francis Grove had dealings with Price as early as 1638, but it is in 1656 that their business relationship blossomed – no fewer than ten Price titles were registered by Grove that year, with another two the next year. Thomas Vere and William Gilbertson appear as purchasers in 1656, on at least one occasion in partnership with Francis Coles and John Wright; so that, apart from one title entered by John Andrews in July, five people appear to have taken all Price could offer between March 1656 and June 1657.

In terms of publishing, the pattern is rather more varied, but all of these first-known exemplars were printed *for* their publisher or publishers, not *by* them, from Margaret Trundle onwards. There was still evidently a division of labour in the trade up to 1660 at least; but sometimes the person who entered a Price song also had it printed for them. This was true of Edward Blackmore, Henry Gosson, Francis Coles, Richard Harper, Thomas Lambert and John Wright the younger in the 1630s. The texts of the 1640s were not entered, and were printed for a variety of what seem to be one-off publishers – except the one for John Wright which, interestingly, includes the initials of a printer who may well have been the second woman to be involved with the commercialisation of Price's songs.[34] The songs entered in the period 1655–7 were also, many of them, printed for the people who did the entering; but a new feature of Price's publication at this period is the jointly-published broadside. Coles, Wright (son of John Wright junior) and Vere formed a partnership on their own between 1663 and 1674, and also with both William Gilbertson and John Clarke, in 1656; while in 1657 we find the names of Coles, Vere and Gilbertson on the same colophon. Francis Grove continued to publish his own entered songs in 1656 and 1657, but he also allowed Coles, Vere and Gilbertson to have one of his texts printed between 1658 and 1664, Coles, Vere and Wright to publish another between 1663 and 1674, and Coles, Vere, Wright and Clarke a third in the years 1674–9. Finally, of the half-dozen texts probably dating from 1660 or 1661, only publishers already involved with Price texts seem to have continued to be so: Coles, Vere, Wright and Grove; while even Price's attributed texts seem not to have strayed very far from these same people. Evidently, Price's texts were progressively monopolised by a very small number of print-trade people, especially after 1655, and it is notable that three of the four re-registered Price texts went from the hands of Francis Grove to those of Coles, Vere, Wright and Clarke, fourteen years after Grove left the trade. Is it possible to clarify how Price's works came to be gathered together in such a methodical fashion?

As it happens, it is.[35] John Wright senior had William Gilbertson as an apprentice, and another of his apprentices, Edward Wright, was later the apprentice-master of Francis Coles. John Wright's son, John junior, was apprenticed to Coles, and in turn went on to be the apprentice-master of Thomas Vere. (Wright the younger's own son, also John, became free of the Company through patrimony.) A later publisher, William Whitwood, was apprenticed to William Gilbertson. As for Francis Grove he had been part of a previous cartel, one of the assignes of Thomas Symcocke, and he took a later publisher of Price songs, William Thackeray, as an apprentice, who in turn took his own son, Thomas, just as Thomas Passinger took his namesake nephew. (Of significant Price publishers, only Henry Gosson, who became free of the Company through patrimony, seems not to have been involved in this ganglion, and in any case he seems to have stopped being active in 1640.) What seems to have happened is that a series of joint arrangements was made between printers and publishers who were connected through apprenticeship, family, or both. Following an idea from Leslie Shepard, and drawing mainly on Blagden's work, Thomson believes these early 'Ballad Partners' operated consistently from the time of the oldest John Wright to that of Thomas Passinger the elder (c. 1624–1692). Then, according to Thomson, there was a period dominated by the 'Successors to the Ballad Partners' (c. 1692–1715), another associated with the Bow Churchyard Press and the Dicey Family (c. 1715–1762) and a fourth based around the Aldermary Churchyard Press and the Marshall family (c. 1762–1795), after which the business inheritance trickled through John Pitts (c. 1797–1844) and William Fortey (c. 1849–1882) to Henry P. Such (c. 1875–1915).[36]

Do the earlier stages of the publication of Price's known texts fit this general pattern? Actually, to some extent, they do. The three John Wrights had their names on fourteen Price texts, either as the person entering it in the Register, or as publisher. Francis Coles had a hand in nine texts, sometimes in partnership with Wright and others. Thomas Vere's name appears in relation to nine first-known publishings, while William Gilbertson does so on five. In terms of republishings of these first-known texts, the relationships become even clearer, as does the continuity to Thomas Passinger. The eighteen texts associated with Francis Grove do, however, indicate that these 'Ballad Partners' did not enjoy a monopoly, either of Price's work or of the trade as a whole. After Grove's retirement in 1661, however, the texts he had controlled were either taken over by Coles and partners, with or without re-entering them (even before 1675), or picked up by Onley. But as William Thackeray had been in partnership with Coles, Vere, Wright, Clarke and Thomas Passinger in the period 1678–80, this distinction of two main strands of Price-publishing was already evidently breaking down. In fact, William Thackeray had several Price texts on his 1688–1689 List; and by the early eighteenth century, what appear to be London-printed broadsides were being sent to places like Newcastle, for the local publishers to add only their own colophon. So while the 'Ballad Partnership' by no means monopolised even Price's texts, let alone the broadside market (even when interests seem to have converged in the 1670s and 1680s, as first Clarke, then William Thackeray and Milbourn entered the fold), one-off publications of Price texts were common enough, suggesting that effective control over individual items was either far from complete, or that individuals could claim the right to publish with or without their normal partners.

Thomson believes that when Francis Grove died, in 1665, his former apprentice, William Thackeray, got hold of his 'ballad stock' and teamed up with Thomas Passinger, who had married his former master's widow, Sarah Tyus – Charles Tyus, apparently, had been Grove's printer for many broadsides. Thomson goes on to speculate that there may have been a rival 'ballad stock', based around Grove, later known as 'ye Antient Ballad warehouse', and that this had been in existence as early as 1656, when as we have seen there was a flurry of registration, including that of many texts by Price. Thomson claims to recognise a 'certain uniformity of typographical style', but since this could easily be explained by rival publishers using the same printer, this idea cannot easily be substantiated. We do know that the Great Fire of 1666 helped reorganise broadside publishers and printers, geographically, and that some refugees set up another 'Ballad Warehouse' at Pye Corner soon after but deaths also helped restructure the partnerships. In the 1680s, Coles, Vere, Thomas Passinger and the third John Wright all died. Passinger left his interest in broadside texts to his nephew, Thomas; but for perhaps two years, between 1688 and 1689, William Thackeray seems to have enjoyed sole ownership (or at least control) of 'ye Antient Ballad warehouse', until he went into partnership with Alexander Milbourn and John Millet, the printer. William Onley, meanwhile, went on printing for a rival cartel (or 'conger'), which included Phillip Brooksby, Jonah Deacon, John Back and Josiah Blore; but when Millet died in 1692, Onley got Thackeray and Milbourn's printing, too. Then, in 1695, Milbourn disappeared, and what Thomson terms a 'chaotic scrambling after copies' ensued, with imprints being frequently vague and general, or non-existent.[37] Certainly, in the early 1700s, William Onley seems to have printed and published almost any text he thought marketable – books as well as broadsides, by one account, after the expiry of the 1662 Licensing Act in 1695 – and his death in 1709 saved him from any Copyright Act repercussions. In any event, at this period chapbooks had come to be a better-selling commodity than broadsides, and the value of the older stocks declined. After all, by 1709, the oldest-known Price song was eighty years old, and only a fraction of his output was kept in print, even in the provinces. In London, the printer Thomas Norris made an attempt to corner the broadside and chapbook trade, entering no fewer than 174 songs from the 'Ballad Partners'' stock in the Registers for 1712; and he and Charles Brown seem to have had a stranglehold on the broadside song trade until perhaps 1720.[38] One of the texts they cornered was Price's *A Warning for Married Women*; another was *Win at first, Lose at Last*.

Between 1708 and 1762, John White of Newcastle published *The famous flower of Serving-Men*, *Loves fierce desire* and *A Wonderful Prophecy*. John Butler in Worcester also issued *The famous flower of Serving-Men*, between 1702 and 1708, and advertised it as being available in another Worcester shop as well as one in Gloucester; while John Turner of Coventry continued into the nineteenth century with his publication of that same song. In London, *The famous flower of Serving-Men* and *Joy after Sorrow* were issued by publishers in Bow Churchyard, between c. 1715 and 1762, and in Aldermany Churchyard, from c. 1762–1795 – *Dead and Alive* also appeared from Bow Churchyard. Thomas Evans – presumably the editor of the 1777 and 1784 editions of *Old Ballads* – published *The famous flower of Serving-Men* and *Robin Hoods golden prize* as broadsides (the former had appeared in Phillips's 1723–1725 work of the same title, and the latter appeared in all Evans editions); and those same two songs were published by a certain L. How in 'Petticoat-Lane, White Chappel', London. Finally, as we have seen, *A Warning for Married Women* started a new life as the truncated text, *The Distressed Ship Carpenter*, in two garlands and on two imprintless broadsides, possibly all dating from the 1780s. Even the most inventive special-pleading could not argue against the thesis that the three songs written by Price and then canonised by Child depended substantially for their circulation and survival on the broadside form; and it is clear that all three were being reissued right up to the point when they were 'collected' from what has traditionally been represented as 'oral transmission'. For my own part, I have no doubt that a systematic search of all eighteenth and nineteenth century broadside collections would only tend to confirm the general pattern that I have established, and might very well make the connection to Lowland Scotland that was there, but not well documented before the nineteenth century, as between Newcastle-upon-Tyne and Edinburgh, especially in the chapbook trade.

Interrogating the text

Having gone this somewhat roundabout route, we can now return to *A Warning for Married Women*, to try to tease out Price's ideas, attitudes and assumptions, so that we can address specific questions to what we know of the wider culture of the period, and begin to situate Price within it. This process can be developed, at a later stage, by an analysis of all his songs – and then his prose – to see if and how his ideas changed through time; but the analysis has to steer clear of both reflectionism (Price's texts are not cultural mirrors) and the autobiographical fallacy (these texts are not his direct account of his life and experiences).[39] And this is hard, given that content analysis is notoriously unscientific. Similarly, we cannot know anything from the texts about how they were produced, disseminated and consumed, since we do not have orally-collected versions or even manuscripts of any of Price's *known* texts from the second half of the seventeenth century. (The manuscript of *A New Game at Cards* is not certainly Price's text or handwriting.) Consequently, we cannot know anything for sure about a given text's performance in singers' repertoire-formation, how it was used on singing occasions, who used it and why. In short, the procedure we have to adopt is one of raising questions to which we may hope to find answers outside the texts, in most instances. And since the first Euing exemplar (no. 377) is the only one which Price may actually have seen in print, I will concentrate on that, making comparisons with later exemplars only when necessary.

(a) Format

At 38cm by 29cm, Euing no. 377 is considerably larger than the later texts – the next largest being Crawford no. 1114, at 38.5cm by 19cm. Euing 377 has four large woodcuts – of a gentleman, a gentlewoman, a man looking in astonishment at a woman riding away on a horse with what look to be long horns rather than ears, and a fourth of a warship at sea with one gun firing – whereas most other exemplars have only two woodcuts, one of a woman, and another of a warship at sea, and the Roxburghe exemplar has no illustration at all. Euing 377 has some decorative borders, but the others have none that in the Roxburghe Collection however, is a later frame, not part of the original text. Euing 377 uses black-letter throughout the text, whereas all later texts have progressively more white-letter; and all exemplars use white-letter for the title and precis. Euing 377 has thirty-two verses, in two columns apiece of seven and nine verses, all separated from each other; and most other exemplars have four columns, two of six verses and two of ten, though the Douce exemplar runs these verses together, and the Roxburghe exemplar has two columns of sixteen verses.

So what? Well, what we know of the song's transmission through the successive partnerships of the broadside trade makes continuities the less surprising – what appears to be the same woodcut appears on two exemplars, for example – but the way in which the focus of the woodcut of the woman goes from full figure to head and shoulders, and the way in which the men disappear and the ships eventually stop firing their guns, would doubtless provide much food for thought for bourgeois psychoanalysts. Considerations of paper size account for most other changes in format: the woodcuts on Euing 377 have obviously been physically altered (in one case) so as to fit the sheet and leave an incomplete margin. However, it is curious that white-letter gets used in the text for James Harris's name and then his speech,[40] suggesting in typographical form his otherness in the story.

(b) Title and precis

A Warning for Married Women is the title which appears on all exemplars up to c. 1720, though Thackeray's *List* refers to the piece by the name of its female character, *Jane Reynolds*. Euing 377 carries a short prose version of the narrative immediately under the title (which is followed, with minor variations, on all other texts):

> By the Example of Mrs. *Jane Renolds*, a West-Country Woman, born neer unto *Plymouth*; who having plighted her troth to a Sea-man, was afterwards Married to a Carpenter, and at last carried away by a Spirit: the manner how shall be presently recited.

Already, there are questions to be asked. Why did married women need to be warned, and against what, precisely? Did a woman named 'Jane Renolds' actually exist, and is this her real story? Did she live at Plymouth? What was the importance of plighting troths at this period,[41] and is there any significance in her doing so with a seaman? What kind of a seaman was he, merchant or navy? Why did she marry a carpenter? And did English people, in London or the provinces, really believe that people could be carried away by spirits? Some of these questions it is comparatively easy to answer; others will have to wait for an analysis of the whole story; and others again would involve massive research.

(c) Tune

Euing 377 recommends that the song be sung to 'a gallant West-country tune, ca'd, *The fair maid of Bristol*; Or, *Bateman*, or, *John True*.' (Three exemplars leave out *Bateman*.) None of the texts has printed music, which is almost always the case on broadsides of this period, and singers could well have adapted other tunes if they didn't know those mentioned. However, Simpson believes that all three titles refer to one tune, which he gives, and tells us was extant in 1597, and associated early on with Antony Holbourne.[42] As early as 1603, the tune had been used for broadside songs, and went on being a 'standard' for over a century afterwards, though this is the only occasion on which Price seems to have used it (if the suggestion was his, and not his printer's or publisher's) presumably because of the aptness of the west-country associations.

(d) Story

The narrative answers some of our earlier questions, though not in any watertight historical way, naturally. For example, we learn that 'Jane Renolds' (sometimes, 'Reynolds') lived 'Neer unto Plimouth stately Town', that she was 'of worthy birth and Fame', and that she had been courted by 'many a proper Youth' as well as one 'Iame Harris', himself a 'comely proper Youth' who was then already a 'Sea-man brave'. Evidently, the couple 'made a solemn vow' which for some unspecified reason was done 'secretly' – they even set a date for their future marriage – but then the narrative addresses the reader more directly, 'outside' the story as it were, to present the 'fatal' lovers almost as in a theatrical tableau. (The other texts print 'fatal' as 'faithful', which may be evidence of an earlier misprint from the manuscript, but which may also be a mistake.) This brings us conveniently to the bottom of the first column of verses – possibly the reason for the format – and leaves us with several more unanswered questions.

For example, did the lovers plight their troth in secret because of a difference in social or economic status – she being 'worthy' and he 'proper' and 'comely' but not necessarily rich – especially if he had to go to sea in order to earn enough money on which to get married? Did her parents disapprove? Or was this arrangement usual, especially when the men were sailors and could be away for years? Did James Harris exist, and what was he, a deckhand or a captain? Why does Price shift attention away from the 'Married

Women' of the title towards both lovers, at this point, and why does he modulate to a first-person narrative in the seventh verse?

The next seven verses form a recognisably distinct segment of the story: Harris is pressed to sea, presumably on one of the king's warships, and Jane Renolds does not try to follow him, as other women are known to have done.[43] Instead, she saw her duty as keeping herself a virgin for three years, at which point she hears of James's death and burial, 'within a Foreign Land'. Even after this news, she kept herself chaste for 'many a day' – 'never was she known at all/the wanton for to play'. Eventually, however, she encourages the addresses of a carpenter – it is Child who christens him a 'ship-carpenter', incidentally[44] – and the couple are then married 'with speed'. For four years, making seven in all since James Harris went away, they 'lovingly agreed', and had three children who made them 'wondrous glad'. So far, the narrative has a matter-of-fact, almost journalistic tone to it; but there are still questions to be asked. How usual was it, for example, for west country seamen to be pressed, and was it always for the king's ships? Could Jane's parents have had anything to do with the pressing? How long would it last, and could he have got free in some way? Why did she not go with him, or try to rush through the wedding ceremony? How did she get news of his alleged death and burial? What land might Harris have been in, and what could he have died of? Why could a carpenter court Jane openly, when a seaman could not? And what significance is there in Price's stress on Jane's long-kept virginity?

The next eighteen verses in Euing 377 do not form two equal narrative segments: in fact, the next fourteen verses form a discrete narrative unit, balancing the two sets of seven verses which set up the basic story, and give us the 'factual' information which is to be set against the unusual events that are to come. Jane's 'Good-man' goes away from home on a journey, which was to last three days, but we do not know why he went or where. While he was away, however, a 'Spirit' came to the window of Jane's house 'in the night' and 'did her sorely fright'. The 'Spirit' is introduced in a matter-of-fact tone, as though such things, while unusual, were not totally unexpected; but we may note that it is the narrator and not Jane who accords the apparition the status of 'Spirit'. In any event, the 'Spirit' spoke to Jane – presumably, through her bedroom window – addressing her as his 'dear and only love', and asking her to 'prepare and come away' with him. He calls himself 'Jame Harris', claims Jane for his wife on account of their betrothal, and maintains that he has travelled for her sake 'at least this long seven year', which is strange, since he is supposed to have died three years after having been *pressed* to sea, hardly evidence of his going for her sake! All the same, he goes on to stress that if she will now go to sea with him, 'all further strife' will cease. Quite what that strife might be is left hanging, but at no point does the 'Spirit' recognise her marriage to the carpenter, even if 'he' knew of it.

Jane's response indicates that, once her initial fright was over, she regarded the 'Spirit' as her 'sweet James'; but she begs the 'Spirit' not to tempt her – clearly, she *was* tempted – above all for the sake of her 'Children small', who she believes would be left without proper care. Presumably, she did not expect (or perhaps trust) her husband to take the responsibility seriously, for all his 'great fame' and the wealth which enables her to think of five hundred pounds as a sizeable enough amount to weigh against his finding out anything of this meeting. If this was a 'Spirit' what on earth could her husband say or do? James matches this imaginary largesse, mentions in passing that he might have 'had' a king's daughter, but that he 'forsook her golden crown' for Jane's sake, and asserts that she ought to come with him in order to fulfil her vow and so enable him to 'forgive all that is past'. It is curiously consistent that Jane's next query is about his visible means of support: she asks what 'means hast thou to bring me to', and as soon as the issue seems to depend on wealth James's confidence increases. He tells her of his 'seven Ships upon the Sea', complete with 'Marriners and Merchandize', that would be at her command, including their silken sails and 'Masts of shining Gold'. That did it: Jane ups and offs with the apparition 'in humane shape', and they go 'from off the English shore', never to be seen again. As she goes, Price has what must be another dig at her materialism, calling her with heavy irony, 'the woman kind' – again, later amended to 'womankind' and so bereft of clear meaning.

The questions that this segment raises are many, but at least we know that the carpenter was well-to-do, and so presumably seen as a proper match for a woman of 'worthy' birth. But why does Price choose to present the apparition of Harris as a 'Spirit' which 'spake like to a man' and to show Jane as taking the appearance for the reality? Did Price believe she was stupid? Is there any magical significance in the 'Spirit' coming only as near as her window and not, as an evil spirit could not unless invited, crossing her doorstep? Has the 'Spirit' got his time-scale wrong; and why doesn't he know of Jane's marriage? Why does he want to take her to 'sea', rather than to some other land? And why did Jane change her mind about her children, once the issue of her own material well-being appeared to have been cleared up? (Did contemporary widowers normally ignore their offspring at this period?) Is the 'Spirit' telling fibs about the king's daughter, and his fleet, and why does it appear plausible to Jane? How could a pressed man get together that much wealth? Is it the case that betrothal vows were generally thought to be stronger than marriage and child-bearing bonds at this period? Why does Jane shift the question from emotional to material concerns – is Price implying that she's simply a gold-digger, and heartless to boot? And is there any non-magical reason why Jane might have been 'never heard of more', other than being the willing victim of a 'Spirit': in what sense might she have been the authoress of her own fate?

The last four verses deal with the carpenter and the children, once the 'Spirit' and Jane disappear from the narrative. The carpenter returns, finds the children alone and Jane gone, then runs out into the street, beating his breast, tearing his hair, making 'heavy doleful cryes' and crying. Price presents him in this 'sad distracted state', and makes no particular fuss about the fact that the carpenter went and hanged himself 'for woe' on a nearby tree. Quite why the carpenter should be sorry to lose such an apparently capricious wife, and why he could not pay to have the children looked after (if he didn't want to do it himself), is not made clear. Instead, Price regales us with a tableau of the suicide, with motherless and now fatherless children 'left without a guide', and with an invocation of 'heavenly powers' which will, he presumes, 'for them provide'. To say the least of it, this is a peculiar end to the narrative.

There are, of course, more questions. Was Jane typical, or atypical: did women leave their husbands for other men, let alone for 'Spirits', at this period? How credible would the carpenter's suicide have been to contemporary readers? Did men behave in public in such ways, then, or was the carpenter going well over the top? What really happened to orphan children? Is Price's invocation of 'heavenly powers' – it is notable that he did not use 'God' – merely token, or is it automatic and unquestioned? Did Price want his readers to feel reassured at the end, or did he simply want a violent climax to his story? Is the story really about materialistic and capricious women, and in what sense would Jane's fate act as a 'Warning' and to whom? Is the story meant to be believable, or is it simply a po-faced spoof, fit to dupe the really superstitious and to delight the worldly? Does Price believe his own propaganda? Or did he knock out a tale for the broadside market for 'wonders' spiced with more than a suggestion of adultery *and* supernatural powers? Obviously, we need to set this long list of questions against what we can glean from all of Price's other known song, – and, eventually, his prose works, but it is educative to look at other attempts to understand the broadside versions of *A Warning for Married Women* before we move on.

(e) Other analyses

There is remarkably little written on this song, given its longevity and especially from the 'ballad' scholars of the later nineteenth century. William Chappell, writing in 1880, announced that

> This is a tale of a married woman who is prompted by the spirit of her deceased lover to leave her husband and three children, and to go with him. She had waited three years for her lover, and heard that he was dead, before she married; so, this being the seventh year, she was badly treated by this member of the spirit world. Her husband hanged himself, and she was never heard of more. The warning to other married women herein conveyed (unless it be against the tricks of evil spirits) is rather obscure. Of course, it did not occur to any one that the old lover could have returned in the flesh. The miracle saved Mrs. Jane Reynold's reputation.[45]

In other words, Chappell gives a late Victorian British slant to Price's tale, hinting at adultery, a clever cover-up, and a sustained public 'reputation', as though Jane Reynolds were a crafty gold-digger of his own time, when divorce remained somewhat problematical, even for the well-to-do, not to mention the religious proprieties.

A dozen years later, Child picks out the name of the 'Spirit' for his title to a broadside which he admits was originally called *A Warning for Married Women*, and makes the following perfunctory judgement: 'Two or three stanzas of A are of the popular description, but it does not seem necessary to posit a tradition behind A.' Thus, he feels unmoved to date the various broadside texts he cites, let alone discover the earliest, and contents himself with noting correspondences with later manuscript versions, and with giving a potted account of the tale:

> Jane Reynolds and James Harris, a seaman, had exchanged

> vows of marriage. The young man was pressed as a sailor, and after three years he was reported as dead; the young woman married a ship-carpenter, and they lived happily together for four years, and had children. One night when the carpenter was absent from home, a spirit rapped at the window and announced himself as James Harris, come after an absence of seven years to claim the woman for his wife. She explained the state of things, but upon obtaining assurance that her long-lost lover had the means to support her – seven ships upon the sea – consented to go with him, for he was really *much* like unto a man. 'The woman kind' was seen no more after that; the carpenter hanged himself.

Child's italicisation of '*much*' suggests he shared Chappell's belief in a cover-up for elopement and adultery, but he leaves the matter there, except to add a footnote:

> Why the ghost should wait for four years, and what is meant in st[anza] 18 by his travelling seven years, it is not easy to understand. The author would probably take up the impregnable position that he [sic] was simply relating the facts as they occurred.[46]

And that's that. Child sees no need to historicise the story, to question other apparant anomalies, or to follow up cultural issues which must surely have seemed strange, especially in late nineteenth century Boston. He admits the song had an author, but doesn't trouble to find out a name, as easily he might. What seems mysterious is allowed to remain so. As with Chappell, of course, such comments (and failures to comment) tell us much more about those who make them than about what they purport to analyse.[47]

Price's ideas in verse

This is not the place to produce an exhaustive content analysis of all of Price's known songs; but we can glean a little from them about what were his ideas on key issues raised by *A Warning for Married Women* and how they may have changed. For example, we would like to know more about how he represents women, as wives and mothers, spirits and the supernatural, wealth and the lack of it, social status, London and the provinces, to mention only the most obvious. Then there are questions about his own role as a songwriter – his responsibilities and possibilities, occasions for singing, support for political, religious, civil and related ideas – which may connect with the little we have been told about his life. Were his songs of the 1630s different to those of the 1640s? Did any of his ideas change after the execution of Charles I in 1649? Or after Cromwell's death in 1658? Or at the Restoration? Did the defeat of the Levellers at Burford, or that of the Diggers at St George's Hill, leave any traces in his songs? Or did he steer clear of any overt political position-taking in his songs – as distinct from his prose pamphlets – and concentrate on personal and moral questions in his choice of narrative themes and his treatment of them? Such questions need to be raised: getting reliable evidence from songs is, of course, a rather problematical procedure; and we have space, here, to concentrate on only a few of them.

(a) Money

Price's first-known song is *Oh Grammercy Penny*, and sets out to 'prove that a penny is a man's best friend', because everything has its price – friendship, good neighbourliness, justice, hospitality, women and, of course, 'Musitioners' at a 'Taverne' or 'Ale-house'. Sexuality is subject to the cash nexus – 'Sometimes you may have a desire to a Wench' – and the deal will be struck once 'she your gold and your money did see', just as any 'Rich Merchant' would treat you with respect on seeing your 'purse well lined and gold in your fist'. To Price, the 'good penny' is more useful in the city than 'Pape *Gregories* blessing or curse', because it can transform lesser mortals into 'Gentlemen'; conversely being without cash makes a person a 'moneyless mate' in a tavern company. This world-weary cynicism is carried through to *Rocke the Cradle, John*, whose 'hero' is a 'Country Gallant' who has wasted his money by coming to the city to court a woman worth £60. But the tables are turned, and she has him as though 'Prentise bound', doing the household chores and minding her children while she gets her breakfast in bed. The want of money, says Price, can un-man you, according to the assumed criteria for manhood, which evidently included frequenting brothels, as in *Newes from Hollands Leaguer*, where inappropriate spending power would result in a dip in the Thames, 'responsible introduction' or no. And even *A Warning to all Lewd Livers*, while pretending to condemn a rake's progress, tots up the £800 and more that is wasted.

Towards the end of the 1630s, however, Price begins to lean towards the honest tradesman, and away from the spendthrift 'gallants', echoing the general criticism of Charles I but at a safe social level; yet he ends *Round boyes indeed* with a personal appeal for the 'gallant gentlemen' in the 'company (presumably, of an ale-house) to give the singer a 'hansell' for a drink to make his throat 'more shrill and clear'. If he was writing for tradesmen, and not simply about them, they must have been well-to-do if 'a crowne' was a possibility, even for an evening's entertainment: but, of course, entertainment was a commodity to be bought and sold in the marketplace, too, as were the favours of the 'lewd Queans' Price so often satirises.

The songs thought to be from the later 1630s and early 1640s certainly treat money seriously, but, as in *Good Ale for my money*, not for the same status audience. His appeal to 'some good fellowes here' is at the more modest level of asking them to 'joyne together pence a peece,/to buy the singer beere', and to get in another round of 'Jugs' to 'drink to him that pen'd' the song, suggesting that the two were not always one and the same person, if they ever were. The 'we' of the song is not patronising and, as yet, not assumed to be opposed entirely in (*A new Spanish Tragedy*) to the state taking plunder from Spanish ships which used coin as shot; though Price appears reluctantly impressed by the 'hog-faced gentlewoman' from Holland's silver, gold and pearls valued at over £60,000, not to mention corn and cattle, in *A Monstrous Shape*. That Price was directing his commodities down-market, however, seems clear: *Good Ale for my money* is all about the economy of buying a dozen bottles of ale for the same price as a quart of imported wine from a tapster; and the price of an evening's drinking – two shillings – isn't half the tip he once expected for the singer. Moreover, though the anti-heroine of *A Monstrous Shape* might lure a husband because of her wealth, Price proclaims she is not fit to be a 'nurse' in England.

If Price did in fact stop writing songs between 1646 and 1654, it must be said that his ideas seem to have changed very little during that decade. In *The dainty Damsel's Dream*, the woman is clearly influenced by the 'purse of gold' her dream-lover brings, and by his promise that she 'should never want such Coyn' while he lived. In *The famous Woman Drummer*, Price explicitly asks his audience to buy copies to send to women; but he returns to the supposedly insatiable demand of women for cash in *Strange and wonderfull news*, where the woman sells her soul to the Devil, who calls in his debts in a suitably brutal fashion. Even the Devil is subject to the cash nexus! And property has to be defended: *A Warning for all wicked Livers* takes for granted that robbing the wealthy and stealing a woman's clothes (and anything else that can be converted into cash) deserves hanging, be the culprits 'high or low, great and small'; but that property seems also to include wives. The husband of the woman in *Strange and Wonderful news*, for example, may have left 'means and money' while he went away overseas to make some more, presumably by trading, but he also left her 'without a guide' – his investment was not secured, and she was free to treat herself as a commodity with the Devil! Just so were the women who sold their bodies in the brothels of London, a tour of which Price makes the subject of *The Merry Man's Resolution*, a song which exudes no confidence that a libertine with such purchasing-power would ever reform. Nor is it at all sure that Price believed that women could change: *The Maydens of London's brave Adventures* is ostensibly about a long list of 'London girls' being invited to sail for a 'new plantation' overseas, and being promised not only food and male company in transit, but gold, silver and other treasure at journey's end; yet there are hints that these women either have been prostitutes (was their journey voluntary?) and would be, effectively, overseas, as tied domestic labour.

The bargaining power – as Price represents it – of women in regard to their sexuality is made wholly clear in *The Maid's Revenge upon Cupid and Venus*, as the woman exerts her leverage in the marriage market and decides neither to buy nor sell: 'Shall I be bound, that may be free', she asks, rhetorically, after rejecting all her tradesmen suitors. On the other hand, once women offered their sexuality on the open market, as in *The Merry Man's Resolution*, a man could buy in the cheapest and safest place – in this case, one of the 'Country Mopseis'. Yet there is something disingenuous about the way in which the hero of *Robin Hoods goulden pryse* seeks to alter the real relations of priests to wealth, after they lied about having no cash about them. Robin makes them take an oath to be 'charitable to the poor' – an interesting contradiction to his attitude towards highway robbers in *A Warning for all wicked Livers* – and forces them to pray for some cash, which miraculously appears! *The Maidens Delight* introduces a somewhat different emphasis, in that an 'honest Trades-man' is held up as the salt of the earth as compared to a 'Vaporing Gallant', not only morally, but also materially, since the former had more earning power. What we know as the Protestant Ethic was seen to pay. Yet even 'country' lovers, like those in *A New merry Dialogue between John and Bessee*, have an eye for expensive fashion, John to wear and Bessee to admire – beaver hats, gold rings, and silk ribbons, not to mention servants and 'any fine fare that can be bought for money' – and 'pretty witty Nancy of the Citie' ridicules 'Dick Down-ryght of the Country' for *not* mending his uncouth appearance, in *The two Jeering Lovers*. Yet none of Price's men and women, including the 'country' people, seem to lack a house, land, goods and at least a modicum of cash: he does not write of landless peasants or unskilled labourers any more than he does (usually) of aristocrats and plutocrats; but *The Seaman's Compass* is perhaps his first song to treat the non-tradesman as socially useful according to cash criteria, and arguing with rich and poor that it is in their interest to support sailors.

By 1660, Price's alleged evolution back towards pre-war attitudes to property rights seems to have been considerable. His *Win at first, Lose at Last* may have been modelled on the mid-1640s *A New Game at Cards* (which has been attributed to him), but it is by no means similar in its ideas. For example, Price openly regrets that the nobility were beaten into submission, economically as well as militarily, and that 'Coaches gave the way to Carts'. He criticised what he saw as the greed of the 'Rumpers' in Parliament in trying to get hold of tithes and college lands; and he noted that some of those who foreswore Christmas on religious grounds did not scruple to 'follow Gameing all the Year' for their individual profit. As to material aspects of relationships between lovers, Price's ideas seem not to have changed though, as in *The True-Lovers Holidaies*, his scale of expenditure does, as the 'lusty Souldier, being one of the Auxiliaries' offers his purse to buy 'a new kirtle, wrought waistcoat & beaver/A dainty silk Apron' for sole rights to the commodity of the woman's person – 'So no body else shall enjoy thee but I.' (Promises are, however, made about future servants, a purse 'cram'd with gold crowns, & rich tresure'.) What makes the woman in *The faithful Maids Adventures* unusual is her valuing of her lover to the tune of several thousand pounds, though she offers to sell her smock to 'march' with him around Europe if need be; and it is interesting to speculate as to whether women following soldiers fell outside Price's customary assumptions about the mercenary city female. There is a hint in *Welcome Merry Christmas*, too, that the cobbler with his groat represented the social class of such an audience as remained to Price after the Restoration, and that, as with his attitude to lower-class women, he was ready to give that stratum of society the benefit of the doubt, particularly since he was unlikely to be welcome in the Music-House at the Mitre, near St Paul's, to write or sing the kind of reactionary and monarchical drivel that could be purchased in print at John and then Henry Playford's shop by the lawyers in the Temple.

(b) Women

The link between money and women might seem to have been made sufficiently clear already, but Price also represented other aspects of 'femininity' which usually dovetailed into his sour mysogyny, and which can be set against our provisional analysis of *A Warning for Married Women*. For example, even so early as *Oh Grammercy Penny* he recounts the offhand treatment of the penniless not only by men, but also by those women who acted as tapsters and hostesses at taverns and ale-houses; and in *Rocke the Cradle, John* he represents the worldly-wise and sexually experienced woman as being in league with the midwife to dupe the 'country Gallant' who is made to believe that twins born one month after their wedding are his responsibility. In general, especially in these early songs, Price sets himself up both as the warner of 'bashful youths' from the country *and* the entertainer of street-wise townsmen.

Paradoxically, for Price, only country women are capable of faithfulness in love; and when,in *A compleate Gentle-woman*, he finds himself called upon to celebrate a woman's 'willto chastitie', he does so in idealised (and perhaps tongue-in-cheek) fashion. Certainly, by the time of *The Bachelor's feast*, he despairs of anyone finding a 'vertuous wife' in the City; and even the woman in *Give me the Willow Garland*, who lives in the country, is represented as having tried over twenty men in order to find a satisfactory marriage partner. The masculinism of his attitudes, and the customary address to a male audience (even when women are being nominally written to) have at least the merit of consistency; and the sub-title of *Cupid's Wanton Wiles*, 'The Young Man's friendly advice', represents Price's assumed role as City-living wiseacre, or man-about-town, especially in relation to wine, women and, of course, song, which are linked in Price's way of seeing to the issue of 'wanton marriage' to anti-heroines such as the woman in *The merry-conceited Lasse*.

The songs from the mid-1650s (if so they are) carry on using women as both butt and a source of titillation, as in *The Dainty Damsel's Dream*; but at least Price never denies female sexuality –

in fact, it is the pivot of many of his songs. Was he pandering to the fantasies of war-weary soldiers with his tale of *The famous Woman Drummer*, and to sexual sadism in his detailed account of the bloody end of the anti-heroine of *Strange and Wonderful News*, where a formal admonition to 'take warning by her fall' is barely masked by an obvious relish for the sanguinary detail, enjoyed by many: 'The blood run all about the place,/as many folks can testify'. So end, according to the pamphlet said to be based on the song, all those guilty of being 'Proud or unfaithfull to God or their Husband'. Naturally, in Price's view, a woman could sin on her own – 'To Mallice, Hatred, Lust and Pride,/and wantonnesse shee was inclyn'd' – once out of sight of her husband and 'guide'. Yet, as *The famous Woman Drummer* reminds us, for Price a woman could only be really admirable when she was a *man*: when she showed masculine qualities by dressing as a soldier, following her man into 'valiant action, honest carriage, and excellent behaviour' in battle. That 'every one supposed that she had been a Man' is intended as a complement to this *honorary man*; but, of course, she is the exception – 'There's hardly such another to be found' – and generalising her behaviour remains at the level of a pious wish – 'I wish in heart and mind/That women to their Husbands were every one so kind'. (Such a celebration presumably also served to reinforce the attitudes towards military campaigns in Ireland, France and Spain that the 'noble-minded Souldiers' Price addresses were meant to have.)

And for all the abstract praise of country people, when it comes to something like a representation of country life, Price's values undergo a strange shift. *The Countrey peoples Felicity* may seek to celebrate an idyllic version of rural courtship, but Price evidently knew enough of land-work to describe the 'Maidens brows' dropping 'a pace with sweat' as she buckled down to work in the fields, and what really cheers him is the women's reconciliation to their lot. Their 'ready way of sweet content' and 'wholsome' life depends on the continuation of the practice that 'each one did their labour/and did no white repine'. Moreover, they are ideologically sound because they are not subject to the City's lures. Price wishes that 'every one in London were,/as pure in Deed and Thought;' but of course his representation of country work and courtship is outrageously idealised, to the point that he claims no one commits any 'hurt', or 'ill act' or did any 'ill business' in the cornfields. This is the more strange because Price appears to have known something about the day-to-day realities of country life, as in *Dead and Alive*, where he writes familiarly of 'fatling pigs', foxes and chickens, and notes the fact that the sheep belong to the woman who drank wine and then beat her husband until the tears 'ran down his hose'. This subtly named 'Simple Simon' from Gloucestershire can be laughed at, precisely because he failed at the major test of establishing male power in the home: he '*could not Rule his wife*'. And since he could not sort out the appropriate relationship Price does it for him, magically, and the couple go to bed 'with speed'.

Flora's farewel confirms that not only was the 'country' of Price's songs simply a convenient and fashionable setting, but that the women (and men) in that landscape were essentially townies, speaking in a metropolitan idiom. More, if the man can protest, 'Why should I to one love be bound', so the woman can exercise her right not to get involved in casual sex, and to spurn his 'cunning tricks of policy' to use her body. And for all its unsubtle irony, *The Maydens of London's brave Adventures* does in some ways appeal to the women's sense of adventure (and also, of course, to men's fantasies about reckless women). In *The Maid's Revenge upon Cupid and Venus*, Price's woman-figure speaks like one of his men: 'Shall I be bound, that may be free', she asks, and vows never to wed a 'false dissembling cogging man' so long as 'reason' rules her 'raging mind'. In other words, she treats men as men are represented as treating women: she is an honorary libertine, but one who could avoid the risks of gettig 'vapouring scabs' in Bloomsbury if she chose her lovers from respectable tradesmen, and not from the gallants represented in *The Merry Man's Resolution*.

Sometimes, as in what appears to be the allegory of *The Matchless Shepheard*, Price could represent 'female' powers in a more political manner. According to Rollins, the 'Shepheard' of the song is the Church of England, and the 'Schismatical Mistress' is none other than Parliament, who manages to 'Overmatch' the established church through the forces of 'English Schismaticks', the forces of Hell, catholicism, calvinism and presbyterianism.[48] In other words, the 'Mistress' is any other Price anti-heroine, writ large. Sensible women, of course, really wanted to be men, like the young woman who dresses up as a man and does 'manly' things in *The famous Flower of Serving-Men*! And if they won't do that, then women should behave like the woman in *A New Merry Dialogue betweene John and Bessee*, and service the man's needs in the time-honoured country way, letting him into her room at midnight so she can 'entertaine' him before he does the decent thing and agrees to marriage. Against the 'contrariness' which Price represents as typical in *The two Jeering Lovers* – where a townswoman first slights her suitor as 'Sir Lobcock' and then agrees to marry him – the heroine of *The Maidens Delight* is the exception which proves the rule, the drops of pure water which *A Wonderful Prophecy* sets against that 'very Sink of Sin' and 'Puddle of Iniquity' that is the world, and above all in its metropolitan manifestation.

The comparative lack of acerbity we have already noted in Price's later songs is borne out to some extent by the way in which they represent women. *The Seaman's Compass*, for example, is said to be 'made by a Maid that to Gravesend did pass', though her role is primarily to bolster up the status of 'brave Sea-men' by giving them privileged positions as suitors! '*There's none but a Sea-man/shall marry with me*', she tells us, in italics. So, in *The faithful Maids Adventures*, the woman has to prove her affection by first submitting to the demands of the man's life, just as she does in *The True-Lovers' Holidaies*, and as the anti-heroine of *Seldome cleanly* does not by her wilful refusal to stop being a slattern. In truth, there is almost nothing in Price's songs to suggest that he ever had more than a fear of strong women, and a contempt for weak ones, though that contempt might sometimes be masked by his 'common-sense' attitude towards his chauvinist conception of a woman's place.

(c) Religion and politics

These issues were so closely interwoven in the history of Price's lifetime that it makes little sense to seek to separate them in an analysis of his songs. Presumably, he was no Catholic: his very first song derides the value of 'Pape *Gregories* blessing or curse'; and though his songs of 1633 may have adopted their strenuous moral tone to suit a perceived audience, *A Wonderful Wonder* invokes a 'Lord' who is 'angry with this sinfull land', 'full of envy and debate'. Later, *A Warning to all lewd Livers* offers to castigate someone who accumulated a small fortune through debauchery, though against 'God's word'; and there is little sense of irony in the story of *A Wonderful Wonder*, when a man swears a 'rash' oath, and Price recounts the 'judgment of God' on him when he choked to death for his 'Vile blasphemie'. Yet beneath the moral tale lurks the wider ructions in church and state, to which those thunderings, visions and startling events are implicitly linked. Price puts himself on the side of the godly, and, in *Bee Patient in Trouble*, advocates Job's patience for 'greedy worldlings' – a position he says he reached himself when 'like you', he was 'troubled for a while', before becoming convinced of the 'great goodness of God'. Quite how this squared with his invocation elsewhere of 'God Cupid' – not to mention the 'Fates' and the 'Phoenix' – is, of course, problematical; but his presentation of religious fatalism is of a piece with his current dutiful reference to 'Our noble king'. Even in London, amongst respectable petty-bourgeois men, the fissures that were to open up before the Civil War had yet to rive Price or, presumably, his audience; and even in the early 1640s, Price could be as chauvinist as Martin Parker, when it came to xenophobia against the Dutch, as represented in *A Monstrous Shape*, or the Spanish, in *A new Spanish Tragedy*. In fact, Price takes more than journalistic relish in recounting how Spanish seamen 'had their very braines dasht out' in a naval engagement, and is scrupulous about wishing Charles I to stay 'in health, and wealth, and peace' in opposition to Catholic Spain, '*Gods Gospel to maintain*'. That last crack might have been subtly ironic, since some people felt that the king's encouragement of the Dutch fleet's attack on the Spanish vessels driven on to the English Downs was itself part of an attempt to 'crush English liberty'.

By 1641, however, Price felt called upon to make a song about an explicitly political internal affair, in *The true manner of the Life and Death of Sir Thomas Wentworth*, the Earl of Strafford, who was executed in May of that year. Like many another, no doubt, Price wanted to believe that Strafford's judicial murder was the result of 'his own folly', and had nothing to do with Charles or state policy in Ireland. Strafford's ambition is said to have caused him to act like a 'tyrant' in Ireland, where he made new laws and 'dealt most cruelly,/To men in misery'. There is, however, a certain ambiguity, in that Price's wish for the king and queen to flourish is associated with a warning about how even the most noble can 'catch the greatest fall' unless they enjoy 'True peace of conscience'; and it might be that Price was chiming in with the Long Parliament's strong hint that the impeachment of one of Charles's protégées could be only the beginning. And then, of course, Price goes silent for almost a decade, in terms of his printed songs.

When his work came into print once again, in the mid-1650s, 'Adonis' and 'Venus' get invoked as often as the Christian God, who is present in Price's songs almost as a formality, even in

Strange and Wonderful News. There, the 'Dear Lord' is asked to take note of 'this sinfull world', where 'The Divill doth like a Lyon go'; but the fact that this 'seeming Gentleman all in black' draws up not a contract but a 'Covenant' with the woman, just like the Scots had done not long before, could not have been ignored by Price's audience. Similarly, in the pamphlet said to be based on the song, Price dissociated himself from 'these *ranting*, *roaring* and most disloyall times', and this too could easily be read as distancing the author from both the regicides and the Ranters and other progressive sects. But this is speculation, especially given his ability to switch from a Christian God to a Heathen Pantheon at the twitch of a goose-feather!

How close Price was to the state in the mid-1650s is not clear, but it is interesting that the earliest broadside song known to Rollins that was 'Licensed according to Order' under the new regulations – four years before the practice was recorded in print on all such texts – was Price's piece, *The Quaker's feare*. According to Rollins, the story had been retailed in a prose pamphlet. The Quaker in question had starved to death in a prison in Colchester, Essex, and both the pamphlet and Price 'grotesquely departed from the truth'. It may be that Price was the victim of propaganda, and so 'merely repeats contemporary falsehoods';[49] but that he put his name to such a piece at all reveals a lot about his religion and politics. According to Price's song, the man Parnel 'set at naught' the teachings of 'Good Ministers', made 'disturbance up and down', and uttered 'wicked blasphemy'. So the fact that Parnel was put in a twelve-foot-deep pit, and died of injuries sustained when he fell back after trying to reach his food placed at the surface, can be righteously ignored by Price as he inveighs against the man who refused to conform:

> He in the midst of plenty starv'd,
> No matter if such hypocrites
> For their deserts were all so served.

And neither Price nor his printer showed any scruple in labelling a woodcut of the Pope with Parnel's name; so if Price did write on behalf of the state at this period, we have to understand that he no more felt it necessary to tolerate sects any more than Catholics, and that any smear was politically acceptable, however inaccurate or dirty. A people who 'learned the living Lord to fear' must necessarily fear the Lord's chosen representatives on earth.

Such blatant black propaganda makes *The Matchless Shepheard* seem sophisticated, if Rollins's reading is correct.[50] The burden of the piece is that the 'solid Shepheard' the protector of the flock, – presumably, an allusion to Cromwell – was wrong to put his trust in Parliament, a 'sort of Swains' who allowed his 'Sheep' of a people to 'scatter' and so fall prey to 'the ravening Wolf and Fox', those forces of Hell, Catholicism, Calvinism and Presbyterianism – not to mention the politically progressive Ranters and Levellers, and their successors – who had fouled up a 'democratic' experiment rather than prolong a benevolent dictatorship. Price sings a lament for Cromwell:

My Shepherdesse is gone,
  my Herds are run astray,
My pretty Lambs are stragled
  from me another way;
My Sheep-crook from me tane,
My Oaten Reed is lost;
  no Shepherd under Sun
  hath been so strangely crost.

If this analysis is correct, Price was by no means the 'vigorous Dissenter' Rollins proclaims him to be;[51] and, as for his political attitudes, the implicit conviction that Cromwell should have taken the crown parallels the representation of Robin Hood as a greenwood Enforcer on a smaller scale. Price's politics were probably hierarchical, not in any modern sense democratic, and this fits with what we know of his attitudes towards 'human nature' in general. And it is as well to remember that when Price wrote these two songs, and *The famous Flower of Serving-Men*, the state was beginning to drift back towards monarchism through the half-way house of personal dictatorship, to that patronage system celebrated in the song, when kings were kings, and had both courts and chamberlains – and, though this isn't said, minstrels too.

The logic of this counter-evolution in Price's political ideology leads, of course, to that revised version of *A New Game at Cards*, whose title sums up his attitude towards the 'democratic' experiment, *Win at first, Lose at Last*. Price openly rejoices that the king had 'recovered his Crown, and Traitors lost their Heads'. Was this Price being a turncoat, or had he always regretted the regicide, and held the 'Knave of Clubs', 'Old NOLL' himself, responsible? And did he always feel uncomfortable at the way in which '*Clubs were better Cards than Hearts*' at a time when aristocratic culture was being crushed, and that of any group who were not

Independents – '*all Cards but Black*'. Neither Oliver nor Richard Cromwell goes uncriticised: The 'Rumpers' are accused of hypocrisy; and the dissenting voices within the army and the chapels – 'such as preach in tubs', or 'bold Phanaticks' who '*every day broacht new Opinions*' – are treated with scorn. Had Price moved to the right, to keep pace with his market, or had he been covering-up a basic conservatism with writings which gave him enough left-cover? We may never know.

Songwriting in the seventeenth century

The discussion of money has already brought to light some clues as to Price's attitude towards writing songs: certainly, they were commodities to him, and the singing of them was an exertion of labour-power which deserved financial reward, albeit in the form of a tip, perhaps, rather than a wage with a rate for the job. There were suggestions, too, that his audience may have shifted from men-about-town in the 1630s, to tradesmen and then soldiers in the 1640s and 1650s; and he wasn't above pushing his products in and through his songs, in the commodity-form of broadsides. But while he seems to have associated songs and singing with ale-houses and taverns, there are hints that he knew at first hand not only the 'Musitians' who played in those genteeler places, but also those who worked the moated grange on the Bankside, the 'Store of musition' mentioned in *Newes from Holland's Leaguer*. Indeed, *Friendly Counsaile* speaks feelingly about the dangers of gambling and whoring, and ending up dead on a dunghill, without friends.

Of course, it may be that Price simply tailored his songs to what he perceived to be a likely market, irrespective of ideological consistency. *A Wonderful Wonder* can be read as being aimed at the market for the 'most strange and true', and other songs of his – *The Young-man's Wish*, for example – seems aimed at those familiar both with tennis balls and classical allusions. Certainly, his songs deal with issues of particular interest to the young, single, urban and skilled male, not only in their themes – the ubiquitous wine, women and song – but also in their attitudes, which are sometimes fiercely masculinist, and sometimes ironically defensive. Nor does this change too much as his audience moves from the city gallant to the 'honest tradesman' of his later songs, any more than do his attitudes towards religion and politics.

Though London may have supplied the country with broadside texts, it is hard to think of Price's assumed audience as anything other than metropolitan, or at least metropolitan-oriented. Thus, while he introduces the odd idiomatic word into *Dead and Alive* – 'wambles' and 'malifies', for example – this 'Gloucestershire' ditty is very similar to the 'Loamshire' of later years. Time and again he might use a little 'local colour', but his songs are often explicitly addressed to 'you London lasses' and to London men. London is at the centre of most of his songs, in one way or another, and *Dead and Alive* itself had to be 'sent/To London, for to have it put in print'. Whether, as Ebsworth opined, Price had first-hand knowledge of Bristol or Gloucester may never be known;[52] but the list of certifying witnesses' names appended to *A Wonderful Prophecy* indicates that Price liked to present himself as one who had contacts in the country, and who knew the latest news, as in Christian James's Padstow story which is 'Continued in Meter by L.P'.

Several of his songs first published in the mid 1650s speak of non-London stories: Price takes us to Padstow in Cornwall, Colchester, Nottinghamshire (by implication) and, of course, to Plymouth, in *A Warning for Married Women*. Sometimes, as there, he points us overseas, to America or other lands, with plantations – the places from which come all those commodities dependent on the merchant marine and *The Seaman's Compass*. At the same time, at this period Price was addressing an adult population who had known decades of civil upheaval and years of war, which involved thousands of young men being uprooted and marched up and down England, or sent to Ireland or elsewhere in the service of the state – all those places mentioned in *The faithful Maids Adventures*. It is interesting to speculate, then, about why so many of his songs were felt to be ripe for repeated publication in the 1670s and 1680s, before the Glorious Revolution, and at the high point of Restoration reaction. Who would buy them? And especially such overtly political tracts as *Win at First, Lose at Last*?

Of course, though we have so far ignored the political problems of being a songwriter in those interesting times, Price could not. Indeed, the Company of Stationers whose Registers contain so many of his songs was set up in 1612 as a monopoly 'ostensibly in order to control the publication of unlicensed and offensive ballads', a subject close to monarchs' hearts since at least 1543; and while the Star Chamber ceased prosecuting printers in 1641, when it was abolished, it was still the case that the licensed and entered texts represented perhaps as little as one quarter of the published titles. (Of Price's known songs, only twenty-six were entered, and none of those for the years 1640-1655.) The House of

Commons issued an order in March 1643 authorising a Committee of Examination to appoint people to look for 'scandalous pamphlets', and to seize presses or printers, so we may never know whether the texts attributed to Price for this period were in fact his, and especially anything he may have written between 1649 and 1655, when all unofficial news pamphlets were suppressed in order, initially, to keep alternative accounts of Cromwell's military massacres at Drogheda and Wexford off the streets. Though licensed books were permitted from May 1650 – a fact which helps explain why Price's output may have switched completely to prose during the next five years – we have no way of knowing whether Price made use of any illegal presses that may have been operating. Probably, however, he was constrained more than the cadre of royalist songwriters, whose patrons protected them from persecution; and he may well have rendered himself liable to prosecution, just as his printer would have been liable to fines and imprisonment, and any street-singers to floggings and the confiscation of their property, at any time between 1647 – when the Commons empowered a Committee to suppress oppositional songs – and 1655. Little wonder, then, that Price chose to write only on safe subjects, after the Bishops' Wars of 1639-1640 turned songwriters' attentions to journalism in verse form, or to prose pamphleteering.[53]

At the same time, the abolition of the Star Chamber meant that it was difficult for the Stationers' Company to enforce their privileges; and even after 1656 printers were not above occasionally forging a licence to get over the new regulations. Once again, Price seems to have been punctilious, since one of his songs was perhaps the first to bear the official licensing. The tightening noose of the previous decade had clearly exerted appropriate pressure. First, many of the white-letter presses were suppressed. Presumably because their royalist owners had the capital to invest in the new technology, while the London cartels stuck to their antiquated black-letter founts. Throughout 1648, printer after printer was arrested; and in London the army was used to winkle out offenders. In 1649, a Treason Act provided the full panoply of state butchery for persons convicted of having written, printed or openly declared that the Commonwealth was 'tyrannical, usurped or unlawful', or that the Commons was not the supreme authority in the state. A critic would have to be hardy indeed to risk putting pen to paper under these circumstances; and the practice of collecting printed matter – as done by George Thomason and

John Selden, the beginner of what became Pepys collection of broadsides – involved serious risks. Even in the provinces, hawkers and singers did not escape floggings and finings; while in London, from January 1653 to midsummer 1654, things got worse for dissenters, and eighteen printers went to Newgate. Singers and sellers were being 'sharply puneshed' at Devizes in 1655, and whipped in Yorkshire in 1656; but from 1653 songs began to make a cautious appearance, sometimes in prose pamphlets, until they too were almost totally wiped out by a further Act in 1653. Price, interestingly, kept on writing and publishing both prose and verse in 1656 and 1657.[54]

The songs of this period tend to be either 'wonders' or coarse – the first a handy way of disguising social comment, and the latter a form of moral dissent in their own right, which tended to be drawn together in booklet form, under titles such as *Wit and Drollery*[55] or *Choice Drollery*,[56] where the anti-Parliamentary feelings of their authors and compilers could be wittily coded. Cromwell ordered their suppression; and perhaps this accounts to some extent for the upsurge in licensing and entering that took place generally in 1656, in which Price's works formed a significant element. 1657 brought further repression, with an Act aimed at vagrants, including 'fiddlers and minstrels', and a staunching of the flow of new songs in the Registers; but Cromwell's death in 1658 saw the virtual end of state censorship, especially for that distinct market for polite and royalist songs which had separated itself out in the capital.[57] Broadsides were no longer of polite interest there, except to antiquarians like Samuel Pepys; but they were of interest to the state after the Restoration, and the Licensing Act of 1662, with its appointment of a Surveyor of the Press, who acted as political watchdog until 1688.[58]

The Licensing Act was allowed to expire in 1695, thereby effectively breaking the Stationers' Company's monopoly;[59] but there were those in the trade who could recall that a printer called John Twyn had been hanged, drawn and quartered so recently as 1663 for publishing a pamphlet deemed to be seditious.[60] Still, even before 1695, the processes of slackening state control had begun: a patent to license ballad singers granted to Sir Charles Killigrew in 1675 was soon after rented out to John Clarke, possibly the son of the broadside-publishing partner of an earlier period.[61] The final blow to this form of incipient monopoly – and to the 'Ballad Partnership' – was, of course, the Copyright Act of 1709, which transferred copyright from the publisher to the writer.[62] The logic of bourgeois individualism had worked itself through even to these backwoods of the publishing trade, and opened up the possibility of provincial publishing, which was quickly responded to by someone like John White in Newcastle.[63] 1709 was, of course, rather too late for Laurence Price to get the full reward for his labours, but the commodities he produced and sold to the trade went on being reprinted for a hundred years and more after his death.

A reading of *A Warning for Married Women*

A Warning for Married Women was a song produced in the form of a broadside 'ballad'[64] and so one of the earliest commodity-forms of song in England – the earliest mass medium. There is no significant evidence (only hints) that it was in existence before it appeared, probably c. 1657–8, in fact, it seems to have been produced specifically for sale to the broadside trade and, through them, to the market for broadsides, above all in London. The text passed through an orderly sequence of publishers, who had control over large numbers of such commodities, until just after 1710, or possibly later. There is absolutely nothing 'traditional' about it in this period; and its popularity has to be seen in the context of a very limited, metropolitan-oriented trade and market. Labouring people may never have had any significant part in the marketing of this text.

The song was written by Laurence Price, who also wrote two other songs canonised by Francis James Child. Price was at least a part-time professional songwriter,and he *may* have sung his and other people's material in London taverns after 1628. The audiences for his texts (and perhaps his singing) seem to have been different from those of a man like Martin Parker, and the other known songwriters who espoused the royalist cause. Price was something of a radical, and his other songs seem targetted at an audience which was predominantly male, single, and likely to be either involved in craft work, as journeymen, small masters or apprentices, or of men training to be professionals, especially in the law, where music, song and dance were endemic at this period, and were beginning to be institutionalised through the shop of the Playfords (father and son), and the various informal arrangements for music and song associated with certain London taverns. Price may have been somewhat down-market in this context, where competition would have been less strong; and we know him to have had a friendly rivalry with Parker, in spite of their apparent ideological differences.

The text does not represent a startling departure from the ideas, attitudes and general ideology implicit in Price's known earlier songs. In it, he continues to downgrade women and to harp on materialism and individualism, and yet to maintain an ambivalent moral position at the same time. Likely, Price was on the right-wing fringes of the Parliamentary movement; and though he may have gone along with the cause (and even with the army at one point), once the king had been executed and the genuinely revolutionary elements inside the army (notably the Diggers) had been crushed, Price, like many others, seems to have lurched back towards royalist assumptions and away from all the ideas and practices associated especially with the more progressive people at the vanguard of cultural and moral (as well as economic and political) developments. In other words, once the absolute monarchy had been crushed, and dangerous democratic tendencies had been put to the sword, Price saw the need and the possibility for a settlement involving a reformed monarchy tied umbilically to the consolidated bourgeoisie. This Parliamentarian fellow-traveller, like many another, reacted strongly against Diggers, Levellers and other tendencies in the army, once the labouring men who formed its backbone had served their historic purpose. In terms of relationships between men and women, and especially of the family, the Interregnum's tendencies towards the emancipation of women now became a positive threat to the new order, and there was a need (from an economic, as well as a more generally political and cultural point of view) to try to turn back the clock from those disturbing days when women came to enjoy some autonomy in public as well as in private life.[65] Part of the ideological offensive necessitated the attempt to reimpose male-dominated families and human relations, and to drive women back into the domestic servicing of men and the rearing of the next generation of workers for capitalists to exploit, by any means which came to hand. Price's song, consciously or otherwise, fits in with this ideological reaction, in the way it presumes to issue a *Warning* to women, accompanied by smears as to the faictitious Jane Reynolds's materialism, her unfaithfulness, her lack of 'proper' (bourgeois) concern for her children and her husband – who has to commit suicide rather than take on the responsibilities of child care, a revealing statement! – and her generally undisciplined will to get what she can out of her life. Bourgeois individualism, in other words, had to be constrained by bourgeois 'morality', and the women were the ones who had to pay. If they refused, and committed adultery (even with a spirit), then they could be marginalised and used as a *Warning* to others, as a representative of all those smears associated by right-wing Parliamentarians and royalists alike with the attempts of women and men on the left to reconstitute human relationships and to adjust (if not yet to abolish) the sexual division of labour. The man – our James Harris – can, of course, do exactly as he pleases with his sexuality!

The apparent lull in publication of this song can be partly explained (in the absence of surviving texts from the years after the restoration and before the Glorious Revolution in 1688, and the consequent establishment of a limited monarchy under strict bourgeois control) as the result of the virtual suppression of right-wing non-royalist writers – even writers of songs. But the commodity was still there, and was passed down the 'ballad inheritance', until the song once again fitted in with the 'new' dominant ideology of the years 1688–9 and after. Yet once the major opposition to the bourgeois state had been cut off at the knees in 1715, and finally liquidated in 1745, the reformed dominant ideology's need for cultural products like Price's text was largely past. It could then become the property of the genteel antiquarian, or of serious historians with an eccentric interest in what the majority population may have sung, thought and felt – people like the entirely untypical selection of English and Scots people who collected black-letter broadsides, and hoarded them up in private collections, which in later years were to become commodities in their own right.

This song has come down to us in its broadside form not because of the agency of working people, or of oral transmission, but because it was bought (often at inflated 'antiquarian' prices) by people like the state official, John Selden, the Admiralty senior bureaucrat, Samuel Pepys, the Gray's Inn-oriented scholar, Douce, a Glasgow businessman called Euing, and the eminently proletarian Duke of Roxburghe, amongst others. In a real sense, what we have of exemplars of this text (and those thousands of others) are the result not only of chance and casualties of all kinds, but also of the mediation of such people – seemingly, all of them men – and it would be proper for us to address the question of what were *they* (rather than Price, or the broadside publishers) up to, and why? Francis James Child was hardly a representative figure in British culture, either, for that matter; and so it is important to know the part he played in the transmission and mediation of these and other texts. Yet not only did he not bother to look at all the broadside's exemplars known to him, or to have the task done for him by an assistant – had he done so, he would have discovered the initials 'L.P.' on one of the Euing texts – he positively did not care for whoever may have written it, because to have done so would have completely subverted his compulsion to posit a 'tradition' of songmaking which could not be 'scientifically' located in a real historical culture at a particular period. In the end, the importance of research into people like Child, Pepys and Roxburghe lies in the way it helps us produce a pathology of bourgeois culture, and of that culture's imperialistic attempts to mediate workers' culture, whether through the agency of antiquarians and scholars, or of the owners of seventeenth century broadside publishing firms.

The parallels to the study of popular music today seem to me, then, to be both striking and important. Just as we cannot expect to understand popularity in the late twentieth century without fully understanding the role of the owners and controllers of song-related media, and their relationships with the dominant ideology – east and west – so we cannot fully understand how our present situation was arrived at, was historically produced, without research of an analogous kind to that which has so far gone into developing a preliminary understanding of *A Warning for Married Women*.

Notes

1 Gillett 1972: 101.
2 Child 1882–98: IV: 360–9. For Child's methods, see Harker 1985: 101–20. Mr Frank Browne's version, sung in Belnagare, Co. Roscommon, in June 1983, is to be heard on Munnelly and Shields 1985.
3 Child 1882–98: IV: 360–9, 524.
4 Rollins 1924: 247.
5 Bagford Collection, British Museum, shelf-mark C 40 m 10 no. 2. Copies are in Chappell and Ebsworth 1871–99: I: xxiv–xxvii, and in Ebsworth 1878: LIII–LVIII.
6 Blagden 1954.
7 Thomson 1975: 75ff, Chappell and Ebsworth 1871–99, Crawford 1890. For an account of Crawford, see Barker 1877.
8 Euing 1971: 628–9.
9 These texts are reproduced with the permission of the Librarian of Glasgow University Library; the Master and Fellows of Magdalene College Cambridge; The British Library; the Earl of Crawford and the Librarian of the John Rylands University Library of Manchester, and the Librarian of the Bodleian Library, Oxford, to all of whom I am grateful.
10 See, for example, the imprintless text in St Bride's Library, Broadside SS 196.

11 Child 1882–98: IV: 360–1.
12 *DNB* 1967–8 edn: XVI: 333.
13 The rest of this paragraph is based on Rollins 1922: ix, xii, 399, 406, 443–4, 449–50, 455–6.
14 Rollins 1923: 16, 20.
15 Rollins 1923: 20–1.
16 Rollins 1922: ix, Chappell and Ebsworth 1871–99: VI: 69, *DNB* 1967–8 edn: XVI: 333. Cf Hazlitt 1867: 479–81.
17 *DNB* 1967–8 edn: XVI: 333.
18 Hazlitt 1867: 479–81.
19 Chappell and Ebsworth 1871–99, Ebsworth 1878, Ebsworth 1880.
20 Wing 1945–, *NUC*, *ECBB*, *BMC*.
21 Rollins 1920, 1922, 1923, 1924, 1927, 1929–32, Ashton 1883, 1891, Collier 1840, 1847.
22 Crawford 1890, Simpson 1966: 368–71.
23 Crawford 1890: no. 1407, Chappell and Ebsworth 1871–99: I: 634.
24 Chappell and Ebsworth 1871–99: VI: 65, Ebsworth 1878: I: 265.
25 Child 1882–98: II: 428, III: 208, 210, 518, IV: 519.
26 Evans 1777: 160–4 (and later reissues), Percy 1765 (1858 edn): III: 70–4.
27 Phillips 1723–5: I: 216, Percy 1765 (1858 edn): III: 87, Ritson 1783: II: 244–9.
28 This task is not yet complete, but I would like to acknowledge the help of colleagues in those British and US libraries, without whom it could not have been attempted. In particular, I would like to thank Mrs M.I. Anderson-Smith and Mr C.A. McLaren of Aberdeen University Library; Mr R.J. Roberts, Ms Sue James, Ms Kathy Firkin and Ms Sheila Edward of the Bodleian Library, Oxford; The Keeper of Printed Books, Ms E.A. Riley and Mr C.S. Rawlings of the British Library Reference Division, London; Mr John Bidwell of the William Andrews Clark Memorial Library, University of California, Los Angeles; Mr Brian Jenkins, Cambridge University Library; Mr Michael R. Powell of Chetham's Library, Manchester; Interlibrary Loan, Columbia University Libraries, New York; Mr A.J. Mealey, Coventry City Libraries; Mr Barr, The Mitchell Library, Glasgow; Mr Philip K. Escreet and Mr David Weston, Glasgow University Library; Ms Jennie Rathbun, The Houghton Library, Harvard University; Interlibrary Loans, The University of Iowa Libraries; Mr D.W. Riley, The John Rylands University Library of Manchester; Mr Peter Van Wingen, the Library of Congress, Washington; the staff of Manchester Central Reference Library; Mr Ian Rogerson, Ms Kate Morrison, and the staff of Manchester Polytechnic All Saints Library; Dr Richard Luckett, Mrs E.M. Coleman and Dr Day of Magdalene College, Cambridge; Mr Tom Burnett, Hatcher Graduate Library, University of Michigan; Mr Alastair Brodie, The National Library of Scotland, Edinburgh; Mr Douglas Bond, Central Library, Newcastle-upon-Tyne; Mr Daniel Tierney, Rare Books and Manuscripts Division, The New York Public Library; the Librarian, Plymouth City Library; Mr Peter Carnell, Sheffield University Library; Dr Louise Craven, Dr James Mosely, Ms Sue Heath, St Bride Printing Library, London; Mr Malcolm Taylor, Ms Janet Bowcott and Ms Kate Callen, Vaughan Williams Memorial Library, London; and Ms Annette Dixon, The Beinecke Rare Book and Manuscript Library, Yale University.

In addition, several colleagues and correspondents have given me help and encouragement, including Mr Ian A. Anderson, editor of *The Southern Rag* magazine; Mr Colin Barker, Dr Alan Bruford, School of Scottish Studies, Edinburgh; Ms Norah Carlin; Mr E.M. Dring of Bernard Quaritch Ltd; Mr David Horn, editor of *Popular Music*, Professor Jan Kleeman, Brown University, Rhode Island; Dr Emily Lyle, School of Scottish Studies, Edinburgh; Mr John J. Morrison, Wing STC Revision Project, Yale University Library; Mr Tom Munnelly, Department of Irish Folklore, University College,

Dublin; Dr Paul Needham, Pierpoint Morgan Library, New York; Ms Katharine F. Pantzer, The Houghton Library, Harvard University; Mr John Renbourn; Mr Steve Roud; Dr Ian Russell, editor of the *Folk Music Journal*; Dr Hugh Shields, Trinity College, Dublin; Mr Paul Smith; and Mr Michael Yates.
Russell, editor of the *Folk Music Journal*; Dr Hugh Shields, Trinity College, Dublin; Mr Paul Smith; and Mr Michael Yates.
I apologise if I have missed anyone off this long list!

29 For White, see Hunt 1975: 95.
30 Chappell and Ebsworth 1871–99: VII: Part 2: 688.
31 Laslett 1983: 107–11 speculates on longevity at this period.
32 Chappell and Ebsworth 1871–99: VII: Part 2: 616.
33 Rollins 1924.
34 i.e. Elizabeth Purslowe, though this is a conjecture.
35 This paragraph is largely based on McKerrow 1910, Plomer *et al.* 1907, 1922 and 1932, and Blagden 1954.
36 Thomson 1975: 39.
37 Thomson 1975: 64, 73.
38 Shepard 1967: xiii.
39 I am grateful to Thomas Pettit, Odense University, for reminding me of this danger.
40 I owe this point to Professor Charles Hamm, Dartmouth College, New Hampshire.
41 See Opie and Opie 1985: 148–9. I owe this reference to Thomas Pettit.
42 Simpson 1966: 368–71.
43 Neale 1985: 122–9.
44 Child 1882–98: IV: 361.
45 Chappell and Ebsworth 1871–99: III: 200.
46 Child 1882–98: IV: 361.
47 This remains true of modern accounts such as Burrison 1967, Gardner-Medwin 1971 and Lyle 1971.
48 Rollins 1923: 439.
49 Rollins 1923: 402.
50 Rollins 1923: 439.
51 Rollins 1923: 439.
52 Ebsworth 1878: 484.
53 Shepard 1973: 34, 58; see also Rollins 1920: xxii, and Rollins 1923: 26–49.
54 Rollins 1923: 13, 38–43, 48–50, 54–5, 58, 63, 64. The song in question was *The Quaker's Fear* – see Rollins 1923: 402–8.
55 See Rollins 1923: 65–6.
56 See Rollins 1923: 66–7. The text was republished in Ebsworth 1876.
57 Harker 1985: 3–7.
58 Shepard 1973: 60.
59 Shepard 1973: 62.
60 Holloway 1971: vii.
61 Rollins 1919: 321.
62 Shepard 1973: 62, Thomson 1975: 81–2.
63 Bell ND contains dozens of White's broadside song publications.
64 For a critique of this term, see Harker 1985 passim.
65 For the link between women's liberation and political struggle see Cliff 1985 passim.

Select bibliography (place of publication London, unless stated)

Ashton, John (1883), *Humour, Wit and Satire of the Seventeenth Century*.

Ashton, John (1891), *Real Sailor Songs*.
Barker, Nicolas (1877), *Bibliotheca Lindesiana*.
Bell, Thomas (ND), 'Reliques of ancient poetry', Newcastle University Library.
Blagden, Cyprian (1954), 'Notes on the ballad market in the second half of the seventeenth century', *Studies in Bibliography* (Virginia), vol. 6, 161–80.
Blagden, Cyprian (1960), *The Stationers' Company: A History, 1403–1959*.
BMC = The British Museum Catalogue of Printed Books to 1955, 1967 edn (New York).
Burrison, John (1967), '"James Harris" in Britain since Child', *Journal of American Folklore*, vol. 80, 271–84.
Chappell, William and Ebsworth, Joseph Woodfall (1871–99), *The Roxburghe Ballads, Illustrating the Last Years of the Stuarts* (Hertford).
Child, Francis James (1882–98), *The English and Scottish Popular Ballads* (Boston).
Cliff, Tony (1985), *Class Struggle and Women's Liberation*.
Collier, John Payne (1840), *Old Ballads from Early Printed Sources*.
Collier, John Payne (1847), *A Book of Roxburghe Ballads*.
Crawford, James Ludovic (Earl of Lindsey)(1890), *Catalogue of a Collection of English Broadsides of the XVIIth and XVIIIth Centuries*.
DNB = The Dictionary of National Biography, 1967–8 edn.
Ebsworth, Joseph Woodfall (1876), *Choyce Drollery*.
Ebsworth, Joseph Woodfall (1878), *The Bagford Ballads: Illustrating the Last Years of the Stuarts* (Hertford).
Ebsworth, Joseph Woodfall (1880), *The Amanda Group of Bagford Poems, circa 1668* (Hertford).
ECBB = Eighteenth CenturyBritish Books: An Author Union Catalogue, 1981 edn (Newcastle).
Euing (1971), *The Euing Collection of English Broadside Ballads in the Library of the University of Glasgow* (Glasgow).
Evans, Thomas (1777), *Old Ballads, Historical and Narrative, with Some of Modern Date*.
Fawcett, F. Burlinghame (1930), *Broadside Ballads of the Restoration Period from the Jersey Collection known as the Osterley Park Ballads*.
Gardner-Medwin, Alisoun (1971), 'The ancestry of "The House Carpenter"', *Journal of American Folklore*, vol. 84, 414–27.
Gillett, Charlie (1972), *Rock File*.
Halliwell, James Orchard (1841), *Early Naval Ballads*.
Harker, Dave (1985), *Fakesong: The Manufacture of British 'Folksong', 1700 to the Present Day* (Milton Keynes and Philadelphia).
Hazlitt, W. Carew (1867), *Hand-Book to the Popular, Poetical, and Dramatic Literature of Great Britain, from the Invention of Printing to the Restoration*.
Hindley, Charles (1873), *The Roxburghe Ballads*.
Holloway, John (1971), 'Introduction' to Euing 1971.
Hunt, Christopher J. (1975), *The Book Trade in Northumberland and Durham to 1860* (Newcastle).
Jackson, W.A. (1957), *Records of the Court of the Stationers' Company, 1602–1640*.
Laslett, Peter (1983), *The World We Have Lost – further explored*.
Lyle, Emily (1971), 'The visions in St. Patrick's Purgatory, Thomas of Erceldoune, Thomas the Rhymer and the Daemon Lover', *Neuphilologische Mitteilungen*, vol. 4, no. LXXII, 716–22.
Mackay, Charles (1863), *The Cavalier Songs and Ballads of England*.
McKerrow, R.B. *et al.* (1910), *A Dictionary of Printers and Booksellers in England . . . 1557–1640*.
Munnelly, Thomas and Shields, Hugh (1985), 'Early ballads in Ireland,

1968–1985', a cassette published by European Ethnic Oral Traditions, CLCS, Trinity College, Dublin 2, Ireland.

Neale, Jonathan (1985), *The Cutlass and the Lash: Mutiny and Discipline in Nelson's Navy*.

NUC = The National Union Catalogue Pre-1956 Imprints.

Newman, Susan Aileen (1975), 'The broadside ballads of Martin Parker: a bibliographical and critical study', unpublished PhD thesis, University of Birmingham.

Opie, Iona and Opie, Peter (1985), *The Singing Game* (Oxford).

Percy, Thomas (1765), *Reliques of Ancient English Poetry* (1858 edn).

Phillips, Ambrose (1723–5), *A Collection of Old Ballads*.

Plomer, Henry R. *et al.* (1907), *A Dictionary of the Booksellers and Printers in England . . . from 1641 to 1667*.

Plomer, Henry R. *et al.* (1922), *A Dictionary of the Printers and Booksellers . . . in England . . . from 1668 to 1725*.

Plomer, Henry R. *et al.* (1932), *A Dictionary of the Printers and Booksellers who were at work in England Scotland and Ireland from 1726 to 1775*.

Ritson, Joseph (1783), *A Select Collection of English Songs*.

Ritson, Joseph (1795), *Robin Hood*.

Rollins, Hyder E. (1919), 'The black-letter broadside ballad', *Publications of the Modern Languages Association*, vol. 34, 258–339.

Rollins, Hyder E. (1920), *Old English Ballads 1553–1625 Chiefly from Manuscripts* (Cambridge).

Rollins, Hyder E. (1922), *A Pepysian Garland: Black-Letter Broadsides of the Years 1595–1639, Chiefly from the Collection of Samuel Pepys* (Cambridge).

Rollins, Hyder E. (1923), *Cavalier and Puritan: Ballads and Broadsides Illustrating the Period of the Great Rebellion 1640–1660* (New York).

Rollins, Hyder E. (1924), *An Analytical Index to the Ballad Entries (1557–1709) in the Registers of the Company of Stationers of London* (North Carolina).

Rollins, Hyder E. (1927), *The Pack of Autolycus or Strange and Terrible News . . . Broadside Ballads of the Years 1624–1693* (Cambridge, Mass.).

Rollins, Hyder E. (1929–32), *The Pepys Ballads* (Cambridge, Mass.).

Shepard, Leslie (1967), 'Foreword' to 1967 edition of Rollins 1924.

Shepard, Leslie (1973), *The History of Street Literature* (Newton Abbot).

Simpson, Claude M. (1966), *The British Broadside Ballad and Its Music* (New Brunswick, New Jersey).

Thomson, Robert S. (1975), 'The development of the broadside ballad trade and its influence upon the transmission of English folksongs', unpublished PhD thesis, University of Cambridge.

Wing, Donald (1945–), *Short-Title Catalogue of Books Printed in England, Scotland, Ireland, Wales and British America, and of English Books Printed in Other Countries, 1641–1700* (Columbia).

CONVENTION AND CONSTRAINT IN WORKING LIFE

Popular music and the law – who owns the song?

Avron Levine White

Introduction

The purpose of this section of the monograph is to examine the conventions and constraints which create systems of interrelationships controlling musicians as individuals and in groups. In particular the articles in this section will consider the ways in which the production of musical sound; personal expectations of musicians; the demands of the venue; and the laws of contract and copyright, critically shape habits of work and the character of the eventual musical performance.

The organisation and presentation of the work in this section reflects the substantial theoretical influence of Howard Becker's discussion of 'Art as a Collective Action'. The article, appearing in the American Sociological Review (vol. 39 no. 6 December 1974) identifies the parameters of interaction crucial to the organisation of artistic work and as such has provided theoretically relevant models useful in the discussion of original ethnographic material.

Legal developments over the past fifteen years regarding the law of copyright relating to songwriting and the recording of original material have imposed considerable constraints on the working habits of professional and semi-professional musicians. The purpose of this discussion is to look at several leading law cases which have influenced the music business and consequently the way in which individual musicians and musical groups approach professional and semi-professional work. The legal factor has many consequences for the social organisation of work within a musical group particularly as musicians become aware of the eventual ownership of the commercial product. For example, semi-professional musicians often write material in groups until they receive a professional contract which awards 50 per cent of the publishing royalities to the writer of the music and 50 per cent of the royalties to the writer of the lyrics. When this is discovered musicians usually write in pairs or alone in order to monopolise the copyright.

In professional circles songwriting partnerships of two individuals are often formed and all publishing royalties are shared equally between them. Furthermore, any additional musicians who may be required for live performance work are then recruited on a session basis. If specialist instrumental expertise is required in the recording studio, session musicians will either require a hefty 'session' fee or alternatively a percentage of the royalties from future sales of the recording will be awarded.

However, this awareness of ownership and eventual control over the commercial end-product by the musician has been achieved through many legal contests each of which has highlighted social and judicial prejudices which are significant for sociological understanding. Furthermore, this awareness of ownership and eventual control over the commercial end-product by the musician has substantially shaped the conventions of working life amongst musicians. But equally important is the way each legal contest throughout the years gradually overcame prejudices in favour of a new respectability and status for the craft of 'pop' music.

In the following pages I will discuss several law cases, the texts of which are primarily concerned with 'pop' music. However, the legal issues which arise have wider application to any form of music intended for a mass market.

The very first case I will discuss, Christie v. Davey (1892), serves as a useful introduction to the underlying judicial and social attitudes towards the production of certain kinds of musical sounds. Furthermore, the case illustrates the aesthetic prejudices which have been carried through the ages as to what has been classed as 'music'. The importance of this first case will be seen when the reader becomes familiar with the remaining cases (late 1960s and early 1970s) which together illustrate that in the absence of institutional credentials, degrees from academies of music, the commercial musician has had very little bargaining power in marketing his craft and has consequently been exploited without sympathy or respect for his abilities until quite recently when legal confrontations have occurred to produce a new awareness of the value of their craft and have resulted in the legal professional awarding the musician greater economic control over his work.

By way of introduction then to the legal aspects of commercial music I will now describe, in detail, the text of one of the very first cases involving professional music teachers and performer, the Christie family (1892) and the opposing party living immediately adjacent, a Mr Davey. Subsequent to this I will discuss the law of copyright and its development in relation to commercial music.

Christie v. Davey

In 1892, when music was still far from being amplified, a Mr Davey found his neighbours, the Christies, who lived in the adjoining household, and were practising music teachers, to be a problem. Evidently, Mr Davey found the actual sounds coming from the adjacent household to be very distracting and causing disruption in his personal life. After some communication with the Christie family over a period of time he decided that the only way he could cope with the disturbance was to begin creating one himself. It was at this point that Mrs Christie, a teacher of pianoforte, whose home and place of work adjoined that of Mr Davey, filed for an injunction to restrain Mr Davey from making annoying and interfering noises of a kind that were detrimental to the professional activities of the Christie household. The parties involved had been living side by side harmoniously for some time until the arrival of a Miss Kennedy, a musician friend of the Christie family who added to the already lengthy schedule of practising. The activities of the Christie household, then, not only involved Mrs Christie's lessons to pupils, but also her son's late night practice of the violincello, her daughter's practice of piano and giving of violin lessons, and now, in addition, the practising of Miss Kennedy. Mrs Christie's daughter and friend, Miss Kennedy, were orthodox musicians and were described as medallists of the Royal Academy. It would appear, however, that despite such laudable qualifications, the defendant, Mr Davey, had reached a critical threshold of tolerance for these activities. On 30 September 1892 he wrote a letter of complaint to Mrs Christie which I will quote in part:

> During this week we have been much disturbed by what I at first thought were howlings of your dog, and, knowing from

> experience that this sort of thing could not be helped, I put up with the annoyance. But, the noise recurring at a comparatively early hour this morning, I find I have been quite mistaken, and that it is the frantic effort of someone trying to sing with piano accompaniment, and during the day we are treated by way of variety to dreadful scrapings on a violin, with accompaniments. If the accompaniments are intended to drown the vocal shrieks or teased catgut vibrations, I can assure you it is failure, for they do not. I am at last compelled to complain, for I cannot carry on my profession with this thump, thump, scrape, scrape, and shriek, shriek, constantly in my ears. It may be a pleasure or source of profit to you, but to me and mine it is confounded nuisance and pecuniary loss, and if allowed to continue, it must most seriously affect our health and comfort.[1]

The Christie household chose to ignore Mr Davey's complaint and his unprofessional assessment of their talents. At a later stage Mr Davey began to respond to the sounds coming from the Christie household with what he considered a musical accompaniment. That is to say, when he heard them practising he would knock on the adjoining wall, keep the beat on trays, whistle and shriek in a manner which Mr Davey felt was imitative of the sounds coming from the Christie household. Mr and Mrs Christie then brought the matter to the attention of their solicitors.

The Christies' solicitors wrote to Mr Davey informing him that in their view his behaviour was relatiatory and 'outrageous'; that his so-called musical sensitivity was questionable, and that the original letter Mr Davey had sent to the Christies was so insulting that it did not deserve a reply. Consequently, under threat of obtaining a court injunction, the solicitor urged him to discontinue these activities as it was interfering with the Christies' professional life. On 13 October 1892 Mr Davey replied to the letter of the Christies' solicitors with the following text:

> Your favour of the 12th to hand in re Christie, in which you talk of 'outrageous systems of annoyance &c., hammering and beating trays &c.' This I emphatically deny. I have a perfect right to amuse myself on any musical instrument I may choose, and I am quite sure I should be the last person to do anything knowingly to annoy my neighbours. What I do is simply for recreation's sake, and to perfect myself in my musical studies. You express your opinion about my letter, which is quite

contrary to my own. I see nothing coarse or insulting in it; but I look upon it as showing my desire to be on friendly terms with my neighbours, for I wrote in quite a jocular manner. However, each one to his taste. Your third paragraph questions my musical taste. Well I believe from my past musical training, that I am qualified to distinguish the difference from music and noise. Now, seriously I put it to you, is it not most excruciating to have constant repetitions of five-finger exercises, and only receiving the higher notes of the vocal efforts? I do not for one moment think there are no graduations, but they don't reach me. I am quite thankful, I can assure you, for your eminently legal opinion as to your clients' non-responsibility for the thinness of the party wall. . . . It is my intention during these winter months to perfect myself on the following instruments – Viz., flute, concertina, cornopean, horn and piano, which my child is learning to accompany me. I used to play them at one time, both in a church band and an amateur troop; but I have been out of practice lately, but I hope soon to regain my former proficiency.'[2]

On 20 October a writ was issued whereby the plaintiff (Christie) claimed an injunction to restrain the defendant (Davey) from making any noise in a manner to annoy the plaintiffs. The action came to trial and in the judgment of the court, it was pointed out that:

> The plaintiff's family consists of the husband, who, perhaps fortunately for himself, is very deaf; the wife, who is admitted to be a skillful musician and an excellent pianist; and a daughter, a young lady who has received *a good musical education and has taken a very good musical degree*.[3]

Subsequently it was determined that the amount of acual playing and practising was not excessive and within the rightful domain of gainful employment. Consequently an injunction was granted to restrain the defendant, Mr Davey, from 'making noises in his house so as to vex and annoy the plaintiff'.

Concluding remarks

It would appear from the text of this case that the extensive musical qualifications of the professionally trained musicians were a significant factor in the final decision. For this reason two issues here are at stake. One of them is the law of nuisance, and the other, which is clearly embedded, is some aesthetic valuation of music. For on the one hand Mr Davey insists that what is played in the Christies' household is something less than music, e.g. 'dreadful scrapings on the violin', 'vocal shrieks', or 'teased catgut vibrations'. On the other hand, the plaintiffs insist that what Mr Davey produces is still less valid as music, or rather that it is 'noise'. Now it would appear that Mr Davey is being antagonistic and that the Christies' superior qualifications and degrees in music give their judgment as to what constitutes music far greater weight. However, it is perhaps this kind of judicial and social attitude towards institutionally accredited music which, years ago, fed the original prejudices so many individuals held against musicians playing other kinds of music. For years the majority of pop and jazz music was classified by the institutionalised musical establishment as nothing other than noise. To be sure, the noise of Mr Davey in 1892 was far less distinguishable as a musical form than anything of the pop variety commercially available in the mid-twentieth century. Nevertheless the weight of the musical establishment's criticism of so-called pop did much to discredit the practice of pop and jazz music as a legitimate professional occupation. A musician's status and viability were dependent upon demand in commercial terms alone. There were no institutions or degrees to guarantee his craft. This is not to suggest that Mr Davey was a budding pop musician held back from stardom; but rather that until the mid-1960s there was no institutional recognition of individual musical skill and consequently it may well be that this lack of accreditation gave the pop musician very little bargaining power when he entered into contractual obligations with publishers, management and record companies. It was more often the case than not that management and recording contracts were so unfairly written that as soon as the musicians could afford to get out of them they did.

The combined judicial and social attitudes which might have carried over from earlier historical periods could well have been one of the factors which left unconventional musicians with very little leverage in the contracts over their work. Certainly, when various kinds of music boomed in popularity and recording companies and managements were fighting over the rights to material of the artists, the highly disadvantageous position of individual musicians became very apparent to the legal profession which gradually sought to redress the balance. One consequence of well-known test cases has been the systematic review of the law(s) of copyright as they relate to popular recording artists, most notably in the field of rock music.

In the pages that follow, I discuss the law of copyright in relation to the legal structures within which the music industry operates to negotiate the mutual and conflicting interests of musicians, management and publishers. In this connection I discuss several leading cases of contract law which illustrate judicial attitudes towards relations of musical production.

Copyright law and the musician

The law of copyright was ushered into its initial stages of existence in this country in 1556; when by virtue of the Star Chamber Decree, the Chartered Stationers' Company was invested with constitutional powers to act on behalf of religious and secular institutions in the regulation and distribution of printed matter. Membership of the company was compulsory for all individuals connected with the printing trade, which included bookbinders and booksellers. The company's role apparently was to register the 'right to copy' and control domestic and foreign distribution of any form of printed matter. The author's implied rights were comparatively insignificant although guaranteed by 'common' law. According to R.F. Whale in his discussion of the law of copyright:

> copyright for some 150 years was quite simply the right to copy and, except for the implied right to publish, nothing else. It was accordingly not an author's right but a publisher's right, and indeed it was the booksellers (publishers) who created this right for themselves as a necessary protection for their business. It was this right that the statute (Statute of Anne) adopted and limited in 1709, and although under the statute the author became entitled to hold copyright, the right protected was still essentially the publisher's right to copy.[4]

Copyright law, then, which appears to have been heavily weighted in favour of protecting the interests of publishers against financial loss rather than the authors,[5] has led to interesting samples of exploitation of musicians by music publishers. The two cases I now discuss were heard within weeks of each other in 1974. They are typical examples of publishing agreements offered to unknown artists. The first case I discuss is *Instone v. A. Schroeder Music Publishing Co. Ltd.*

Instone v. A. Schroeder Music Publishing Co. Ltd

In the case of Instone v. A. Schroeder Music Publishing Co. Ltd (1974) 1 ALL ER, a young composer of 'pop' music, Anthony Gordon Instone (also known as Tony Macauley), the plaintiff, and his collaborator Mr McLeod approached Schroeder Music Publishing Co. in the hopes of getting into the production side of the record industry. In the course of their dealings with a Mr Schroeder, the composer signed a contract assigning to the publishing company exclusive copyright 'for the whole world' in all existing compositions as well as works produced during a five-year period. The contract further stipulated that the publishers would pay Instone the sum of £50 as an advance again the royalties received by the publishers. If and when the £50 had been recouped through royalties the publishers then agreed to pay another £50 to Instone. Assuming all went well and an average of more than twenty transactions occurred per year yielding a total sum greater than £5,000 over a five-year period, then the agreement would be automatically renewed. However, the publishing company was under no obligation whatsoever to publish the writer's works or take any steps to exploit the composer's material during the five-year period. Consequently the only payment which Instone was guaranteed during the entire period was £50. Furthermore, the composer had no right, at the end of the five-year period, to recover the copyright of a composition not used by the publishers. The inequitable conditions of this agreement were further compounded by the stipulations that:

(1) the publishers could, at any time, terminate the agreement with one month's notice, and
(2) the publishers had the right to assign the entire agreement or the rights to any particular composition to any other party of their choosing.

These conditions were not reciprocal. The court judged in favour of the composer on the grounds that there was unjustifiable restriction of trade in that:

(a) there was no obligation on the defendants to exploit anything composed by the plaintiff throughout the five-year period, and

(b) the restrictions combined a total lack of obligation on the side of the publishers with a total obligation on the side of the composer.

In the words of the actual judgment, 'The contract was therefore restrictive of the ability of the plaintiff to turn to account his compositions to an extent and in a manner that was against the public interest.'[6] A. Schroeder Music Publishing Co. appealed against this decision and in the case of A. Schroeder Music Publishing Co. Ltd v. A. Macauley the court ruled against the appeal.[7]

Remarks

The contract which the composer signed occurred without legal consultation. As we can see, it was written entirely in favour of the publishers whereby they retained virtually complete control over the composer's material. In effect what this case exemplifies is a practice known as 'shelving'. The combined effect of being under no obligation to 'exploit' or 'place' the material on the market, along with the provision that the publishers could restrict the artists from going elsewhere to sell his material, is, indirectly, a method by which a publishing company takes material off the market or, figuratively speaking, puts it on the shelf. In effect, this technique has been used as a device, for a long time, to reduce competition in critical areas of the music business. With such methods recording and publishing companies have been able to back more than one horse as it were, and then shift the bet to the winning runner or effectively eliminate competitive opposition from the race.

Musicians at this particular point in time had very little awareness of contract law or the more complex aspects of business organisation in the recording industry. Consequently, many talented and creative musicians had careers destroyed or held to a virtual standstill. The Musicians' Union, however, has taken active steps to publicise a general legal knowledge of business practice. In this area most professional musicians today acquire legal representation in all negotiations of contracts. Further, it has been through the periodic links between semi-professional musicians that a greater awareness of the legal implications has been aroused. This awareness has had considerable impact on the attitudes of musicians towards songwriting and the structure of actual musical groups.

I would like now to discuss another case of similar type which occurred only one week after the previous case was heard by the court of appeal. The facts that both cases occurred within such a short space of time, and that this second case involved a very well-known group, Fleetwood Mac, brought considerable public and professional attention to the matter of contract law and the law of copyright. The first case I discussed illustrated how a songwriting contract constrained the artist and was deemed by the judiciary to be 'restrictive of trade'. The second case illustrates an example of an infringement of copyright, this time, however, involving a combined publishing and management agreement.

Clifford Davis Management Ltd v. WEA Records Ltd and Another

On 27 of September 1974 a writ was issued on behalf of the plaintiffs Clifford Davis Management Ltd, bringing an action against WEA Records Ltd., and CBS Records Ltd., claiming an injunction restraining the defendants from infringements of copyright in the compositions of Anne Christine McVie and Robert Lawrence Welch – two members of a pop group known as Fleetwood Mac. The record entitled *Heroes are Hard to Find* was released in the United States and sold 150,000 copies. The album in question combined eleven compositions by McVie and Welch. The defendants WEA and CBS records sought to distribute the album for sale in England. An interim injunction was granted on 8 October 1974. The defendants appealed against the injunction which was discharged according to the judgment of Lord Denning MR. The conditions of this case were not dissimilar to the one previously discussed, Instone v. Schroeder Music Publishing Company. Again, this particular case, Clifford Davis Management Ltd v. WEA Records Ltd, originates in an unfair copyright agreement.

Initially Clifford Davis, who formed himself into the limited company Clifford Davis Management Ltd, was engaged by written agreement to act as agent and manager of the pop group Fleetwood Mac of Fleetwood Mac Promotions Ltd. In January of 1971 Clifford Davis Management Ltd secured a publishing contract with two of the group's members: Anne Christine McVie and Robert Welch. The publishing agreement was a professionally prepared document of a standard format which the individual musicians signed without having received independent legal advice. The agreements gave Clifford Davis Management Ltd English and world copyright in any composition throughout a five-year period – renewable for a further five years at the publisher's option. An initial consideration of one shilling was to be paid for each composition with additional royalties payable for those works Clifford Davis chose to exploit. Yet he was in no way bound to publish any of the work submitted. It was agreed that Anne Christine McVie would produce at least one composition per month which could be rejected without payment, at the discretion of the publisher. Furthermore, the management had the right to assign the copyright of the works to any third party.

The group became successful and did several tours of America. However, personal disagreements between Clifford Davis and the group eventually led to their disassociation. Clifford Davis Management Ltd subsequently assembled a completely new group of five musicians which he promoted on tour in America under the same name Fleetwood Mac. The original group brought an action against their former manager, Clifford Davis, and were granted an interim injunction restraining Clifford Davis from promoting a competitive group under the same name. Subsequently, the original group worked for new management in America and produced the aforementioned record album entitled *Heroes are Hard to Find*. Upon the album's intended release in England, former manager Clifford Davis tried to retaliate, as one might expect, and proceeded to invoke the original publishing agreement claiming that his company was entitled to copyright of this album despite his lack, now, of professional involvement with the group. Nevertheless he succeeded in obtaining an interim injunction preventing the distribution and sale of *Heroes are Hard to Find* in England. After an unsuccessful attempt to have the injunction discharged, the original Fleetwood Mac sought to overrule the injunction in a Court of Appeal. In October of 1974 it was determined in the judgment of Lord Denning that, 'The agreement is of the same class as the agreement considered by the Court of Appeal in Instone v. A. Schroeder Musical Publishing Company Ltd. and by the House of Lords last week' (Macauley v. A. Schroeder Publishing Co. Ltd).[8] Hence, in a similar context to Instone v. A. Schroeder, the contractual restrictions were considered to be unjustifiably restrictive of trade in that the agreement required exclusive obligations to one individual over a 'long term of years'. The critical features of this inequitable agreement are summarised in Lord Denning's judgement.

> . . . (1) That the terms of the contract were manifestly unfair. Each composer was tied for ten years without any retaining fee and with no promise to anything in return save for a promise by the publisher to use his best endeavours. Such a promise was so general as probably to be of little use to the composer. . . . (2) The property (the copyright in every one of the works over ten years) was transferred for a consideration that was grossly inadequate. It was one shilling for each work. It is true that if the publisher chose to exploit a work, he was to pay royalties but if he did not do so, he got the copyright for it. . . . (3) That the bargining power of each of the composers was gravely impaired by the position in which he or she was placed *vis-à-vis* the manager. . . . (4) That undue influences or pressures were brought to bear on the composers by or for the benefit of the manager. The manager did not condescend to say how the agreements came to be signed. But from the internal evidence much can be inferred. They were cyclostyled and hence came from a stock of forms. They were very long and full of legal terms and phrases. Hence they were drawn up by lawyers. Some spaces had been filled in by typewriters, others left blank. Hence done by clerks in the office. Both the composer and the publisher signed in the presence of the same witness. It may be inferred that the manager took a stock form, got the blanks filled in and asked the composer to sign without reading it through or explaining it. One thing is clear from the evidence. The composer had no lawyer and no legal advisers. It seems to me that if the publisher wished to exact such onerous terms or to drive so unconscionable a bargain, he ought to have seen that the composer had independent advice. For these reasons it may well be said that there was such inequality of bargaining power that the agreement should not be enforced and the assignment of copyright was invalid and should be set aside.[9]

As can be seen this far, the popular musician had been ensnared in a variety of agreements which are clearly unbalanced from the point of view of fairness to the artist. This has to some extent been a result of conventions established in the original laws of copyright which assign the ownership of intellectual property, in real economic terms, to the publisher rather than the author. This goes some way to explaining the expectations of publishers, and in some respects it has set the trend for management agreements as well. One might assume that the musical project in the eyes of management is more or less viewed as a form of property potentially yielding a return on the principal investments. It may also be argued that this view is not entirely unreasonable given the technological developments of sound and light production which have made the promotion process of 'pop' groups progressively more capital-intensive. From the standpoint of individual musicians, however, these aims, which are partially of mutual interest, may well conflict with a broad range of professional opportunities relevant to the goals of artistic development rather than being in the interest of mutual financial gain; alternative opportunities may present themselves which are financially advantageous only to the artist. Consequently the musician's contract with management is now facing a great deal more scrutiny than in previous years. Furthermore, the publicity surrounding these events has made the professional musician all the more aware of his legal position. This has produced some degree of reaction in the management sector.

In many instances management seek to eliminate opposition to their control by signing up members of a given group on totally independent contracts rather than on a group basis. In this case each musician must negotiate on his own behalf rather than on the strength of the entire group and it is easier for management to limit claims and conditions on a sort of divide-and-rule basis. It is my general view, although further research is needed here, that this new approach may be of benefit to management initially, however, all too often it leads to the break-up of the band. The unequal terms upon which each musician is individually signed can instigate a breakdown of a good working relationship. In one example a nationally known band was signed on a group contract basis so that each player benefited equally from royalties of any song published and recorded. From a group point of view each member felt at ease to contribute musical ideas freely for the benefit of the entire musical project. In later years, however, when management of the group changed hands, they were signed individually and solely for their independent musical contributions. This, of course, led to immediate conflict over the ownership of songs and consequently members of the band began to work separately. Furthermore, each player would be financially motivated to want to feature as much as possible of his original material on forthcoming recordings so as to collect the greatest possible share of royalties from record sales. The musicians would argue as to whose material was best, each making grandiose aesthetic claims for the superiority of their own material whilst emphatically denying financial incentives. Ultimately the conflict would yield a deadlock which would leave the group suitably vulnerable for management to intervene and take a decisive role in the conflict.

In the case of this aforementioned band which had switched from a group contract with split royalties to individual contracts, the lead guitarist/vocalist and the saxophone player/vocalist monopolised the majority of the writing until the bass player eventually came up with a song which the band agreed to do – it was very successful and reached the top ten in American music charts. However, this success created great disturbance within the band. The bass player's role was suddenly reversed from that of being a backing musician to that of being a front man. The band of course objected and he eventualy left to form a band of his own. Replacement auditions were held and bass players from semi-professional rock bands were potential candidates. Although the replacement player eventually selected was already professional and working with another band, the interaction that this professional outfit had with members from the semi-professional circuit brought the subject of copyright, songwriting and royalties into discussion on the semi-professional scene.

My major aim here has been to illustrate to what extent the action and reaction of management in the area of professional music can upset or establish conventions which in some instances affect the attitude and group interaction on the semi-professional scene. I continue now with my discussion of legal cases in order to illustrate another dimension of management control – the personal service agreement.

Page One Records and Another v. Britton and Others

Another level on which the management side of the music business seeks to restrict and control the musicians is through personal service agreements. Here control of musicians is achieved through the role of agent and personal manager. An interesting case in this context is the case of Page One Records Ltd and Another v. Britton and Others (trading as The Troggs) and Another (1967) 3 ALL ER. This particular case features a personal management contract in which a group known as The Troggs signed an agreement in February of 1966 appointing Larry Page of Page One Records to manage all affairs relevant to their professional careers. A term of the contract was that the The Troggs would not engage any other person, including themselves, to act as manager or agent. The agreement also stated that the plaintiff, Larry Page, would be paid a commission of 20 per cent of all money received by The Troggs through the period of the contract. Several months later in May of 1966 an additional recording contract and copyright agreement was signed with the plaintiff. The Troggs were to receive 20 per cent royalties. Subsequent to this a three-year publishing contract was signed with Dick James Music Ltd assigning first option of world copyright on all musical compositions. The Troggs then became very successful. Approximately one and a half years later The Troggs became interested in new management. In their efforts to extricate themselves from the management and publishing contracts, they informed Page One Records Ltd via their solicitors that they were in breach of contract on the ground that The Troggs had not been made aware that there was a business connection between management – Page One Records Ltd – and publisher – Dick James Music Ltd. As it was the intention of The Troggs to enter into contractual obligations with Harvey Block Associates Ltd in a way that was in breach of the agreement with Page One Records Ltd, the plaintiffs began action against The Troggs and motioned for interlocutory injunction restraining The Troggs from engaging new management.

The legal action against The Troggs is essentially a response to the breakdown of a personal services agreement. Hence, the matter falls within the area of contract law. The remedy prescribed by a court of law is either to award 'damages', i.e. financial remuneration, or an injunction restraining either party from entering a service agreement with someone else. As a general rule the courts will not enforce a personal service agreement where either party no longer wishes to be held by it. In the more traditional terms of legal description, the courts will not grant an order for 'specific performance' of 'positive covenants' in contracts for personal services. Cheshire and Fifoot's *Law of Contract* (8th edition) clarifies the judicial outlook:

> 'Since it is undesirable, and indeed in most cases impossible to compel an unwilling party to maintain continuous personal relations with another, it is well established that a contract for

> personal services is not specifically enforceable at the suit of either party. (p. 608)[10]

This general view leads to another important point relevant to this case, that is, the relationship between 'negative stipulation' and 'positive covenants'. Contracts are generally two-dimensional in that they contain 'positive covenants' – obligations to be fulfilled; and 'negative stipulations' – restrictions imposed upon either party, usually limiting their involvement with third parties. The most common form of a personal service contract is marriage. Since the court will not enforce personal service contracts, they will also not enforce 'negative stipulations' which indirectly coerce a party to fulfil a personal service contract he or she no longer wishes to perform. In the case of THE TROGGS, Page One Records persuaded the musicians to sign contracts with two negative stipulations relevant to the case:

(1) that they would not engage any management other than Larry Page;
(2) that they would not manage themselves.

Hence, in the judgment of the court it was shown that the 'negative stipulations' of the original agreements were indirectly coercive in the manner previously mentioned. To wit:

> For the purposes of consideration of equitable relief, I must, I think, look at the totality of the arrangements: and the negative stipulations on which the plaintiffs rely, are, in my judgment, no more or less than stipulations designed to tie the parties together in a relationship of mutual confidence, mutual endeavour and reciprocal obligations.[11]

However, injunctions in cases of personal service agreements are additionally considered on the basis of a still broader legal principle which takes into account whether the defendant who is restrained by an injunction is indirectly coerced, by the threat of penury, to continue working for a party with whom he no longer wishes any further association. Cheshire and Fifoot summarise the matter as follows:

> If, for instance, A agrees to give the whole of his time to the services of B and not to serve anybody else in any capacity

> whatever, an injunction will not be granted, for its inevitable result would be to compel A to work for B or otherwise starve.[12]

In the case of The Troggs this broader rationale for refusing the injunction did seem to apply. Evidently the plaintiff, Page One Records Ltd, made a point of the naivety, inexperience, and simple mentality of The Troggs and their consequent need for supervision and management. The court took judicial note of this fact and it was partially on this basis that the injunction was refused. I quote from the text of judgement.

> Indeed, it is the plaintiffs' own case that The Troggs are simple persons of no business experience, and could not survive without the services of a manager. As a practical matter on the evidence before me, I entertain no doubt that they would be compelled, if the injunction were granted on the terms that the plaintiffs see, to continue to employ the first plaintiff as their manager and agent.[13]

Consequently, it would appear that the court dismissed the injunction on the grounds that The Troggs would be indirectly forced into a relationship of an undesirable and highly personal nature due to the facts that:

(1) the injunction would prevent The Troggs from undertaking alternative management, or from managing themselves; and
(2) in the face of these closed options, their simple mentality, lack of business experience and general need for supervision would give them no alternative, from the standpoint of survival, other than to remain with Page One Records Ltd.

It seems apparent from the proceedings of this case and others that financial arragements based upon personal service agreements are to some degree uncertain. Apart from the undesirability of enforcing such an agreement unsatisfactory to either party, it would be extremely difficult for a court of law to supervise such a relationship, particularly if it is of highly personal nature.

As mentioned earlier, one of two remedies are available for breach of such agreements: (1) damages, e.g. financial compensation, or (2) an injunction restraining the party from entering a similar agreement with others. The latter, of course, however, may be seen indirectly to coerce a party to remain bound to the plaintiff who anticipates profit from the continued association. The judicial attitude here is quite unsympathetic. Alternatively, an entrepreneur may seek an injunction in order to protect expected profits based upon earlier joint business activities which may be jeopardised if the defendant party enters into association with another party which will be competitive with the plaintiff's and defendant's original joint venture. The judicial attitude in these circumstances seems to be substantially more sympathetic in relation to awarding an injunction. In the case of Warner Brothers Pictures Inc. v. Nelson,[14] Warner Bros was awarded an injunction preventing film actress Bette Davis from appearing in another film production. The injunction was awarded partially on the basis that Bette Davis might appear in competitive films at a time which would depreciate the value of previously made Warner Bros films that were in the market for sale or hire but had not yet been shown.

This then is a further example of the way in which management has played a fairly important role in the musical project. It is worth noting that the level of involvement and financial remuneration in this capacity is somewhere equivalent to the earnings of the actual band member. In effect the personal manager is like an additional member of the band.

I would like to point out at this stage that the kind of group contract offered between a band and management would imply to a greater or lesser degree a personal services agreement between the actual musicians themselves. That is to say that each musician is very much tied to playing with the others exclusively unless special permission is granted to undertake the work with another band. This kind of contractual arrangement, not entirely unlike marriage, places a great amount of emphasis on maintaining the quality of the personal relationship within that working group. This is one reason why even successful groups who have been together for a long time apparently undergo intense periods of hostility. In some instances when the personal relationship breaks down irretrievably the personal services agreement must be terminated even though such an action may cause serious financial loss.

The frustration created by restriction of musical interaction with third parties may lead members of a professional group to seek some kind of outlet on the semi-professional scene on a strictly casual basis. This kind of activity, which occurs often in the form of 'sitting-in' or 'jamming', creates lines of communication which significantly influence the semi-professional music circuit.

The case I have just discussed illustrates the judicial attitude towards personal service agreements involving musicians and management. One feature of the case was that there had been a deviously contrived connection between management and publishers which was unknown to The Troggs (or perhaps it would be more realistic to say, not understood by The Troggs). In the next case I will discuss a similar disagreement involving a connection between management and publisher.

Denmark Productions Ltd. v. Boscobel Productions Ltd

This next case involves the principal instigator of the events in the case of The Troggs – Larry Page. He appeared in court once again through his involvement with the well-known pop group The Kinks. This case shows, among other things, the critical ties between management and publisher through copyright agreements. In the case of Denmark Productions Ltd v. Boscobel Productions Ltd, the pop group The Kinks was embroiled in a battle between themselves and Larry Page through various levels of management and publishing contracts. Originally, two entrepreneurs, inexperienced in the pop industry, became interested in managing a then unknown pop group called The Kinks. In view of their inexperience they involved the comparatively more experienced Larry Page who was, at that point in time, employed by a large American publisher of pop music, headed by Edward Kassner, and called the Edward Kassner Music Publishing Corporation. In 1963, Edward Kassner and Larry Page formed the plaintiff company, Denmark Productions Ltd, through which Larry Page conducted all his activities. In 1964, Wace and Collins, the original entrepreneurs, formed the defendant company, Boscobel Productions Ltd, and contracted with The Kinks to be their 'personal manager' entitling them to exclusive publishing rights and 40 per cent of the group's gross earnings.

On 26 February 1964, an aggreement between the plaintiffs, Denmark Productions, and the defendants, Boscobel Productions Ltd, provided that:

> '(1) The [plaintiffs] will through Mr Larry Page, one of its directors, act jointly with the [defendants] as manager of The Kinks in the same manner and to the same extent and subject to the same liabilities as if the [plaintiffs] had joined in the said

three agreements as a manager jointly with the [defendants]. (2) This agreement shall subsist for the duration of the said agreements. (3) The [defendants] shall during the subsistance of this agreement pay to the [plaintiffs] by way of remuneration for their services hereunder 10 per cent of the gross earnings earned by The Kinks from all sources. . . . (6) The [defendants] hereby assign to the [plaintiffs] all their rights of placing any and all musical compositions or lyrics for musical compositions that are written wholly by The Kinks or by any one or combination of them.'[15]

In effect, Larry Page, through Denmark Productions Ltd, agreed to act as personal manager for the pop group, an area in which Wace and Collins had no expertise, for 10 per cent of the gross earnings and the right to assign or place all musical composition to a publishing company. The idea was for Page to channel all the publishing rights to the Edward Kassner Publishing Company, of which Page was an employee, and the head of which, Edward Kassner, was Page's partner in the plaintiff company Denmark Productions Ltd. There was, however, the possibility of indirect profit to Denmark Productions Ltd, if the Kassner Publishing Company enhanced the group's reputation through its efforts.

> All his [Raymond Davies, leader of The Kinks] compositions were handed over to the Kassner organisation in accordance with Mr Page's obligation to his employer Kassner, and it was significant that Mr Page's remuneration for that activity was largely increased in August 1964.[16]

This agreement obtained for some time during which The Kinks became quite successful earning a gross salary of £90,000 per year and a world-wide reputation. However, despite such notable achievements there was considerable personal tension within the group itself, and in particular between Raymond Davies, singer-songwriter of the group itself, and their personal manager, Larry Page. During a peak point of The Kinks' career, while engaged in an important tour of the United States, there occurred a substantial breakdown between management and The Kinks. I quote the following passage from the text of the court proceedings issued in a statement of facts from the judgment of Harman L. J.

> In the early part of 1965 it was proposed that The Kinks should

undertake a tour of the United States of America. They were advised that such a tour was immensely important to them, the American market being the biggest outlet both for performances and for recording. Kassner, in particular, was in favour of the venture because it would enhance his publishing profits. There had been, however, great stresses between the members of the group (on one occasion there had been a fight on the stage in Cardiff), who behaved in a thoroughly prima donna-ish manner, and it needed all Mr Page's tact and care to keep it together. He did, in the early days anyhow, the lion's share of the promotion activities, the defendants attending to the bookkeeping side. Raymond Davies was unwilling to go to America, but was eventually persuaded by Mr Page to go on the footing that Mr Page himself should go as personal manager. Apparently, on a foreign tour young pop musicians took with them not only a tour manager, who acted as a kind of courier, but also a personal manager, who was there to look after them in their personal difficulties, to smooth over the troubles arising from day to day, to collect money at the box office, to ward off the dragons of the revenue, to see that the programme of engagements was either kept or cancelled as the case might be, and generally act as a kind of guide, philosopher and friend to the members of the group.

Mr Page was anxious to go on tour, having possibly in his mind that he might pick up other business there; that was in fact what he did, as he was entitled to do, The Kinks having no exclusive rights to his services. It was agreed between him and the defendants after some discussion that he, rather than they or some nominee of theirs, should perform this most important task.

The tour was planned to last from June 28th, 1965 to July 10th, 1965, and was of a most arduous nature, involving a number of one-night stands and, in particular, three days at Los Angeles.

Things did not go at all smoothly and the tour was afterwards described by Mr Page in a trade paper has having been a disaster, but the judge's impression was that on the whole it did not go too badly. Raymond Davies was particularly unhappy and demanded that his wife should be flown out to help comfort him and that was arranged by Mr Page by cable and she arrived on the night of July 3rd at Los Angeles. Mr Page in the meantime had decided that his other activities made it desirable

> for him to return to England. On July 3rd he told the other members of the group of that, but not Raymond Davies. He gave as his reason that that would only produce an outburst of temperament by that young man. He, therefore, departed on the morning of July 4th, just before the group were due to take an aeroplane to San Francisco, where the remaining activities of the tour were to be performed. His departure was a great shock to Raymond Davies, who relied on the advice and countenance of Mr Page in his distress, and the whole group held an *indignation* [sic] meeting on the airfield on the morning of July 4th and then and there decided to have no more to do with Mr Page and to get rid of his services if they could. The question whether any of the group objected to Mr Page's departure when he told them of it was not explored at the trial except with Michael Avory who said that he had no objection because he thought that Mr Page had important matters pending in London, The judge found that Mr Page left for some private reason which he had not revealed.[17]

Subsequently when the group returned to London they engaged Wace, of the defendant company, Boscobel Productions Ltd, to act on their behalf in helping The Kinks to extricate themselves from legal ties with Larry Page. Wace organised a solicitor who encouraged The Kinks to repudiate their agreement. This move, on the part of Wace, was, as we shall see, a significant intervention complicating the termination of the contract binding Larry Page to The Kinks. On 2 September, the solicitor representing The Kinks sent a letter to the plaintiffs, Denmark Productions Ltd, expressing The Kinks' dissatisfaction with Larry Page and their intention to have no further dealings with him. The solicitor claimed that The Kinks were unaware that Boscobel Productions Ltd had assigned Larry Page, via Denmark Productions Ltd., both composer's and management rights under the agreement of 12 February and that these arrangements were not binding because The Kinks were 'infants'. This claim was not accurate. A copy of the same letter was sent to Boscobel Productions Ltd terminating the agreements of 12 February 1964. However, in the copy of the letter to Boscobel Productions Ltd a statement was added suggesting that a new contract with Boscobel Productions Ltd be drawn up assigning full management and publishing rights to Boscobel and renouncing any obligation to Larry Page. Consequently, Denmark Productions Ltd threatened legal action in the event of a breach of contract.

Subsequently, Boscobel Productions Ltd informed Denmark Productions Ltd that The Kinks had now terminated the original contract linking the two companies and that, furthermore, they had now renegotiated a new contract which excluded obligations to Denmark Productions Ltd.

Denmark Productions Ltd received no payment after June 1965 and they filed for an injunction restraining Boscobel from placing the rights to compositions with anyone but themselves. They also claimed for the original 10 per cent management fee. The court, however, dismissed the injunction on the ground that the contract between Boscobel and Denmark had been 'frustrated'. That is to say that since the original contract between The Kinks and Boscobel Productions Ltd had been terminated (due to The Kinks refusal to have any further association with Larry Page), the related contract between Denmark and Boscobel could no longer be fulfilled. However, the 'doctrine of frustration' only applies when the performance of a contract becomes impossible through factors for which neither party was responsible. Consequently, on appeal it was determined that the doctrine of 'frustration' did not apply because, in fact, the defendants had assisted in terminating the contract when Wace, of Boscobel Productions Ltd, had intervened, introducing The Kinks to a solicitor for the purpose of repudiating the original agreement in order to eliminate Larry Page. Further to this, the appeal decision awarded Denmark Productions Ltd 10 per cent (the usual management fee) during the period of June to September 1965, as damages for wrongful dismissal as co-managers. As far as the injunction restraining Boscobel Productions Ltd from assigning publishing rights to anyone but the plaintiffs was concerned, this was again dismissed as the claim for these rights were of benefit to a third party (the publishing company of which Krassner was the head and Page the employee) and not of direct benefit to the plaintiffs in their form as Denmark Productions Ltd.

The case between The Kinks and Larry Page illustrates, through the text of this case, the role played by management. Essentially there are two functions: the role of agent and the role of personal manager. The agent's role, apart from keeping the group name as well known in professional circles as possible, is to be a clearing house for all enquiries concerning the group, to accept bookings selectively, to negotiate fees and generally deal with any problems arising in the terms of the contract and negotiations with the managers of venues. The other role of personal management service, such as Larry Page had been involved in with The Kinks and The Troggs, involves taking charge of a group's entire career, recording dates, contracts and all manner of personal difficulties that may occur in the band. For this extra service they claim a considerable percentage of monies earned.

Conclusion

The various cases I have discussed employ doctrines of 'frustration', 'undue influence', 'restraint of trade', and the law of 'copyright' in negotiating the conflicting interests of musicians and management. In an overview, it would appear, in some fundamental respect, that the aims of management have been to divest the artist of rights and control of his work, so as to ensure a return on their investment. Hence, in some superficial way the relations of musical production seem to encourage a view of the performing artist, in this context, as some kind of private property owned and displayed for profit. This characteristic of the relationship between musician and management is partially held in check by legal constraints. There is perhaps another, less obvious factor which militates against the total ownership of the music and musician by management. This, I think, is in the nature of the art form's necessity for an almost ritual event of the 'live' performance. Although the musical product yields its greatest source of income in recorded and written form, its authenticity, or validity, is very much dependent upon the music's being on view in the live performance. In this context the musical product is being produced and consumed in the same moment; there is an inextricable association between the musician and his music. Consequently the entrepreneur has difficulty in entirely alienating the musician from the product of work.

Finally, then, the areas of commercial law relevant to musicians more or less stipulate limits as to how much of an artist's right over his 'intellectual' property can be taken in exchange for capital. It would appear that over the past decade the courts of law have taken an increasingly sympathetic view. Certainly the Musicians' Union has played an important role in advising and informing contemporary musicians of their rights. As a consequence of many court decisions current management and publishing contracts now require independent legal advice for all musicians before final commitment.

This series of legal confrontations has resulted in creating new conventions regarding the expectations and obligations of those involved at various professional levels of the musical project. Furthermore the legal developments described have led to changes in the structure of recording and management contracts generally. There is now a tendency for management to sign musicians within a group individually rather than collectively, negotiating separate financial arrangements for every member of the group. This kind of contractual procedure enables more of a 'divide-and-rule' tactic but it also means that songwriters who perform as well are in a considerably stronger economic and legal position than other members of the group. The result of this development has changed the nature and meaning of band identity. The 'band' phenomenon which highlighted essentially collective activity with high morale and individualism within a setting of general group cohesion is a dying art form. Songwriters/performers are 'pairing off' or working as a solo artist employing a 'band' as it were, on a strictly session basis, reducing individual players to nameless backing musicians.

These developments also change the action at the bargaining table. The conventions and constraints involve new sets of variables. A songwriter/performer, for example, who is after a 'publishing' or 'recording' deal may not have the cash 'up-front' to finance recording demonstration material or to pay professional musicians to play the backing track. Where cash is limited percentage points of potential record sales are awarded instead of session fees, musical ideas are traded for skill required for another project, recording studio engineers exchange studio time for percentages of future sales, and so on.

Finally, in conjunction with the legal conventions and constraints are technological developments which also dramatically change the labour structure of musical production and enable still smaller groups of individuals to monopolise ownership of musical material. These devices number among them rhythm machines and computerised backing which replaces the usual range of live studio accompaniment.

David Harker, in *One for the Money: The Politics of Popular Song*, describes the pattern of demise of the big band era. Perhaps this was only a foreshadow of things to come.

> Singers soon came to realise that the mike and the amplifier enabled them to produce more noise than an unamplified band. . . . Big bands came to be economic albatrosses and were

> undercut by small groups and solo artists. In fact, we can date the rise of the solo performer in North America from the early 1940s.

The vocalist and his computer backing band is already with us. The business of 'convention' and 'constraint' will inevitably involve the ownership of the computer and the ownership of the computer 'program'. The legal profession will have a considerable headache presiding over the relative value of these levels of ownership. Furthermore, infringement of copyright will not just be a matter of musical analysis but also a matter complicated by the multiplicity of computer languages.

Notes

1 Christie v. Davey (1892), 1 Ch., p. 318.
2 Ibid., pp. 319, 320, 321.
3 Ibid., p. 324.
4 R. F. Whale, *Copyright: Evolution, Theory and Practice*, Longman, London, 1970, p. 18.
5 Ibid., p. 12 It is interesting to note in a comparative context that whereas English copyright law seeks to incorporate concepts of real 'property' and identifies the author's work as a separate entity with all the implications of commodity production, German and French copyright law aim at protecting the author's exclusive relationship to his work.
6 Instone v. A. Schroeder Music Publishing Co. Ltd (1974), 1 ALL ER 172.
7 This case in particular features the application of the doctrine of undue influence to a situation of inequality of bargaining power. Cheshire and Fifoot identified its comparatively wider use in the American legal context and in 1972 foreshadowed its use in this country. See Cheshire and Fifoot, *Law of Contract*, 8th edn, Butterworth, London, 1979, p. 282.
8 Clifford Davis v. WEA Records (1975), 1 ALL ER, p. 239.
9 Ibid., pp. 240–1.
10 Cheshire and Fifoot, op. cit., p. 608.
11 Page One Records Ltd and Another v. Britton and Others (trading as 'The Troggs') and Another (1967), 3 ALL ER, p. 826.
12 Cheshire and Fifoot, op. cit., p. 610.
13 Page One Records, p. 827.
14 Warner Brothers Pictures v. Nelson (1936), 3 ALL ER, p. 160.
15 Denmark Productions Ltd v. Boscobel Productions Ltd (1968), 3 WLR, p. 845.
16 Ibid., p. 845.
17 Ibid., pp. 845–6.

Bibliography

Carlen, Pat (ed.), *The Sociology of Law*, Sociological Review Monograph No. 23, University of Keele, 1976.

Cheshire, G.C. and Fifoot, C.H.S. *Law of Contract*, 8th edn, Butterworths, London, 1979.

Denning, Rt Hon. Lord, Master of the Rolls, *The Discipline of Law*, Butterworths, London, 1979.

Harding, Alan, *A Social History of English Law*, Penguin, Harmondsworth, 1966.

Harker, D., *One For the Money, the Politics of Popular Song*, Hutchinson Group, London, 1980.

Heydon, J.D., *The Restraint of Trade Doctrine*, Butterworths, London, 1971.

Podgorecki, Adam, *Law and Society*, Routledge & Kegan Paul, London, 1974.

Whale, R.F., *Copyright: Evolution, Theory and Practice*, Longman, London, 1970.

A Professional Jazz Group

Avron Levine White

So far musical projects have been investigated, albeit minimally, in terms of their economic parameters, social conventions, practical objectives, and to some degree aesthetic criteria. They have been seen to be an essentially group activity which provides scope within its structure for individual expression and achievement. The purpose of this investigations is to identify conventions and constraints which operate in the functioning of a professional jazz group which I will refer to as RJ and his Jazzmen. In particular the text will consider the ways in which the production of musical sound, personal expectations of musicians, and the demands of the venue critically shape the eventual musical performance. Furthermore, that conventions and constraints in these areas create factors which control artists as individuals and in groups.

I have selected RJ and his Jazzmen for a case study because of my involvement with the group as a professional drummer. Apart from this there have been several advantages in studying this particular jazz group. First, it was an essentially acoustic ensemble having no technically complex electronic equipment designed to augment sound. Second, because the residency was a professional engagement over a period of two months, I was able to have close contact with the entire group and there were no extraneous factors such as day jobs or domestic obligations which might have interfered with identifying an established routine. Furthermore, the repertoire which the group played was composed of well-known jazz classics that were performed as close to the original recording as possible. In the terms used by Bennet, the musical outfit might be referred to as a 'copy group' (Bennet, 1980, p. 153).

There was no 'songwriting', as such, because the entire repertoire was composed of already recorded material. Further, there were only minimal legal issues regarding the musical performance as there was no contest over the ownership of intellectual property e.g. the rights to the song.

The contract

The Casa-Bar in Zurich, Switzerland is a well-known jazz club and has been operating for over thirty years. The club features traditional jazz groups as this style of music, the managers claim, is the most popular for European tourists and residents in the locality. The resident band, that is the band which performs there most regularly, is a band which had its heyday in the traditional jazz boom in this country in the 1950s and early 1960s.

According to Swiss law foreign employees may only work in the country six or eight months of the year depending upon the nature of their employment. They must reside outside the country for a period of four months before they are permitted to return to work and live in Switzerland.

This very practical constraint dramatically shapes the lives of the musicians of the resident band. It also creates six months' work a year for other bands. Three of them are given to RJ and the remaining three to other bands recruited by the bandleader.

The accommodation provided comprised a flat above the club. The times of playing were between 8 and 12 midnight with three twelve-minute breaks. Breaks between sets were monitored carefully by the management and late starts were accumulated and subtracted in cash terms from bonus awards if they were achieved during the month.

During the intervals the musicians were discouraged from sitting down in the venue unless there was a minimum of 40 per cent of the house seating available. This was not a rule but an expectation. The reason for this practice was that the bar staff were paid entirely on commission for the drinks they served. If seats were taken by musicians rather than customers it immediately cut into the salary of the bar staff. There was a curious relationship that developed between the band and the bar staff. In addition to the salary of each musician there was a potential pay bonus which was paid to the band if the monthly bar takings were over 70,000 francs. It was therefore in the interests of the band that the bar staff served quickly and efficiently. If the venue was poorly attended or there were complaints made about the quality of service, the band and the bar staff had reason to complain about each other. The bar staff would occasionally complain that the music was too loud or unpopular and that it was affecting their income negatively. Alternatively, the band would sometimes complain that bar staff were serving drinks too slowly or inefficiently and therefore reducing the band's potential for earning a bonus.

The bonus factor had other effects on the relationship between band members and bar staff. The original contract of employment stipulated that musicians were to receive a quota of free drinks throughout the evening. These were to be served by bar staff to band members upon request. The bar staff had little incentive to do this, however, particularly as the evening trade picked up. The bar staff would obviously prefer to spend their time serving drinks from which they would derive a commission than attend to a band member. Further, the band member would be considering the potential effect of customer loss on his bonus potential if by chance a sale was missed while a barman was serving up his free drink. Consequently, if the club was crowded during the interval, and bar staff were either unwilling or unable to stop serving customers in order to bring musicians their quota of free drinks, the band members were encouraged indirectly to go to the bar next door. Although this meant purchasing a drink, it did also mean that one could sit down and relax without the feeling of depriving anyone of their income.

We were officially due to arrive at the venue at 7.30 p.m. in order to start at 8 p.m. prompt. However, the usual routine was to arrive ten minutes before showtime. Upon arrival drinks were offered to the band and if a musician turned down a drink at any time of the night he was considered by the management to be suffering from illness.

The audience were generally attracted to the club by the street volume of the band playing as they passed by the club. Enthusiastic bar staff quickly ushered potential clientele from the door to their seats whereupon they were required to buy a drink at rates even the Swiss thought high. The pressure to buy drinks was largely responsible for the turnover in the club. The entire audience of approximately 150 changed nearly three times in the evening. The band never played beyond midnight. Contractual agreement stipulated that any overtime was to be paid for at a higher rate. The only occasion we played beyond midnight was New Year's Eve when we played until 1 a.m. Further to the contractual restrictions on playing beyond midnight there were licensing laws for that particular club which prohibited loud music after midnight. This was not the case in all venues in the area. Consequently, in order to compete with later music venues, the bandleader played solo piano for an additional two hours for which he received extra money.

The atmosphere during the actual performance was intense and full of excitement. The audiences were always very appreciative, religiously applauding individual solos. As the night progressed and the audiences became more wound up by drink, their enthusiasm became aggressive with dancing and wild screaming not dissimilar to rock audiences in this country. The enthusiasm for jazz in Switzerland is one reason why there is a regular rota of jazz bands working in Zurich. Another reason, however, is that English jazz musicians are poorly paid by Swiss standards and their moderate expectations therefore explain their popularity with Swiss music venues.

Furthermore, foreign musicians are not only cheaper but are considered more authentic jazz musicians and very few of the venues will employ Swiss musicians for this reason. Additionally, the Swiss venues are reluctant to employ foreign musicians who live permanently in Switzerland as they are then considered to be local.

During my stay in Switzerland I heard of several musicians who married native Swiss and discovered that although the legal bar to their permanent residence and employment in that country had been lifted, the local venues would no longer employ them because they were no longer considered 'foreign' musicians.

Getting the 'gear' to the venue

The band members had their own instruments well before being contracted for the engagement. The problem of transporting them to the venue was greatly alleviated by the fact that the engagement was for a jazz group; an essentially acoustic ensemble. The bass player did, however, use an electric Fender jazz bass as opposed to a string bass (i.e. a double bass). He also hired the necessary amplification for the engagement from a local music shop near the venue in Switzerland. Consequently he had then only to transport the guitar from London to Zurich. The actual amplification he used was a 100-watt amplifier which was more than adequate for the performance.

If he had used an acoustic string bass the cost incurred in transporting such an instrument would have made the job uneconomical. Furthermore, there were considerable constraints regarding space on stage. The stage was extremely small and could barely accommodate live players. Apart from the advantages of space conservation there were other advantages of a musical nature. The electric bass guitar lends itself to other types of jazz-based music more fluently than a string bass. Although a string bass provides more traditional tonal qualities known to jazz it is very difficult to play on it what is known as crossover fusion music. As a result of the bass player's equipment and of course his ability it was possible to vary the evening's playing format more widely, I suspect, than otherwise.

The banjo/guitar player had to bring two instruments but his equipment was amplified through the house PA along with the vocals. The advantages of the moderate amplification were that it enabled the group to perform a broader range of material than if we had been exclusively acoustic. The acoustic guitar was equipped with a pick-up which went straight into the house PA. The Swiss like guitars but are very partial to banjos. Many banjo solos are expected throughout the evening and they are very enthusiastically received. The banjo player in fact brought two banjos so that when strings broke he would get through a number without having to repair strings immediately.

The trombone player had only to bring his trombone and this was a fairly easy matter. He rarely used amplification – it was hardly necessary as the microphone used for the vocals picked up the brass sound on the periphery and helped to throw it out. The feature player RJ (saxophone/clarinet/vocals), brought with him a clarinet and saxophone – again relatively easy to transport. Although he used amplification for his voice he only periodically used amplification for soft clarinet features such as 'Jacqueline' (Sidney Bechet).

There were occasional moments throughout the month when the wind players overused the vocal microphones to amplify their equipment. This usually occurred when either of the front line instruments felt the other was drowning them out or if the audience was particularly enthusiastic and encouraged the player to play at greater volume. Invariably, the management and bar staff complained when the band increased in volume regardless of whether the audience were enjoying or encouraging them to do so. The employees of the establishment found it difficult to converse with customers when the band played too loud. The bar staff consequently sold fewer drinks and there was some degree of customer dissatisfaction.

The bandleader (sax/clarinet) insisted that volume was necessary to play loudly at the beginning of the evening so that passing trade would hear live music in the club and be drawn in. Subsequently as the evening progressed the gradual increase in volume and intensity of playing was, in the mind of the bandleader, a 'way of winding people up' and 'getting them into the music'. Further, he argued that the more enthusiastic the audience the more they would drink. The entire month was riddled with arguments over band volume. Evidently, all bands playing there had similar difficulties.

Finally, as the drummer, I had made other arrangements regarding equipment. A drum kit is, of course, expensive to transport. When I was originally asked to do the residency I anticipated having to transport my entire kit. The bandleader in fact offered to drive to Switzerland with the drum kit tied to the car roof. This, however, seemed inordinately complicated and I was fortunately able to arrange a loan of part of a drum kit from the resident drummer of the club. This meant I only had to bring my snare drum, bass drum pedal and cymbals.

Apart from the basic drum kit the only other item I used on the job was an electronic drum synthesiser. I never used this during any of the ensemble playing. I only used this on my drum solo. I was required to play a twenty-minute drum solo every evening and it was during this period that I used the synthesiser – more as a sort of gimmick sound, e.g. jazz with a bit of contemporary spice. The other members of the band and the audience welcomed the diversion.

Sheet music and the running order

Methods of notation varied from player to player, but each one had a songbook with collections of chord charts and bass lines for each number. During the time we were there, we played some seventy numbers but the actual songbooks of the trombone player, bandleader and guitar player contained over 300 numbers. Most of the material was played from memory, unfamiliar in structure and and expectation only to me as I was a generation behind in playing experience and familiarity with the idiom. When the bandleader called a number that anyone was unsure of they simply consulted their chord book and followed it. This, however, created some disturbance on several occasions between the bandleader and different players in the band. In the majority of disagreements, numbers in question were standard and the chord charts, structure and sequence were settled without question. However, on some numbers different parts were in different keys, and the bandleader's way of playing it was different from the written notation of other players. Technically speaking the bandleader should have provided the music on all numbers so that there was no ambiguity over chord structures and arrangements. This was a considerable fault in the entire musical organisation of the engagement. The bandleader's chord book was in conflict with the guitarist/banjo player's and this of course had something to do with the choice of keys in which to play certain numbers. It became necessary consequently for the guitarist and bandleader to meet regularly to discuss differences. However, in many instances the bandleader would simply play the part incorrectly. If anyone did go wrong it was considered, in his view, invariably to be someone else's fault. At the beginning of the month, the bandleader seemed to create many confrontations which encouraged a degree of uncertainty. It was argued by some that he was using the dissimilarity in people's methods of notation to retain his authority over the band.

In contrast to the others I had no methods of notation, and there were no written drum parts. The bandleader was nevertheless fairly decisive in the kind of drum part he wanted on each number. In some instances he was uncertain what he wanted me to play and he might suggest different approaches to certain numbers on different nights. I often found, however, that I was caught between conflicting demands – between the rhythm section and the front line – as to how they wanted me to play. Occasionally the bandleader might directly object to what the other members of the band would suggest for a drum part on individual numbers. Sometimes he would say to me, 'Don't listen to what they tell you to play, play what I want you to play – I'm the bandleader.'

Learning to play jazz

Learning to play jazz was always presented to me as a mixture of mysterious visitation (genetic or spiritual) and some kind of total dedication to achieving unobtainable goals. Listening has always been the key piece of advice. Different jazz players have said different things. The independent study of technique at text book level was always considered a necessary evil. Transforming technique was gained through, first and foremost, listening, and subsequent to this, playing live with different musical groups.

Nearly every jazz musician I've spoken to was old enough to be my father and it was not uncommon for them to give professional advice. I did, of course, actively seek their advice whenever they were prepared to give it. Here are some of the comments made to me.

A	How do you learn to play jazz?
Sax Player	Listen to it!
A	What would you advise a drummer to learn in order to develop his ability?
Session jazz drummer	Play in as many different bands as you possibly can. Don't ever tie yourself down to one kind of band. Listen to records of course, watch how musicians play in the live gig. Also listen to the sounds of engines, machines, clocks, industrial conveyor belts, etc.
RJ bandleader	When you're learning to play listen! But don't copy! Never copy another player's technique, melody lines, notes – copy his attitude, his approach, the way he is feeling the music. This is where you learn the most. There's nothing worse than listening to a solo which is initially original-sounding and then all of a sudden a line or two from a well worn tune drops in – something everyone recognises immediately. Maybe it'll happen for only a few bars, but it will ruin the solo.

A.	What about learning from books?
R.J.	You can't learn anything from books!
Unsolicited, bass player in Zurich	You're doin' all right now, the thing you've gotta do is listen to some of these old jazz records so you pick up all the little fills and stops and all that bit. You ought to learn to read as well as you can do the shows and the cabaret thing – there's a lot of bread in all that game.

To the majority of players, reading music disrupted one's ability to feel the music. A loose structure with plenty of room for improvisation enabled the soloist to play as he felt. Most of the material we did had plenty of room for this.

With regard to rehearsals, in my years of playing jazz there have never been any. However, the groups I have worked with have all rehearsed during previous formative periods. Therefore I think my experience is unusual and partly due to the age difference between myself and other players. When I first approached local jazz musicians to discover possibilities for joining a group, rehearsals were something of a taboo. Consequently all my learning came from listening and doing what I was told to do only minutes before a number was played, with the expectation that I would forever remember the arrangement. Even in Zurich, which was ostensibly a professional engagement, there were no rehearsals. In my contract that was sent to me by the bandleader it was stated specifically that all rehearsals called by the bandleader were to be attended unpaid. Certainly, some of the sparks that flew on stage could have been avoided if the band had had a rehearsal but the thought of rehearsal during the day was absolutely taboo. The closest the band came to rehearsal was drinking or eating together before performing when the bandleader would say what was wrong or right or what changes might be made in a particular number. Everyone did take note very carefully and did their best to oblige the bandleader's requests or for that matter the request of any other player who had a reasonable criticism.

The business of rehearsal in Zurich was also hampered by the fact that the management really didn't want anyone in the club unsupervised during the day. Presumably there was some worry that the ease of access to alcohol might be a temptation. Hence the fact that a rehearsal had to be supervised by the managment of the club, in addition to the fact that the musicians viewed such an activity as unpaid work, was a great discouragement to the organisation of a rehearsal. In fact the standing joke, at the time, for any musical errors was the threat of a band rehearsal at 9 a.m. the next morning.

Nevertheless there was still another kind of rehearsing that went on in the form of 'chat' which I grew to see as far more significant preparation for the evening's performance than I originally realised. Quite often it would occur late at night after the performance. The musicians would swap chord books and go through numbers and try to sing them to one another. This might go on for some time. Occasional references to different numbers in the band's repertoire would be the subject of criticism and one player or another might be advised with regard to his playing. As a rule the bandleader encouraged everyone to simplify his part.

Cassettes were sometimes used – particularly with me. The bandleader recorded five hours of jazz classics for me to listen to. The other band members would hang around while I was listening and point things out. I was forever being warned about not copying other players and creating my original style, but this was to be achieved through playing unobtrusively and playing all the arrangements correctly.

Publicity and promotion

In my experience of jazz groups the venue advertises the band in terms of the lead vocalist or instrumentalist, usually brass (although sometimes guitar and keyboard), and this individual arrives with his backing band which he makes a fuss over while the audience make a fuss over him. In some instances the star player or bandleader may have an additional share of the money compared to everyone else. For that he is responsible for bookings, publicity, musical notation and arrangements, and the general on-stage responsibility of fronting the band. When it is a good night and the audience is with you the bandleader has an enjoyable time along with the rest of the band. If the venue is bad, the audience unresponsive, or if the band plays badly, the bandleader gets the majority of the criticism from the audience and the management. I think it is a genuinely difficult role to play.

With regard to the gig in Zurich, the band was billed as R. J. and his Jazzmen. There was no question about this as R. J. had acquired this engagement through his former association with the resident band, and his playing in Germany on the jazz circuit. In Germany and Switzerland he is very well known. In this country he is not a bandleader and apparently has no desire to be. The actual transformation in his personality given the change in role is quite dramatic. Likewise, it was for another player who changed his role from bandleader to front line musician. On the first occasion we went to Zurich the trombone player was a bandleader in this country. In fact RJ regularly worked as a sax and clarinet player in his band. When I spoke to RJ over the telephone regarding the line-up in Zurich he said to me that he was taking PA (trombone player) to Zurich because PA had given him so much work in this country. PA had been a bandleader for years and runs a local band. He employs approximately fifteen musicians who do different jobs with him as and when they are available. RJ worked with him regularly for six months prior to going to Zurich. Since PA went to Zurich they hardly ever play together. In this case the roles were reversed with RJ being the bandleader and PA being the backing musician. The ramifications of this role reversal I will discuss later. However, for now, let me say that all the advertising was in RJ's name. The Casa-Bar prepared a special placard and in their showcase window several pictures of RJ were displayed.

The band was advertised in the local press and in the national press. There were usually two write-ups throughout the course of the engagement invariably featuring RJ and with a brief mention of other players in the band. Apart from this there was the odd mention on radio broadcasts but there was no sale of tickets for performances.

The audience

The audience at the Casa-Bar has been cultivated and recruited over a period of thirty years of jazz groups performing in this venue. Currently the main draw locally is the resident band. It is this outfit, once famous in England, who have cultivated the greatest local following. They perform in the club six months out of the year.

RJ performs at this venue approximately three times a year and has done so for the last seven years. His crowd of supporters has been cultivated over the years as well, but it is not as strong an audience as that of the resident band. Discussion of the difference requires several factors to be taken into consideration. First and foremost, there is consistency of playing dates in the venue. Second, the relationship between bar staff, management and the band can greatly affect audiences. Third and perhaps most important are the differences in the jazz following. The resident band plays strictly New Orleans jazz. RJ and his jazzmen is a predominantly traditional jazz outfit although additionally the band will play mainstream, blues and jazz funk. Audience recruitment is therefore affected by these factors of taste. The other dimension of audience recruitment is the musicians' involvement in the local social scene and their willingness to relate to customers in the Casa-Bar. The management are particularly keen to have band members fraternise with customers particularly when customers buy them drinks. There is also a lot of tourism in the area and English-speaking business clientele are grateful to have English-speaking musicians to chat to. All these factors together help to create audience atmosphere and contribute to audience recruitment.

Another dimension of audience recruitment was the preparation and sale of audio tapes. The first edition of these tapes was recorded five years ago. When we play at the venue RJ contacts the recording studio where the tapes were made and orders up to 100. Now, in the particular instance these tapes feature jazz standards as played by RJ and his Jazzmen and RJ has retained the copyright. That is, the musicians who backed him in the recording of the tape were simply paid a session fee and were not offered royalties on any further sales of the tape. Since the actual changeover in personnel in this band is so great, the original musicians who recorded the tape are no longer with the band. I remember on one occasion a customer who purchased a copy of the entire tape wanted autographs of the entire band who were ostensibly RJ and his Jazzmen. Because RJ had copyright and there was no mention of the original players on the tape he simply handed the cassette copy around to the existing band and asked them to sign it. He offered the band nothing for promoting the tape or actually signing it. However, he did offer a commission to anyone who sold the tape to a club customer.

The tape served an additional purpose in publicising the band. That is, a member of the audience could take the tape and play it to friends who might then be persuaded to attend for an evening at the club. At the very least, the sale of the tape certainly helped to make people more aware of the band's existence and invariably this had an impact on audience numbers.

There was always some spillover from the audiences attending the resident band engagements. We always took over the very next day after they had completed their monthly residency. Consequently the audience they built up during their stay would more than likely come to the next night expecting the usual band to be in residence. Inevitably some of them would be disappointed and would not attend the club on future occasions until the resident band returned. However, some of the audience became devoted fans of RJ and his Jazzmen.

Audience numbers were affected therefore by several factors: confusion as to which band was playing; curiosity about the new band playing once they discovered there was a change; the relationship between the band and the audience; the relationship between musicians, bar staff, and management; the sale of pre-recorded tapes; and media publicity.

During the course of the month there was an initial surge of audience attendance motivated by the confusion, curiosity and musical style factors. Then over the next two weeks the RJ and his Jazzman audience would begin to develop more selectively and a hard core of regulars and newcomers would establish a pattern. Audiences were reasonably consistent in numbers throughout the week except for Saturday night when it was so crowded it was difficult to get off the stage. People would begin to arrive between 8.30 and 9.30 p.m. there would be a gradual build-up between 9.30 and 11.0 p.m. when audience numbers would peak. At approximately 11.30 p.m. audience numbers would begin to taper off as individuals would travel home by trans-local transport – which ceased operating at midnight.

The 'gig'

The performance started promptly at 8 p.m. Depending on the mood of the bandleader, he would either ask the band what they wanted to start with or simply announce the first number (usually 'Rosetta'). This was a medium tempo tune which gave the band a chance to loosen up and gradually ease into the evening's performance. If there was a large audience during the first set the material he selected would tend to be more on the up-tempo side. However, more often than not, what determined the numbers we played was how energetic he felt, what he had had to eat, and when he had eaten it, whether or not he had slept that afternoon, or whether he had been drinking. Food and alcohol late in the day always slowed him down, in which case we did a lot of slow tempo material in the first spot. It was, nevertheless, well received. The bandleader's mood affected everyone dramatically and we could always tell by his behaviour in the first set whether the night was going to be fairly easy going or fraught with arguments about musical arrangements.

At the very beginning of the evening the hardcore alcoholics were propped up at the bar applauding almost everything in a hilariously enthusiastic way. A few of the local prostitutes would come in for a quick drink before work. The atmosphere had a combined quality of indignity and desperation about 'starting work'. It was always at this time that arguments about volume occurred. As mentioned earlier the band is basically acoustic and not very loud to begin with but, alas, the club is small. The management wanted some kind of volume to attract passing trade. The bar staff wanted little volume so they could hear the requests for drinks. Also, in the early part of the evening when there were very few people in the club, some of the customers complained about volume levels. Although the band would play at volume levels primarily to attract crowds from the streets, the other extreme of trying to play especially quietly at the beginning of the evening would make the band behaviour tense and would affect the fluidity of the music. Initially this problem affected the choice of material, until after the first week, when the bandleader had a full-scale confrontation with the manageress and the bar staff. He claimed the volume levels would have been tolerated in the earlier part of the evening in the interests of filling the club and the overall quality of the music. After that, we all simply carried on without further attention to volume. It never really became very loud.

The first set, known to some people in the trade as the 'dinner' set when people were still feeling pretty delicate from just eating or feeling their way through the first few drinks, was always beset with these tensions. Like the first part of any job it was the most difficult to get through. It was also the longest of all sets, lasting an hour and fifteen minutes. After the first set everyone in the band except the bandleader went next door for a drink and there were occasions when the band returned late from their interval visit to the Castel Bar next door. This created a great amount of anxiety for the bandleader and in fact it became a counter-weapon for the band if he became too unreasonble during playing time. It was also at this particular point that the band members had to be very careful how much they drank. Upon arrival for the first set musicians were handed a drink. Then, during the interval everyone had a drink next door at the Castel Bar. Further, the barman, who liked the band personnel using his bar, would quite often distribute free an expensive round of 'schnapps' which could not be refused without causing insult. This was intended to be consumed along with Swiss beer which together formed what is known as 'Swiss Scotch'. The two drinks together are extremely potent. By the time the band returned to the Casa-Bar a round of drinks had been prepared by the bar staff waiting to be taken on stage for the second set. Furthermore, the band was usually bought a round of 'shorts' during the set by a customer several times during the evening. Consequently it was very easy to overdrink. There was a firm rule, however, that drunkenness on stage was immediate grounds for dismissal.

There was an additional practical aspect of this engagement which encouraged excessive drinking – the total convenience of the accommodation situated above the club. After work it was unecessary to travel more than a couple of hundred feet to arrive at the flat.

It was necessary to drink and play together because the band as a whole played better if they had a little to drink as it reduced tension, and generally made everyone ease up on the instruments and relax. The trouble was, of course, in trying to keep a check on it and not allowing the social situation to encourage drinking beyond one's ability to play. There were several occasions during which the band played badly because they all had had too much to drink. The bandleader would sense this, but since he was a drinker himself he couldn't be too critical of it. Of course on those evenings when the drinking became excessive he generally selected numbers that were less complicated, and so easier to play. For the brass and reed section, too much drink made the lips go numb and they just could't play certain notes. For the rhythm section, chords were missed, beats were dropped and bass lines wavered.

During the second set of the evening one could tell how the rest of the night was going to turn out. The audience numbers increased to their maximum. The band had, by then, settled into their drinking pace for the night; and the bandleader had completed his routine 'keeping everyone in line' effort. Also the volume had settled to a comfortable level by then and people were beginning to get a bit wound up. Every number featured solos from every instrument except the drums. A drum solo was a feature of the third set. The audience applauded the solos enthusiastically and, in many ways, it became a habit for the players, to expect this. If for any reason one of the players didn't get his usual applause he would feel personally affronted and it might put him in a bad mood until the next solo when the audience applause would bring him out of it. In some instances, on a bad night when the audience wasn't responding as well as usual, the front line members would actually solicit the applause. After a while it became laborious. At first so much audience response would encourage each player to play better and still better until a plateau of achievement had been reached beyond which they could go no further. It couldn't get better. The novelty of periodic and momentary stardom began to wear off. Like an adrenalin drug more and more was required to bring on the 'high' feeling, but the supply, which was all created socially and through musical ability, couldn't be increased in doses – you could only stay at the same level. This encouraged all the musicians, eventually, to look around town for a 'sit-in' with another band. A new setting, a new audience, and a new group of players would be temporarily uplifting. Of course any other musicians present at our venue would also 'sit in'. Those that weren't working were always desperate to play – and the band was always sympathetic and invited them to join in. The only player on that circuit who I spoke to who wasn't keen on sitting in was the bandleader RJ. I asked him quite casually once whether or not he was going down to the local venue, the Bacillus Club, one Sunday afternoon for a 'sit-in'. He simply said, 'Why should I play if I'm not getting paid for it? I'd have to get outta bed, shave, put on my stage gear and play for nothin' – no, it's a waste of time.'

As far as letting people sit in was concerned, only those musicians personally known to the bandleader were given this opportunity. Usually it was the front line. The bandleader preferred people sitting in who didn't play his instruments, clarinet/saxophone, but he always let those who did play those instruments have the opportunity. Sometimes several guest players including clarinet, trombone and trumpet would climb on stage and we would have a fantastic sound if they could 'get it all together' and play some 'fat unison passages'. If it didn't come together, the sit-in could be disastrous and tedious – but this rarely happened. Occasionally, a guest spot would bring a competitive element into the playing and on certain evenings individual musicians played some absolutely stunning performances.

I remember one evening the new trombone player who came on the second month's residency found a rival Dixieland jazz band resident a mile from us at a competing venue, the 82 Club. They were called the Harlem Jazz Band. He introduced himself while in band uniform, and asked to sit in. They liked what he played and so they asked him to come along any time he liked. On one occasion I went along to that club to watch LD, the trombone player, sit in with this band. The band were on different terms and conditions than at the Casa-Bar. Their evening's work didn't actually start until 9.30 p.m. and they were booked for five hours a night instead of four. Consequently they were always playing a good couple of hours after we finished. Quite often, LD would race down to this club (as if he hadn't had enough) at this point and join in as soon as the regular trombone player came off stage. Their regular tombonist didn't seem to mind that LD was up there playing for however long he wanted. The regular trombone player seemed glad of the rest and was quite happy to let another player work a couple of hours while he sat quietly chatting to customers and drinking.

The Harlem Jazz Band were an all-American black jazz band – 'the real thing'. LD was so impressed by playing with them that he couldn't stop talking about it for days. He also managed, through his playing with them, to draw some of their regular audience to see him playing with us in the Casa-Bar. In that respect, sitting in can be good for business.

The third spot of the night was the high spot of the evening. Everyone in the club had by then had quite a lot to drink, the place was full, the musicians were warmed up, and everyone was generally in a good mood. This was the feature spot where everybody did their speciality act. Nearly everything in the set was up-tempo and then we would do a trombone feature. This is when we would bring the crossover or fusion element into the band's playing. The bandleader would walk off stage and allow LD, the trombonist, to be feature front line player and we would do a 'funky' version of 'Night Train'. The rhythm section would kick off, and basically the trombone would carry the whole thing through. It was a contrast to more traditional material and it always went extremely well. Then RJ would come back on stage to do a really sensitive Sidney Bechet tune called 'Jacqueline'. This developed even more interest cooling things down with even greater contrast. Then we would begin building up again with a racy guitar or banjo feature. The audience would be getting more and more excited. This was followed by the drum solo. The band would introduce the solo with the number 'Bei Mir Bist Du Schon'. Gradually each player left the stage leaving only myself and RJ, who finally departed after a long wailing note on the clarinet. The audience would applaud him as he moved off stage, which he did very slowly. I would drop the rhythm to something very quiet until he actually finished climbing down from the stage. Then I would do a very explosive roll around the kit. In particular I would play the synthesiser, which the audience hadn't heard before, and this always drew their attention. The solo then proceeded through a series of techniques which began with a jazz rhythm, developed into a Latin American rhythm, moving on to a rock rhythm, disco, funk, ending on an almost modern-day fusion of punk/funk and reggae until it gradually crept into 6/8 polyrhythm which built up in intensity and then stopped. I would then start a Mammy Daddy Roll, and very slowly build it into a fast double-stroke triplet roll until the entire kit was going in counter-rhythms. I would cue the band in and then they would walk on stage, with RJ the last to arrive. The bandleader would count the band in while I continued, and then we were all in.

The first time I did the solo at the Casa-Bar I was quite pleased with it. The bandleader wasn't. He always thought I could do better and I remember thinking at the time that the audience liked it and it was good enough. But he really pushed me to achieve something quite different which was very much an improvement. He said to me on the third or fourth day, 'We've gotta get together on your solo and work something out.' This was about as close as anyone came to having a rehearsal and it basically meant that you sat in the bar with a few drinks while he told you how to improve your technique. His first criticisms were that the solo lacked calculated organisation – it was too spontaneous. He would say:

> 'Sometimes, it comes off with all that spontaneous bit when you're in the right frame of mind and everything is going OK but other times it seems to be all over the place with you almost looking like you don't know what's going to happen next. The thing to do is get a balance between that spontaneous thing and building it up gradually. You see that's the difference between jazz and rock. In rock you explode all the time – that's no good

in jazz – you've got to take it from simple beginnings and build up the intensity gradually and wait for the audience to come with you.'

I asked him to describe how he thought the whole thing ought to go. To my surprise he had in fact listened to my solos quite carefully and could identify each segment of it, and he more or less suggested a re-organisation. He suggested the following:

> 'When the two of us are on stage together and you play that Gene Krupa type of rhythm on the tom toms – that's great. And when I come off stage and you burst into a roll and play the synth, that's showmanship – the audience like that. But you can get a lot more applause out of them if you build it up gradually. After you've done that whole exploding bit drop the volume and tempo of the rhythm, just keep it goin' in your feet and do something light around the toms toms, soft rolls 3 against 2, that sort of thing. Then put a little bit of steam into the thing and build it up tempo. Then as you build it more, start to drive it into those heavier rock beats. Build it up to a crescendo and drop it back to that slow jazz thing and they'll clap. Then stop. Look at 'em hard and start that Daddy Mammy roll. Build it all around the kit then go into the 6/8 thing and let em have it.'

I followed RJ's guidelines and found that some of it worked and other things did not. However, the overall effect was some improvement. I found the business of being left on stage on my own for twenty minutes a bit daunting but I became used to it and I tried to inject as much energy into it as possible. I remember the first night I did my solo, however, and the bass player came to the part where he walked off stage and he turned to me and said as he was going, 'Keep it going for as long as you can I'm just goin' next door for a drink.' They never did that but I remember believing him the first time he said it. I had worked out a signal to cue the band to come back on stage. It was a rhythm on the cowbell which, when I reached the point of exhaustion, I played very loudly. The band, who were all standing around the bar, settling into a drink would jump to their feet. I remember on several occasions I left the cue too long. My hands and wrists were starting to tense up trying to keep this fast double-stroke triplet roll going round the kit while I waited for the band to climb on stage. Consequently I used to start the cue a lot earlier to give the band a few extra minutes without driving myself to total exhaustion. When the band came in at the end we did two choruses then a final eight-bar break at the end. When that was over I could relax. That was always the end of the third spot and it was a relief to have it out of the way.

The bandleader classed the drum solo as a pretty important feature of the night and really pushed me to work it up as much as I could. In some ways I felt the other soloists had it easier, only ever having to carry the can for sixteen or thirty-two bars at a time. The bass player was a borderline alcoholic and RJ used to give him a lot of solos when he thought he was hitting the bottle too much – it kept him on his toes, boosted his morale a bit, and occasionally laid him off the drink.

The band would comment on my solo. They encouraged me and compared it favourably with the others they had heard. In many jazz groups I have played with the solo seems to be almost as important as the ensemble playing. This is, I feel, why there is so much structured solo work. It's all very democratic. Everybody has a chance to play his own thing, and when it's time to do the ensemble playing there's no ego battle the way there is sometimes in a rock band. Everybody buckles down to doing the job right.

I was of course curious to hear about the other drummers who had been there in the past and who were playing elsewhere locally. I heard stories about drummers' solos which were performed in an entirely different way to the kind of thing I wanted to do. Their previous drummer had done quite a bit of show work and cabaret and generally had had more professional experience. His approach to the solo was completely different and one which is used, evidently, by quite a few drummers. They usually start off with a simple rhythm which they play on each drum. Then, while still playing, they get up from the kit and carry on playing on different surfaces, e.g. floors, table tops, bar glasses, human anatomy, and so on. The audience evidently loved this kind of thing.

The last spot of the night varied in quality and attendance. Many people left after the third spot in order to catch local transport which ceased after midnight. At the weekend people would remain in the club long after the band had stopped playing. Often during the week the band would really over-indulge in drinking just before the last spot because everyone viewed the night's work as over. This was a natural feeling which was the inevitable consequence of everybody's feature being over. However, the bandleader quite rightly didn't always see it this way for several reasons. First, because he was bandleader and discipline had something to do with the job; second, the night's work for him did not end until two hours after we all finished. I do believe he would have been in a better mood on some of those evenings if he hadn't had to play piano for two hours after every job. Nevertheless, he wanted the money so he did it.

At the end of nearly every performance, which was at midnight on the dot, the audience invariably asked for an encore which we wanted to do but we couldn't for several reasons. The first was that the bandleader was absolutely firm about overtime rates which had to be double. Second, the law stated that loud music could not be played in the club after midnight. This caused the management some consternation because they lost a lot of business to the club down the road which had a licence for loud music until 2 a.m. The piano playing was light contrast and although the audiences appreciated it, it didn't always hold them. I was required to put a blanket around the drum kit to prevent individuals from the audience trying to play the kit.

On several occasions guest musicians would come in after hours to play the piano. They were usually young Swiss people who were trying to attract custom for their normal gigs elsewhere. RJ was always keen to let them play and the management were always happy about this because they were popular and held people drinking in the club after hours. The guests were never paid, although the management used to give them a drink on the house.

Zurich was very heavily populated with street musicians who worked in pairs and sometimes in groups. They used battery-operated amplification and played mostly loud rocking blues or rock 'n' roll. I remember at first thinking how fortunate I was to have the job at the club until I realised that they quite often earned far more than I did just by playing on the street. The majority of these buskers came from England and America for a few months at a time. It transpired that there was quite a demand for this sort of thing because there were so few working Swiss musicians who would be willing to accept the comparatively reduced standard of living they would have if they played music professionally. Consequently, the Swiss musicians who came into the club were all engaged in some other profession and only played music as a hobby, or, as RJ put it, 'for the birds and the social life'.

During the course of the residency several points of friction occurred apart from arguments over chords and arrangements. As I mentioned earlier, on the first residency in December, PA came along – an already established bandleader in Britain. As I said, the roles between RJ and PA were now reversed. Yet whereas RJ could cope with it in Britain, PA couldn't in Switzerland. In fact, within the first week he had an identity crisis. He kept wanting to announce all the numbers, count the band in, and tell everyone what to do. This of course got on RJ's nerves and everyone else's and they fell out over petty things like where the other ought to stand on stage and how many solos were to be taken in any given number. In my view there was no contest; RJ was clearly the star of the show and he very often had to rouse applause for PA's solo work. The residency, however, unfortunately resulted in a permanent separation of their professional association. Evidently, a member of the audience approached PA with a serious offer of a residential engagement in northern Germany and PA told the individual that RJ's band was called PA and his Allstars. When RJ heard about this he was angry. According to RJ, PA was treading on his patch and would never be asked to work with him again.

The personal lives of the musicians and the intensity of the work situation had an extreme impact on the group as a whole. In many instances pressures caused deep-seated depression and anxiety and in the cases of long-term employees of the club, the work of playing in the Casa-Bar changed people's lives. Graham Collier in *Inside Jazz* (London, Quartet Books, 1973) speaks of the unstable lifestyle of the jazz musician and how certain kinds of work situations are incompatible with stable family life. The pattern seems to be that while in Zurich, musicians who are there on a regular basis conduct a lifestyle of serial monogamy which in some respects is tantamount to polygamy. The wife and children remain in England and the musician is kept indirectly by a female in Switzerland. The situation arises out of periodic separation caused by the residency in addition to the financial necessity of finding a resident partner in Switzerland. There is virtually no possibility of bringing a family to the country because of the expense and Swiss law. Swiss law does not permit an individual to enter the country for work unless special arrangements are made prior to arrival. Consequently, finding work for a spouse is virtually impossible. Further, even if the relationship breaks down through periodic separation Swiss law will not permit a foreigner to reside in the country as an employee for more than six months a year. Consequently, even if an individual wanted a permanent life in Switzerland he could legally work there for more than six months a year only if he married a Swiss national. The greater likelihood is that while working alone in that country he forms an attachment and upon returning to England he simply reunites with his family. Initially, it is in the interests of the musicians to keep the relationship with a new partner on a strictly casual basis – but this rarely happens. Consequently the situation creates marital breakdown and destroys the possibilities of stable family life. If you continue in this line of work a double life is required unless you make a complete break with your roots in this country to live permanently in Switzerland. The problem with this is that even if you decide to remain permanently within the country and marry a national then your employment opportunities are restricted to the trade with which you came to the country. It is then illegal to work as anything other than a musician. Further, in the case where you become resident in Switzerland, many clubs will not employ you because you are no longer an international musician in the eyes of a club manager, but a local musician. The lifestyle is thus very demanding and disrupting. From the employment point of view, as far as the professional musician is concerned, once he is committed to the residency on a regular basis his regular work in Britain tends to be given to someone else. Furthermore, when a musician does return to this country and looks for work he finds that it takes a long time for people in the business to register in their minds that he has returned and consequently by the time work begins to resurface from his home base, the next month in Switzerland emerges and he is off again. After six months of this you are classed as either unreliable or unavailable and the usual outcome of the in-between is that you end up cooling your heels in England waiting for the next engagement.

Another disadvantage, if you have a family, is that very often it is necessary to be working abroad during holiday periods. One player's alcoholism and the breakdown of his marriage was largely the result of playing in Switzerland at the Casa-Bar. He led a double life for as long as he could and now he and his wife are separated. He is committed to the residency in Switzerland over Christmas and is therefore unable to spend it with his family. Furthermore, the woman he now lives with in Switzerland is continually pressurising him to return to Switzerland even when he isn't working, whereas his children pressurise him about his absenteeism. The whole syndrome drives him to fits of intense depression. There really isn't enough work at the Casa-Bar or anywhere else in Zurich for him to make a permanent transition from the marital home and even if he did he would then be a resident in Switzerland and the club then would not employ him.

He's burned his bridges, as it were, with regard to stable work in the UK and he lives a life where he periodically moves from place to place.

Other individuals thrive on this kind of existence. Many of the players in other bands at the Casa-Bar prefer a floating existence without a secure base and are grateful for having an excuse not to establish one. In some instances the Casa-Bar residency provides an escape for some musicians who have already been separated or divorced.

The lifestyle problems of being a professional jazz musician became even more apparent if I compare the personnel on the first and second engagements. The first residency was in December. The bandleader had been offered the residency at short notice after a long break from doing a club on a regular basis. Consequently the bandleader didn't have enough time to get all professionals on the job and it was necessary to bring two semi-professionals along – myself and the guitar/banjo player. The difference between us, however, was that I could do the entire month and I had no family to bring over with me. In fact the month of December was split between two different guitarists. The first guitarist, who was a semi-pro, brought his girlfriend over and would only do half the month at the venue. The second guitarist brought his wife and child. The trombone player, who has his own band, is by all accounts a professional but was not considered as such by the bandleader or the bass player who classed the behaviour of bringing one's spouse to the venue as unprofessional. I thought this was unreasonable, as marital partners had a rough time during separation. As it turned out, during the month of December I was pressurised by both the guitarists who brought family with them to stay in a single hotel room at their expense. They found it was cheaper to put me up in a single hotel room and for the family to stay in the flat than for the family to book a double hotel room during the course of the residency. Both guitarists utilised my co-operation to make the job into a holiday for them. Neither could view it any other way given that the cost of an additional partner in Zurich meant you would save very little money. Furthermore once the Swiss management found out that one of the guitarists had brought his wife and child over they attempted to deduct some of his payment for additional facilities used in the accommodation provided for the musicians. From the bandleader's point of view this was one complication to avoid.

As a result of all these complications the bandleader deliberately selected individuals for the next period in Zurich who had no family or had no intention of bringing any partner with them. In this case the personnel were: a trombone player who, although married to a working wife and with a family, had sympathy from his partner, sufficient to cope with his prolonged absence and the domestic stress which the separation might create; myself, who was single at the time, and the banjo player/guitarist who had recently been separated from his wife. Additionally there was the bass player from the previous engagement with his periodic living together arrangement, and RJ who was single.

The three-bedroomed flat was occupied by four of us; the bass player stayed with his girlfriend. The trombone player and the banjo player shared one room primarily because they were both cigarette smokers, and I stayed in the other room. On the previous visit I expected to share one of the bedrooms. Life in the accommodation provided established a certain routine. As the flat was directly above the club and opening hours were until in the region of 3 a.m. nightly the band didn't usually retire for the night until 4 a.m. People certainly waited until RJ finished his piano playing at 2 a.m. and usually a few of us were still drinking or hanging around while we waited for him to finish. If people were not in the club they were drinking in the flat and listening to tapes of their favourite jazz musicians. At 3 a.m. players began to look at chord books with favourite numbers along with tales of great performances with great players in various parts of the world.

Stage dress

The management of the venue required all resident bands to dress in uniform – a T-shirt bearing the name of the band and dark trousers. There was no possible deviation from this uniform, much to the annoyance of band members. From the management point of view, as well as that of the bandleader, it made the business of visual identification far easier in the crowded venue. Also regular bar staff found it easier to locate and identify individual musicians with changes in the group from month to month. Apart from very practical concerns, the band uniform provided a sense of visual unity which, in the minds of band members, was for the benefit of the audience.

The networks

The networks responsible for producing the residency at the Casa-

Bar are several. First, there is the network of the local professional/semi-professional jazz scene from which players are recruited. This network yields a consistent range of musicians who would be available for the gig. RJ plays regularly on this network as a bandsman rather than as a bandleader and it is through his experiences on this circuit that he finds adequate personnel for his work in Switzerland. What are interesting to note are certain factors governing his selection of personnel for the first line-up in Switzerland. As it turned out, virtually all the players who came on the very first gig, apart from myself and the bass player, were all regular players in PA's band. It was in many respects, therefore, a convention of reciprocity that PA was asked along with the rest of the players in his band to do the performances as well. In fact I distinctly recall my conversation with RJ when he was describing the line-up:

A 'What is the line up for the gig?'
RJ ' I think you know all the players on the gig. At least you've played with them once before locally. We'll have GJ on guitar and banjo, and MD taking over from him half-way through. There'll be TT on bass, whom you don't know, you and me, and I have decided to have PA. I've decided to have PA because he's given me so much work over the past few months.

As mentioned earlier, one of the reasons for PA's identity crisis in Switzerland was the fact that suddenly his status was reduced from bandleader to bandsman, and he now stood alongside all his former employees as an equal rather than as a superior. All the while he was in Switzerland he made the regular point, 'These are my lads RJ is using and this is my band'. It was a convention of professional etiquette, therefore, that RJ immediately reversed his role when he returned to Britain. On one particular occasion I was intending to book RJ and his Jazzmen at a venue where we had formally played with PA under the banner of PA and his Allstars. RJ said we couldn't possibly do the engagement as RJ and his Jazzmen, as this would be a profound violation of professional convention. This convention therefore created a constraint and consequently the convention created an alternative course of action. RJ insisted that the only way we could do the gig at this particular venue was if we played another venue first which was known to PA, and from there it would then be possible to claim that the band had been booked at the intended venue as a result of this prior performance elsewhere.

In this particular example of RJ and his Jazzmen and PA and his Allstars, there is clearly an overlapping of networks which are beset with certain kinds of conventions. In particular, the sequence of events illustrates how 'existing conventions simultaneously make coordinated action possible and limit the forms it can take'. It was possible therefore for RJ as a bandsman to recruit an entire band from the personnel involved with another bandleader. However, it was also necessary to recruit the bandleader. This created some status conflict in another country which was only barely tolerable, and the conventions operating did in fact limit the forms in which RJ could operate when he returned to Britain.

Other networks responsible for producing the engagement at the Casa-Bar were the management and bar staff, each of which had some degree of control in the levels of co-operation in producing the actual event. The management created the terms and conditions of actual employment of the venue and the bar staff were a determining factor in the overall wage of the band. There were clearly points of conflict and mutual interest which enabled the residency to occur.

Convention and constraint

The initial constraint I came up against when wanting to learn to play jazz was having been established in a rock band. There was considerable opposition to the holding of joint identities in local semi-professional circles. However, this was of no consequence or interest to professional musicians who simply wanted players who could do the job for the fee offered.

Other constraints based on conventions were operative. In particular the actual musical format of traditional jazz had to be played in its original versions and the systems of notation had to be standardised where they were different. One of the events which occurred in the second month which did seem to alter several things was that the banjo player was a very weak soloist. This created a problem because it was a convention of the jazz format that many solos in many numbers were expected. The audience were also particularly responsive to the banjo and when the player concerned refused to play solos the bandleader had the bass player do long solos on nearly every number. Consequently RJ gave the bass guitarist many more solo sections.

Other conventions, laws, or conditions of employment created various constraints as well. There were many occasions, for example, when RJ was playing the piano between the hours of 12 p.m. and 2 a.m. and one of the musicians in our band or even a guest musician would have liked to accompany him. However, because of the licensing hours of the venue, RJ had to play acoustic piano unaccompanied. I strongly suspect that if there had been no licensing laws a 'jamming' session would have occurred which would have lasted through the early hours of the morning.

Another constraint which RJ held the band to quite rigorously was overtime. On New Year's Eve, which was the one occasion when the club was permitted a full live sound after midnight, the band were very keen to play, I suspect indefinitely. RJ had contracted for one additional hour and would not allow the band (much to the disappointment of both band and the audience) to play beyond 1.15 a.m. This in fact caused tremendous irritation and ill-feeling between the audience and players who, apart from RJ were entirely in sympathy with them.

It is arguable that small changes within a system of conventions in one area will create the need for change in other areas. For example, in the traditional jazz outfit the musical ensemble is basically acoustic. However, in view of the ease of transporting electronic equipment (particularly in the case of the electric bass) and achieving a greater variety of sound, electric instruments were incorporated into traditional jazz settings. In some instances this caused volume problems, in that wind players played louder than usual in order to keep pace with the volume dimensions of electrical instruments. Alternatively the use of electric equipment influenced the actual choice of material. There were more 'mainstream' numbers included in the set than there would otherwise have been and we did in fact feature a funky version of a jazz number as a result of the electric bass. Further, it was possible to do a few blues numbers which featured electric guitar. The presence of these electric instruments did go some way towards circumventing traditional conventions but my personal interest in electronics and 'funk' fusion with jazz did go some way towards actually bringing these numbers about. Another factor in persuading the other members of the band to do some blues and funky material was that the Castel Bar next door, where we usually ended up for a drink, always played piped-in jazz/funk fusion music.

Conclusion

In my view, it seems clear that conventions and constraints create systems of interrelationships which control artists as individuals and in groups. It does seem reasonably clear on one level that there are certain dimensions of convention which have specific location *vis-à-vis* the production of musical sound (e.g. the correct chords, correct bass lines, correct arrangements), as well as those conventions that have to do with personal feelings and expectations in a professional relationship (e.g. reversal of roles as bandleader and bandsman) as well as the practical needs and expectations of the venue in which one performs. Non-musical factors such as the latter can have as much to do with the final production of musical sounds as can the actual physical act of playing together. It seems clear, however, that this multiplicity of factors is enormously complex and that any form of determinism would only restrict one's view of the totality of the music project.

Convention and constraint among British semi-professional jazz musicians

Harry Christian

Introduction

This article is intended to explore sociologically the conventions and constraints that influence the activities of semi-professional jazz musicians in Britain. It presents ethnographic material on an area of musical activity which is at present unrepresented in the literature and the data are organised in such a way as to make them theoretically relevant to Howard Becker's discussion of Art as a Collective Action.[1]

It is based on a study by participant observation and informal interviewing of British part-time traditional and mainstream jazz musicians in a provincial area of England during the period 1982–7. It draws on my own experience of playing either regularly or occasionally with a total of nineteen bands during that period. Through this experience I was also able to compile a list of more than 100 contacts and interview musicians performing in an area which includes the West Midlands conurbation, Staffordshire, Shropshire, South Cheshire and nearby parts of Wales.

The article is arranged into four sections. The first section outlines the historical background to the recent and current activities of these British semi-pro jazz musicians; the second sets out data obtained in the study about the social characteristics and attitudes of these musicians; the third uses the same data sources to analyse this type of musical activity; and finally the fourth section presents three case studies in which the formation of bands and their subsequent history are discussed in terms of the general concepts of convention and constraint.

Historical background

Jazz is a minority interest in Britain today. In a way it always was but from the 1920s up to the mid-1960s a substantial minority of young people were added to the fraternity of jazz followers and musicians each decade,[2] and in the 1950s there was a particularly strong upsurge of youth interest,[3] but since the Beatles era and the rise of modern rock-influenced pop music the jazz fraternity has recruited a much smaller number of young people. The result is that, whereas in the 1950s and early 1960s jazz, and especially traditional jazz, had a mass audience and was usually played at the local level by young part-time musicians and predominantly for young dancers in soft-drinks-only venues, it is now typically played for middle-aged drinkers in pubs. Jazz players themselves also reflect this generational change. Only a minority of active part-time jazz players are now under 40 and many are over 50.

This demographic fact indicates that at least some of the conventions and constraints which influence semi-pro jazz musicians today arose during the time when they were learning to play jazz and getting their first experience of band playing. Values which they imbibed at that time still affect their thinking and actions, and therefore it is necessary to give some account of the historical background to current activity.

By the early 1950s, the period of stylised and highly commercialised big band swing had run its course, together with a popular music scene which often involved sophisticated 'adult' ballads, many from musical shows. These no longer appealed to the younger generation emerging after the Second World War. A rejection of commercially produced popular music was particularly strongly expressed in the New Orleans Revival, a rediscovery of pre-1930 jazz which began to be influential in Britain in the late 1940s. Eventually this revival itself became partially commercialised by the late 1950s at the height of the British 'trad' boom, but there was a period during the late 1940s[4] and most of the 1950s when jazz, and especially traditional jazz, symbolised for its followers musical integrity, widespread popular participation in music-making, and freedom from the influence of Tin Pan Alley money-grubbing.

The traditional jazz revival in both Britain and the United States was predominantly a white phenomenon and expressed a protest against both the musical and social restrictions felt by white young people at the time. Meanwhile the more sophisticated blacks in America were developing their own quite different musical and social protest in the form of bop (early modern jazz),[5] and their less sophisticated fellows were creating rhythm 'n' blues,[6] later to become the main influence behind early rock music. Traditional jazz did not appeal to younger blacks because it had already been 'stolen' from them by whites, it symbolised their more subservient past and they believed it did not give them sufficient scope for their technical musical abilities.

For young whites, however, it served as a suitable vehicle for musical protest[7] because its relative musical simplicity and its atavism offended their elders, as did its racial connections, and these shocking factors could be reinforced by the myth of the red light origins of News Orleans jazz and the less mythical association with the gangster speakeasies of the prohibition era.

Its basic musical principles, if not its finer points, could be quickly learned by teenage musicians, thus making possible the large-scale participation which steadily developed during the 1950s, when most towns of any size all over Britain produced several jazz bands of varying abilities, and had several jazz clubs running every week, either run by the more competent amateur bands or run by a club committee of enthusiasts and featuring the better-known semi-professional bands visiting from other areas, with local bands doing the interval spots. In nearly all these jazz clubs the bulk of the youthful supporters paying on the door came to dance in the 'jiving' style and were not deeply committed to appreciating the details of the music.

In the late 1950s the beginnings of the trad boom coincided with the arrival of rock 'n' roll, but there was little connection between the two other than the fact that both involved forms of youthful musical protest and both were musically basic enough to make possible widespread participation.

By the mid-1960s the trad jazz boom had spent itself and the next cohort of young listeners and dancers succumbed instead to the impact of the Beatles in the popular field. The jiving-type jazz clubs gradually closed down and trad jazz returned to its former status of being a minority interest, though with a residue of sympathisers with nostalgic memories and of musicians with some experience of band playing but mostly by now getting involved in careers and family obligations. Instruments and records began to gather dust in spare bedrooms, though a small number of clubs survived and a few musicians continued to play to depleted audiences.

Gradually during the later 1970s and early 1980s, with their children entering their teens or with marriages breaking up, former jazz musicians retrieved their instruments from their resting places, and ventured out to 'sit in' with the small number of semi-pro bands that continued to play. Temporary or more lasting 'come-backs' were achieved and new bands came together mainly for the sheer enjoyment of 'blowing' again. The same tunes – many of them in any case dating from the 1920s and earlier – were recalled and new numbers were learned, but mostly the style remained much the same as it had been in the boom years.

The intervening years had brought some changes though. Some former trad jazzmen moved on to mainstreams or modern jazz styles but many stuck strictly to the old style. Amplification now seemed to be much more essential as it was assumed that audiences had become accustomed to louder volumes. It used to be said of jazz musicians that if the power were cut off and the lights went out they could keep on playing just the same. This was no longer the case for those depending on amplification. Bass guitars now often replaced double basses, because of ease of transport. Some bands even contained recruits from the rock and other fields on such instruments as amplified guitar, bass guitar or drums. But in most trad band rhythm sections the banjo was still ubiquitous. Saxophones were now more tolerated by traditional jazz musicians but some of the more purist listeners still regarded them as anathema.

By this time the venues that were available were nearly all pubs and dancing played little or no part in the proceedings. Audiences were also predominatly middle-aged and clearly many of them were the same people who had jived and listened to jazz in the late 1950s and early 1960s.

In the West Midlands region where this research was carried out there were frequent rumours on the jazz scene that a 'new boom' was on the way and one heard tell of a thriving jazz scene further south, but the boom – like affluence in general – did not seem to spread beyond the south!

Musicians' social characteristics and attitudes

The occupations of the musicians studied included a hospital anaesthetist, a dental technician, an income tax inspector, a social security inspector, a carpenter, a window cleaner, two tailors, a barber, a butcher, several teachers, including one who was head of music at an independent grammar school, two head teachers, several other local authority employees, several lecturers in further or higher education, a commercial traveller (in musical instruments), a foreman in the building trade, several businessmen, an RAF technical instructor and an RAF helicopter pilot, and several retired or unemployed men. Apart from a few singers, only three of the musicians were women (a pianist and two sax players). One of these was a teacher, one a lecturer and one a student.

The musicians' ages ranged from the early twenties to the seventies, but approximately 60–70 per cent were within the age range 45–55, reflecting the fact that they had nearly all started playing during the British traditional jazz heyday between 1950 and 1960 even though some now played other styles.

Semi-pro jazz musicians who do not get any benefit from Arts Council-type patronage (and this seems to apply to any style other than modern ones) continue to play for money which is often well below Musicians' Union rates. Many jazz performances would not take place and many venues would not exist if this were not the case. Since most of the musicians involved are not full-time professionals and play mainly for their own enjoyment they are keen to get opportunities to play provided their expenses are covered and they are able to go home a little in pocket.

Some can earn bigger money playing with bands which play for ballroom dancing on Saturday evenings, but are only too glad to get the chance to play something more to their taste and with more freedom of expression even for very little money. An illustration of this was when I rang a Birmingham drummer who did not know me to ask if he would deputise on a Saturday night. His immediate reply was that he could not do it, but when he realised it was a jazz gig, he replied with obvious enthusiasm, 'Right I'll do it.' When told the money would be poor he commented, 'Oh that's all right I'll enjoy it.'

Similarly a bass player who gets regular well-paid work with a well-established folk group in the Black Country expressed his eagerness to be invited to play jazz at much lower pay.

> 'We play the same fifteen to twenty numbers over and over again that we have been playing for years. When we do a new number we rehearse it for weeks before we do it on a gig. It gets really boring. But when I play jazz we work with a chord book with more like 100 numbers in it and we never play the same programme two gigs running. Even numbers we've done before we play differently each time.'

Most semi-pro jazzmen are aware that their experience and ability by now deserve much higher rewards but seem resigned to a scene which at least allows them to play in public with moderate frequency. As an accomplished Birmingham jazz pianist in well-paid medical employment remarked, 'We're playing for peanuts nowadays. If you take the AA's estimate of the real costs of running a car we're subsidising it ourselves.' The same pianist was willing to travel a 120-mile round trip carrying a £1,000 electric piano to play a jazz gig for less than £10.

One factor which militates against well-paid work for semi-pro jazzmen is that their places of residence are typically dependent on their main employment and/or family commitments rather than on availability of suitable jazz-playing opportunities. As a result they have to be prepared to travel considerable distances for the chance to play, especially if they want to play in a style other than the most popular ones. Since jazz musicians and venues are more thinly spread than they once were it is essential to run a car and to have a telephone. It is clear that playing semi-pro jazz is far from being a money-spinner but more in the nature of a hobby which with luck more or less finances itself.

Nevertheless there is an alertness not to be too much exploited. A Shropshire trombonist said, 'I play for enjoyment but I enjoy it just as much when I'm being paid for it.' The same musician, when his band was hired by a wealthy businessman to play for his daughter's 21st birthday party, drove a hard bargain and was able to share out sums which surprised the other musicians involved. But such gigs do not come frequently.

Much resented is the attitude of some organisers of social events that jazzmen will play all night for nothing if you keep them supplied with drinks. Some jazz musicians do drink a lot but others are more like the sax player who said, 'I don't drink unless I'm on a gig and then I spend all evening over half a pint.'

Even full-time professional jazzmen in this area are not playing so regularly that they can insist on full pay in fully professional company. Many are known in semi-pro circles as being prepared to deputise or do guest appearances with semi-pro bands for moderate fees on nights when their diary is empty.

My impression is that Birmingham is a particularly low-pay area for semi-pro jazz. Informants reported that to play all evening at a regular venue for £8 or less each is not unusual. One-off gigs are a little better paid but regular venues are few and jazzmen themselves are keen to keep them and their bands going. One bandleader said that he regularly shares out his band's £40 earnings at one venue by giving £8 each to other five members of his band and taking nothing himself. Yet he does a sixty-mile round trip to play there and is glad to have the gig because there is always an appreciative audience there.

Another musician said he had drawn the line after being expected fortnightly to do a seventy-mile round trip to play for £3 and free drinks. His main reason for leaving the band, though, was that he did not enjoy their style of playing.

So if jazz musicians are not in it for the money, what are they in it for? The most frequent reply was that they are in it for the intrinsic enjoyment involved. But what constitutes this intrinsic enjoyment of playing jazz as compared with other kinds of music? Replies showed that some of the appeal is the same – the sheer pleasure of social music-making and giving pleasure to listeners who appreciate what one is doing, the company of musically like-minded people and the teamwork involved in producing a collective product that could not be done alone. But in addition, in the case of jazz, musicians refer to the appeal of being an on-the-spot composer. An improvised solo within an understood harmonic framework gives a jazz musician a highly appealing combination of creativeness and contextual support. At the same time it provides a satisfying synthesis of individuality and teamwork.

Another factor which can be common to other forms of music too, but which seems to be particularly noted by these musicians, is that in the case of semi-pro jazz one mixes with people from quite varied social backgrounds and modes of life but the only thing that really matters is the shared musical interests. In one band there was a drummer who was a window cleaner and a guitarist who was a carpenter, while the pianist was a hospital anaesthetist and the bass player a lecturer in human biology. In another band one player was one of the most affluent businessmen in the area while another was unemployed. In another band one player was a social security inspector who also usually collected the band's earnings, while at least two other members of the band were drawing social security and were being handed their share – in cash – by the social security inspector.

Analysis

The musical instruments

Most of the jazz musicians studied had bought their first instrument in their teens, either a secondhand one or a very cheap new one, and paid for out it of their earnings from a daytime job. Many had bought them on hire purchase. Some still play the same instruments today. One, for instance, still plays a 1937 saxophone which he bought in 1957. Most, however, have exchanged their initial instruments for better-quality ones several times. Some of the reed players have made a collection of related instruments. One has, and regularly plays, a clarinet, a flute, and soprano, alto, tenor and baritone saxophones. Another has all these except a baritone and a third has all except a soprano and he was seeking to buy one at the time of interview. The cost of purchase is nearly always financed out of daytime, i.e. non-jazz, earnings. The same applies to microphones, amplifiers, speakers, instrument stands, mutes, etc. Because their earnings from playing jazz are limited they tend not to have their instruments regularly serviced but only do so when they find them beginning to be unplayable.

Sheet music

Notation is minimal. Most jazz musicians in small bands make use of chord books which list numbers in the repertoire in the form of sequences of chord symbols which summarise the harmonic structures of the numbers. These are used as a basis for improvision by soloists. Sheet music with formal musical notation is rarely used except by big bands – which means ten or more players. Tunes and harmony parts are normally memorised, and in the case of harmony parts they are quite often improvised on the spot. A considerable development of the ear and the musical memory is therefore involved. Apart from these, some players have memorised famous solos note-for-note from classic jazz records and regularly reproduce these, as well as playing their own improvised solos on the same themes.

Original compositions in the form of new tunes are uncommon among semi-pro bands but new harmony parts are sometimes added to old numbers and in any case an improvising jazz player is composing all the time, since no number is ever played quite the same on successive occasions. If there is too great a similarity in successive performances this is a cause of criticism from discerning listeners.

Learning to play jazz

Most semi-pro jazz players learned the rudiments of their technique and style in their teens. Learning was mainly by ear, particularly by listening to records and playing along with them. A record player was far more important to most of them than a music stand and sheet music.[8] The practising of arpeggios on the chords of numbers was more important than learning scales. Practising by improvising numbers in different keys was central to the learning process. Most also emphasised the enormous value of playing with other learners and more experienced players. Band-playing experience can only be obtained by playing with a band, and to be able to mess about and make mistakes and learn along with others doing the same was seen as being a more essential learning experience than formal tuition in reading music. A training in orthodox music was often seen as a disadvantage for jazz players. 'If you once get hooked on the dots you'll never learn to improvise,' I was told by a clarinettist. Many others repeated the same point in other words. Most thought that becoming a fluent reader was a useful skill but far from essential for them.

Since the early 1960s some part-time jazz players have had a long lay-off and have taken a while to get back into practice again. Others had shorter breaks while a small number have been playing continuously since the 1950s.

More than half were conscientious about their playing today and would like to practise at home regularly with the aim of improving their techniques but daytime employment and family circumstances often restricted this. Fewer, but still a substantial proportion, having reached what they regarded as a satisfactory level of competence, were content to go on playing at the same level indefinitely. Several never touched their instruments between public performances at least a week apart.

Young players trying to enter the scene are few and they have a considerable difficulty in that they have few contemporaries to learn along with as the more experienced players had in their teens. It is nerve-racking for them to sit in with much more accomplished players and to make mistakes in front of often critical jazz audiences. In addition they are unfamiliar with the cues and unspoken, taken-for-granted understandings which ensure musical rapport between older players (see below).

Rehearsal

Musicians varied a great deal in their attitudes towards band rehearsals. some bands, as will be seen later, never rehearse while others are keen to do so when circumstances permit. Most said they would like to have the time and opportunities to rehearse more and one trumpeter said he preferred rehearsing to playing in public.

Promotion
This is usually left to managers of venues or organisers of events but some bands do produce demonstration tape recordings which can be sent to the more sought-after jazz venues in the hopes of getting band bookings. Apart from these, a widely used form of cheap advertisement is the national *Jazz Guide* produced monthly by a bandleader in the south of England. This is a four-page leaflet in which bands, venue organisers and some individuals place standing advertisements. The *Guide* is not circulated commercially but a batch of copies is sent to each advertiser who then distributes them free at their jazz events early in the month. In this way everyone advertises everyone else and circulation is concentrated where the *Guide* is likely to be most effective. Advertising is restricted to the older (pre-bop) types of jazz, in other words precisely the styles which do not get public arts subsidies.

Marketing jazz
This can be a difficult problem since jazz is not currently a young people's dance music. Many pub licensees try to use live music as an attraction and some are of the age group where they may themselves be jazz fans or at least remember how much of a draw trad jazz was twenty-five years ago. Jazz events or series are therefore often attempted, giving bands a chance to play, but frequently a sparse audience responds and young people get up and leave after a few minutes.

There are nevertheless well-established jazz venues where a full and appreciative audience can usually be expected. Some pubs have over the years gained a reputation as jazz pubs and attract people from a wide radius. One such jazz pub in the Black Country has nine jazz sessions every week – every night plus two lunchtimes – and attracts customers from a thirty- to forty-mile radius. It is the sort of small old pub which would be empty or might by now have closed down if it were not for the entertainment provided. Its whole existence is devoted to jazz, its walls are covered with photographs of jazz musicians and even its name has been changed to reflect its jazz policy. Even though the pay is far from generous it is the sort of venue which jazz musicians would like to see much more numerous. Most other jazz pubs can sustain only one or two successful nights a week.

Apart from audiences at such venues, most bands that play regularly accumulate a small enthusiastic following, but these are seldom enough to make a success of an event unless other people can be attracted too.

Playing the 'gig'

Whether or not a jazz band has an official leader there is nearly always one player who leads musically in performance. This role normally falls to the trumpeter unless the band has an acknowledged leader who plays another instrument.

Either a leader has a list of numbers worked out beforehand or, as often happens, numbers are decided by the leader as he goes along or by a quick discussion 'on the stand'. If often surprises the uninitiated that jazz musicians often do not know what number they are going to play until a few seconds before they start. Quite often the first a band member hears of it is when the leader announces it over the microphone, which is frequently followed by the inquiry 'what key?' from behind him. The leader may well call out the key while he is already beginning to 'tap in' the number (indicating the tempo). And they are away.

Once stated they may play a 'head arrangement' which may have been practised in rehearsal but quite often has evolved in previous performances, or one which is simply copied from a famous recording. Otherwise the trumpeter will state the melody line and other instruments will improvise harmony or contrapuntal parts to fit.

Numbers usually have one harmonic sequence which is repeated over and over with improvised solo variations by each front line instrument plus the pianist, guitarist or banjo player. Many traditional numbers, however, have two or three and sometimes more themes with linking passages, on which arranged parts or collective improvisations are performed. Nevertheless there is always a 'main theme' which is used for solo improvisation. Many semi-pro bands often fall into rather too rigid a procedure for solos – there is often little variation in solo order and since these are part-timers who all want their chance to shine, all soloists are given a solo on every number. In jazz a 'solo' normally means one instrument accompanied by the rhythm section.

Where leaders try to vary the solo order this is not usually worked out in advance but 'turns' are indicated in performance by a nod of the head, raised eyebrows or some similar gesture. Sometimes variety is created by the soloists' playing four-bar 'chases', often called 'taking fours'. Still improvising on the chord sequence, each soloist plays four solo bars before handing over to another. This continues until the chorus is completed. This procedure may involve the drummer's playing each alternate four-bar solo sequence interspersed between four bars from a front line player. Again this is often not worked out before the number starts but is signalled to the drummer in the preceding chorus by the holding up of four fingers and pointing to the players who will be involved.

Solos completed, the band then returns to the tune or to collective improvisation on the main theme until the trumpeter or other leader signals 'last chorus', usually by swinging his instrument round to the band. The drummer then often increases his emphasis in some way, which leaves everyone in no doubt that the end is coming. Sometimes this procedure fails – jazz musicians sometimes play with their eyes closed or get carried away by their own playing – but even then the situation can be retrieved by the drummer's taking a momentary decision to create a coda by playing a four-bar 'break' before everyone joins in again for an extra two or four concluding bars. Usually, though, such an ending is deliberate and is signalled to the drummer towards the end of the number, often by his being shown four fingers (a four-bar break).

Original composition

As can be seen from the previous section, musical composition is taking place continuously in a jazz performance both individually and collectively. Nevertheless individual band members may sometimes write a number, which would always involve a harmonic sequence as well as a tune, but such 'off-the-stand' composition is fairly rare among semi-pro jazz musicians. They are seldom involved in issues of copyright and are unconcerned about writing popular 'hits'. Such a 'commercial' attitude would be frowned upon.

On the stage

A few jazz bands do have a 'band uniform' but this is unusual and often thought too 'commercial'. Sometimes evening dress or clothing of a similar style and colour (white shirts, dark suits) is worn for particular engagements where this seems appropriate. But most bands, especially when playing at established jazz venues, affect a completely casual attitude to dress. Nevertheless most semi-pro jazz musicians are middle-aged and dress fairly conventionally, though informally. The same applies to current pop dress fashions and hairstyles. Jazz musicians do not tend to perform looking like punks or hippies. In any case such a stage appearance would strike jazz enthusiasts as being just as 'commercial' as band uniforms and therefore equally unwelcome.

Starting a band – three examples

In this section I intend to outline three different strategies of band formation which I have observed in order to explore the interconnections between the prevailing conventions and constraints within concrete settings. These three strategies can be summed up as: the Topsy method; the formal method; and the personal selection method. The first refers to the experience of Topsy in *Uncle Tom's Cabin* who believed that she did not come from anywhere but 'just growed'. The second refers to the method of advertising for players in a formal way and forming a band from those who respond. The third refers to the personal invitation of players whose styles and abilities have been assessed by on-the-spot observation. The first and third methods led to successful bands which are still playing regularly while the second method led to a band which broke up after six months.

Case I This band grew almost imperceptibly from an assortment of players who converged on an established venue in north Staffordshire which in 1982 was putting on a 'jam session' evening open to all comers. (A jam session is a relaxed and unrehearsed musical session based on a familiar repertoire and primarily for the enjoyment of the musicians.)[9] With the departure of a previously resident band a small nucleus of experienced jazzmen who were playing regularly elsewhere agreed to take part to keep jazz going in a venue otherwise devoted to non-jazz styles. Others who had not played regularly for some years came along for an informal 'blow' to get themselves in practice again.

Over a period of about eighteen months this informal set-up continued but by the end of that time a regular, balanced line-up had emerged accustomed to playing together in a style acceptable to all of them. The more experienced semi-pros gradually dropped out to be replaced by others who had been regaining their confidence and their form in the jam sessions. The newly emerged band, still with no name and no clearly defined leader, were offered, late in 1983, a regular venue in a nearby town where a keen jazz fan ran a pub.

So began a weekly residency which has now lasted for four years, and the band has eventually adopted the name of the pub as their band name. They also continued for several months to play weekly for poor money in their original venue but then decided to concentrate on their new venue where the money was more reasonable and the audience more numerous and more appreciative.

The resulting band is still one with no clear leader. One member usually chooses most of the numbers played and collects and shares out the money, but two others arrange for deputies for absent members, and occasional engagements away from their usual venue can be obtained and negotiated by any member. The band has never had a formal rehearsal but plays mostly long-familiar numbers in a well-understood style, and they have no ambitions of ever reaching the Big Time. Several of their members frequently play for other bands. Their whole approach is casual and easy-going. They seldom meet one another between their weekly sessions and have few other common interests.

The band lacks any ambition even to play outside their immediate locality. A commercial outlook is entirely absent – they have never advertised themselves in any way – and their organisation is informal – no clear leader and for almost four years not even a settled band name. All these features reflect the unplanned nature of the band's original formation. Its members are content to operate within the long-established conventions and constraints of the British provincial part-time traditional jazz scene.

Case II This band was formed in 1983 by a young teacher of music who had recently moved into the Black Country area. He had played jazz at university and wanted a chance to play jazz as well as conducting school choirs, orchestras and bands in performances of western orthodox music. His local contacts were very limited and so he advertised in the nationally circulated monthly *Jazz Guide* for volunteers to join his band. After a month or so he was contacted by a more experienced older jazz musician who wanted to play the style mentioned in the advertisement. Through him a pianist was also recruited. A school colleague of the leader also asked to join in and finally a local dance band drummer was obtained to make up a five-piece band. A band name was chosen which identified it with the Black Country area.

A local brewery, one of whose pubs was already an established jazz venue, was contacted and the new band was offered the chance to play at a refurbished pub in the Black Country. No funding was provided but it was understood that the band would pass round a hat and the landlord would supply them with free drinks. Brewery funding might be provided later if the venture proved successful. Band members saw it as a chance to get started as a band and perhaps develop a new venue.

A series of carefully drilled rehearsals was held before the first public appearance and notation was provided by the leader in the form of sheet music with chord symbols added.

The band then played fortnightly for about six months but the hoped-for musical style did not fully materialise. Although most of the band had formal musical qualifications – three were music teachers – the jazz experience of all but one band member was very limited and rapport in performance was often unsatisfactory. The drummer tended to get drunk and either lose tempo or drown the others with noisy outbursts.

The audience was small and it was clear that both the venue and the band did not attract much local interest. A few people who travelled around to hear different bands came regularly but their numbers were insufficient to make the sessions a success either socially or financially.

Finally the band broke up in early 1984, primarily over dissatisfactions with the band's musical style.

Case III This band was formed in 1984 by an experienced player who had become dissatisfied with playing traditional jazz and wanted to play in the mainstream or swing style. Having become convinced that his best chance of playing in this style was to form his own band, he had spent approximately eighteen months listening to and sitting in with bands in the area, making contacts, becoming known, making his own assessment of the styles and abilities of the players he heard, inquiring about their likely availability and compiling an extended list of telephone numbers.

Having discoverd that a number of suitable players were willing to play with him on nights when they were not committed to their existing bands, he approached a nucleus of likely musicians with a view to forming a band. It became clear to him that if he could obtain gigs on appropriate evenings he could get a potentially good band going.

He then carried out a systematic survey of public houses over a large area accessible to the intended players, pinpointed likely venues and approached their licensees. After a while he was offered fortnightly engagements at two pubs and then set about producing an advertising leaflet to distribute to existing jazz venues in the area.

In spite of this thorough preparation the band played its first public performance without having any rehearsal and with some of its members having never met before. The poorly attended first session, with the band having some difficulties over rapport, was followed by several in which the personnel settled down and began to play well together and a repertoire was built up.

After several months of playing at non-established jazz venues to sparse audiences but building up both musical rapport and a settled line-up, the band was offered an engagement at a venue with a discerning jazz audience. Several rehearsals then took place but involving only the three core members of the band to cut down expense since the band was drawn from a widely dispersed geographical area. Also their time was limited because all band members including the leader were playing regularly with other bands.

Their first appearance at the established venue was judged a success musically and they were offered a monthly booking. Soon another established jazz venue offered them a fortnightly and eventually a weekly engagement and the band was able to settle down to playing together regularly. Though this residency lasted only five months, they have since gained regular return bookings at two other well-known jazz pubs in the West Midlands and a pool of players familiar with the band's style has been built up so that anyone who is unable to play on a particular date can be replaced by a regular deputy. In effect the band's leader forms the node of a social network which he contacts by telephone. Some of the other members play together elsewhere but the particular combination assembled by this leader is unique to his band.

Unlike the band in Case I, this band seeks to be known in a wide geographical area and its members live between mid-Staffordshire and north Worcestershire. The band's name also signifies that it is envisaged as a Midlands area band rather than a purely local one. Nevertheless despite this wider focus its members do not see it as aiming at national recognition or professional status. None would consider giving up their daytime jobs to pursue these aims. Though on friendly terms they have no connection with one another outside the jazz scene. They come together to further their basic motivation of musical enjoyment within their chosen style.

Discussion A comparison of the way in which these three bands were formed throws light on the issues of convention and constraint in the socio-musical context of British semi-pro jazz. The way they were formed had a direct bearing on their chances of survival and success and was also reflected in their subsequent characteristics.

The band in Case I arose from a group of people coming together to have informal fun and continuing until they realised they had developed into a settled band with a shared repertoire. For such a process to occur it was necessary that all or most of the participants were from the same locality and that the style of jazz being played was familiar to them – the lowest common denominator as it were – which in this case meant that it had to be traditional jazz.

Since there was no clear leader and no rehearsals were ever even considered, it was necessary that the participants were all familiar with the unspoken social and musical assumptions of traditional jazz. In fact all had 'learned the ropes' in this way some twenty to thirty years previously even though some were 'rusty' through not having played regularly for years. The band's regular members therefore ranged in ages from early forties to early sixties.

They were happy to maintain a low profile so that they could continue to enjoy a more or less self-financing hobby without getting involved in any complications with the Inland Revenue, the Musicians' Union or the Performing Rights Society.

The band in Case II illustrates what can happen when the appropriate conventions and constraints are not sufficiently taken into account by participants. The leader acted in a way more appropriate to the organisation of orthodox musical groups. Where the composer is the ultimate arbiter and the reproductions of his intentions is the primary aim, what is required is the assembly of suitably competent performers who can be assumed to be more or less interchangeable. Their personal styles of performance are not the primary consideration. A formal procedure of advertising for performers and then organising a musical combination from the competent ones that respond is appropriate.

In jazz, however, the performer is the composer – existing compositions are mere vehicles for improvised creation on the spot and the wishes of their composers are of secondary importance if at all. Performers' styles in jazz are typically highly individual to each player and musical compatibility is therefore all-important.[10]

Compatibility in a band can be achieved by self-selection as in Case I or by careful informed selection by a leader, as in Case III. The band in Case II failed musically and did not survive, ultimately because it was not formed in a way which took account of the appropriate conventions. The musicians assembled were ill-assorted. Three were in their twenties and lacked familiarity with the informal norms and shared understandings that were acquired almost subliminally by those who learned their jazz as teenagers in the 1950s. The formal musical competence of the band's players was not in doubt but they just did not 'jell' as a jazz band. Also, a drummer whose main experience is ballroom dance work is highly likely to be a dead weight holding back a jazz group. Those jazz drummers who also do dance work for the money are a different matter – their delight at being 'liberated' for an evening can set a jazz band alight.

A band some of whose members have to travel a distance to play are unlikely to feel tolerant for long of musically unsatisfying performances if their expenses are not adequately covered by their share of the band's receipts. Even when money is not the main motivation it is still a factor that has to be taken into consideration. Semi-pro jazz players play mainly for enjoyment but they do not expect to be 'out of pocket' after helping to provide an evening's entertainment. Lack of understanding of this convention by the band's leader was another reason for the band's demise. In addition the rehearsals involved travelling without provision for expenses. Inadequate financial arrangements are therefore likely to alienate established players who no longer feel they need to buy experience. A combination of these factors led to the break-up of this band after a few months, in which time it had played in public about a dozen times in only one venue.

The band in Case III has never established a long-term weekly residency as did the Case I band, and has gone through some lean periods for bookings partly because it is not a trad band, but it has nevertheless survived and developed musically. There is an established pool of musicians who are happy to play with the band when they are available and the band's core members have developed a sense of identity and loyalty to the band even though they play together on average no more than twice a month and all also play more frequently with other bands.

Its formation was influenced by the need to achieve stylistic compatibility and by the desire to play a less popular jazz style in which there are fewer musicians able or willing to play. This meant the selection of musicians from a wide geographical area. At the same time it was not the kind of avant-garde style which typically attracts public subsidy. From this flowed the difficulty of holding full band rehearsals without any funding from which to pay members' travelling expenses.

There therefore had to be a heavy reliance on the established competence and experience of the players in order to produce acceptable public performances without full rehearsals. This was usually successful given careful choice of members and deputies but it sometimes caused difficulties since some members were venturing outside the strictly traditional jazz conventions with which they were more familiar. What they were attempting often involved more complex chords sequences, more demanding keys and more precise timing in ensemble playing.

Also, because their style was less familiar to the public and to organisers of venues, there was more difficulty in getting engagements, thus necessitating a more deliberate effort on the part of the leader to obtain gigs. He was also hindered by the fact that the substantial travelling expenses of members had to be covered in addition to reasonable payment for playing and he could therefore not afford to offer their services too cheaply even though the market would not stand high payments.

A careful balance had to be struck between the need to have sufficient playing opportunities to keep the band going and the need to ensure that its members were not too unreasonably paid. He also felt it desirable to advertise the band. The result was that he undertook to fund the band to some extent out of his daytime earnings and tried to make it up by his taking a slightly larger 'cut' from any gigs that were better paid and from his earnings playing with another band. He felt this was worthwhile because it meant that he was able to play jazz in the style he wanted.

Conclusion

This article has examined the main conventions and constraints which structure the activities of semi-professional jazz musicians in a British provincial region. I have sought to demonstrate by the presentation of organised ethnographic data the nature of these restraints and to trace some of the ways in which they operate.

The situation can be summed up as being a precarious and fluctuating balance between, on the the one hand, efforts to maintain musical integrity as expressed in the values and conventions held by most jazz musicians – that their music is not primarily a commercial commodity but a creative artistic activity – and, on the other hand, the need to operate within a market situation in order to find opportunities to play. Awareness that they do operate within such a situation leads them to regard their labour as having a value to organisers of venues and to audiences, and therefore they are not prepared to treat their playing as purely a hobby which must be totally financed out of other income. On the other hand they are also aware that they cannot today expect a widespread popular following which will bring them high payment for playing what they enjoy.

Compromises have to be made, sometimes in terms of what they play but more often in terms of the level of payment they can expect. These musicians will play occasional numbers they would not freely choose for the sake of pleasing paying customers, but most semi-pro jazzmen would rather not play at all than completely sell out to popular taste.

Compromises have to be made also between artistic satisfaction and the practical demands of daytime jobs, family commitments, and the costs of travelling and maintenance of instruments and other equipment.

Since some of these musicians are good enough players to become professional if they chose to do so, the further conclusion follows that remaining semi-pro is a deliberate choice they have made which enables them partially to satisfy musical ambitions while minimising the pressures on them which would be likely to make them compromise their musical integrity or their otherwise conventional life styles for the sake of earning a living. Most have long ago decided that the insecurity, unsocial hours and regular long night-time journeys involved in being a professional jazz musician are not for them.

It is clear that these social factors, like any others, operate within a configuration of social conventions and material constraints and have to decide on their strategies in terms of how to achieve their goals by taking account of these conditions, and negotiating compromises of kinds which they find acceptable. Compromises may include some modification of the goals themselves as well as of the material rewards they would ideally like to obtain from their activity, but on the whole aesthetic and satisfaction criteria tend to come out on top. They are mercenary to the extent of not wanting to be 'out of pocket', but beyond that, as one cornet player commented, 'We do it because we love it.'

Notes

1 Becker, Howard S., 'Art as collective action', in the *American Sociological Review*, vol. 39, no. 6, December 1974.
2 Godbolt, Jim, *Jazz in Britain, 1919–1950*, Paladin, London, 1986.
3 Ibid., pp. 263–72.
4 Harris, Rex, *Jazz*, Penguin, Harmondsworth, 1957, pp. 219–46.
5 Russell, Ross, 'Bebop', in Martin T. Williams, *The Art of Jazz*, Cassel & Co., London, 1960, pp. 187–213.

6 Oakley, Giles, *The Devil's Music: A History of the Blues*, Ariel Books, BBC, London, 1983, pp. 208–16.
7 Godbolt, op. cit., pp. 196–211.
8 On the importance of 'mechanical reproduction' for twentieth-century musics, see Wishart, Trevor in Shepherd, J. Virden, P., Vulliamy, G. and Wishart, T., *Whose Music?*, Latimer New Dimensions, London, 1977, p. 137; and on learning to play jazz see Lyttelton, Humphrey, in Harris, op. cit., pp. 228–9, and Bryce, Owen and MacLaren, Alex, *Let's Play Jazz*, Bryce, Borough Green, Kent, 1968.
9 Cameron, William Bruce, 'Sociological notes on the jam session', in his *Informal Sociology*, Random House, New York, 1964, pp. 118–30.
10 Newton, Francis, *The Jazz Scene*, Jazz Book Club, MacGibbon & Kee, London, 1960, pp. 29–30.

RECORDING MUSIC

Technology in the art of recording

Stephen Struthers

The design of the technology used to duplicate sound recordings for eventual 'reproduction', the familiar disc, was not the result of chance decisions, or of technical imperatives. Gramophone discs of recorded sound and pre-recorded tapes satisfy a number of criteria for a commoditised entertainment industry; they can be manufactured and sold relatively cheaply, and in large quantities this can be made very profitable by economies of scale; they are semi-durable, and therefore the consumer purchases a long-lasting good, but may be persuaded to seek replacements; they are portable, and cheaply and easily transported and stored. Lastly, and most importantly, discs of recorded sound can only be made by a process of manufacture that is difficult and costly to set up. This usefully hinders the entry into the market for discs of competitors who might engage in price competition, but more particularly, and what is sociologically important, distinguishes a social division of labour between producer and consumer, allowing producers to maintain control over recorded material, and hence over consumers.

This control of producers has recently been challenged by consumers using the newer technology of the blank magnetic recording cassette tape. The efforts of producers to combat this challenge by technical and legal means is testimony to its financial importance to them.[1]

The chosen manufacturing process also gives producers control over the type of sounds that are available. The sound recording as a cultural artifact bears witness to its origins as an entertainment commodity. To paraphrase John Berger, the term 'sound recording' refers to more than a technique, it defines a cultural form that was developed only when there was a need for a particular way of listening.[2]

The initial impetus behind Edison's invention of a technique of sound recording in 1878 was the commercial potential of the market that a telephone manufacturing company perceived for a telephone repeater machine in government and business offices.[3] However, the market did not materialise and development stagnated. It is a sleight of hand to suggest that this was the source of the contemporary sound recording, as some recent accounts of the history of sound recording have done,[4] for Edisons recorders were designed to permit the operator to make his own recordings. We would argue on the other hand that the real source of the sound recording as a cultural artifact dates from Berliner's invention of the gramophone and pre-recorded discs in 1898. Gramophone manufacturers subsequently made sound recordings as a relatively cheap consumable good that would, by offering varied entertainment at home, encourage the public to purchase their own gramophones.

The sound recording as a cultural form is a socially constructed artifact whose origins, as a product of capitalist business, accounts both for its primary purpose as an object of consumption and for its technical form. It is a means of reifying, packaging and selling sounds. Certain technologies which have been used in recording production have become embodied in the sounds that are packaged and sold.

The rise and fall of realism

In the earliest days of sound recording, both the recording industry and the public subscribed towards an ideal of realism, that is, that recordings should strive towards a faithful reproduction of the original performance; that what went into the recording machine should come out in exactly the same form at a later time.[5] Given our knowledge of the state of the art then, this was a perfectly reasonable but not unambitious objective.

The range of sound capable of reproduction is one measurable dimension where we can trace a path of consistent development and improvement in the quality of recorded sound. This improvement is an important background to other innovations. The earliest phonographs of Edison had given only the barest approximation to human speech, but progress in improving this was steady, if slow. In the first decade of this century, the quality of reproduction had been so poor that almost any room sufficed for recording (which offered some advantages) and it was normally necessary to rearrange a composer's instrumentation to bring the accompaniment within the limited range of the recording process.

Technical advances in improving the quality of sound reproduction, or the manageability of the storage medium, in the period until the 1920s were slow by modern standards. We may attribute this to the relatively limited financial resources available to firms in the industry. Recording was profitable, although not excessively so, and it is likely that this did not encourage risky investment.

At the most advanced stage of acoustic recording, a full symphony orchestra could be recorded without substituting instruments, and the acoustic properties of the recording room could begin to be taken into account, although the frequency range remained limited to between E and triple C (164–2088cs) compared with the 60–8,000cs range of most music. This meant that neither the low notes nor the overtones were reproduced. Recorded music acquired a 'metallic' sound and lost much of its flavour.

A contributory reason for the rapid diffusion in the late 1920s of electrical recording equipment and techniques adapted from radio broadcasting was the noticeable improvement offered in the frequency range of sound reproduced. Musical recordings were still somewhat deficient in bass and treble, with a frequency range of from 100 to 5,000cs, but quite good enough to pick up the ambience of the recording room.

By 1950, when the whole range of sound audible to the human ear (25–20,000cs) could be recorded and reproduced by magnetic tape, it might have been thought that the sound engineer's aims of a faithful reproduction of an original performance had been achieved. However, improving fidelity and electrical recording techniques had, ironically, the opposite effect, for they showed clearly to those who had not already appreciated it, that sound fidelity was only one component of a sound recording, which was not simply the technical reproduction of a given spectrum of the frequency range. These advances in the physical reproduction of sounds have made it clear that the ideals of fidelity and realism in sound recording are chimeras. Successive technical developments which have appeared to improve sound reproduction have, instead, increased the difference between sound recording and sound reproduction. As Read and Welch write, 'The old idea of preserving or storing up . . . gave way to the creation of calculated effects, of a specious and spurious type of reproduction.'[6]

Replicable art

Walter Benjamin argued that the possibility of mechanical reproduction fundamentally altered the meaning of art. He also pointed out that the possibilities of mechanical reproduction have sometimes been taken a logical step further, for in some cases the art-works themselves are indistinguishable from the artifacts called 'reproductions', which should, by definition, be dependent on them. Then, multiple copies are made from a master copy, so there is no original, no unique artifact with the aura and authenticity of an original, no artifact with a better pedigree than any other. It is clearly inappropriate to continue to regard these artifacts as 'art' in the traditional meaning of that term, with its associated concepts of authenticity and aura, or indeed, as 'reproductions' of art.

Benjamin predicts that where works of art are habitually reproduced, they will become, under the inevitable pressure of events, 'designed for reproducibility',[7] or replicable art. The objective in making replicable art is not to make a single work of art whose value derives from its uniqueness, but to make a large number of identical artifacts for mass sale in the marketplace. A step is removed from traditional methods of reproduction, which presuppose the existence of an original which the reproduction is the copy. 'Process' reproduction such as this results in not one original, but ten, a thousand or tens of thousands of identical artifacts, each one an original only in the sense that it does not replicate an earlier form.

This can be illustrated in the domestic example of the difference between cooking a meal for one person and cooking for a dinner party. The latter requires, say, eight meals which have been made with this end in mind using methods and quanitites appropriate for eight servings, rather than making one meal eight times. Hence, there is no original.

The concept of replicable art, art made for reproduction, is particularly apposite for sound recordings. We would argue that the various technological, social and economic pressures have acted in a way to bring about this development. The idea of a contemporary musical recording as a reproduction of a real musical event is not tenable as, using multi-track magnetic tape recording, the final recording is assembled and 'reconstructed' from a number of fragments, and so there is no 'original' of which that published recording can be a reproduction. Indeed a significant amount of popular music has never existed in a pre-recorded stage, being created as it was being recorded, or as a unique combination of previously recorded pieces first heard together during editing. Many recordings today are made with the circumstances of reproduction uppermost in mind, either on the radio or for domestic listening. This represents a considerable change since sound recordings were first made; we now propose to consider some of these factors further.

A collage of perfect details

Contemporary recording techniques are intimately related to the use for recording of magnetic tape. However, it is not a necessary consequence of using magnetic tape that recordings should be constructed out of fragments of recorded sound, nor does magnetic tape, notwithstanding its almost universal use, offer the only possible means of storing sounds.

The ease with which magnetic tape can be edited offers immense aesthetic opportunities, and its use has become a hallmark of recording today. Once the rudimentary editing facility was refined, sound recording was freed from limitations imposed by real time and real place, as temporally and/or spatially separated fragments of recording could be spliced together, and presented as apparently one complete sequential piece.

The technology of magnetic tape recording has been developed in a way that maximises its usefulness and effectiveness for sound editing. The single track tape recorder of the 1940s was succeeded by tape recorders with two tracks offering stereo recording in the 1950s. Editing was feasible to a limited extent, although there is evidence that, in general, recording engineers did not really take advantage of the new opportunities offered by this technology until it was further developed in the four-track tape recorders in the mid-1960s. Subsequent developments, mainly initiated as we have noted, by studios competing for a share of a burgeoning business led to the availability and use of eight, sixteen, thirty-two and more synchronous tracks of tape for recording. The use of magnetic tape enables recording personnel to make numerous artificial modifications to sound sources during recording as a means of widening the range of aesthetic choices, and to construct finished recordings from individual segments recorded at different times, each of which can be modified in isolation.

Recording personnel have chosen to use the facilities to ensure that the finished product includes only what they consider to be the best possible recorded performances. Many fragments are separately recorded and re-recorded a number of times. This search for a 'perfection' is a prominent feature in the process of recording, and has implications for the questions of reproduction and illusion. 'Perfection' is not an absolute quality, but a subjective judgment on the part of the artistic arbiter about the relationship between what has been recorded and what might have been intended. Recording is one of a number of cultural products where production personnel are seeking to achieve a perfection, for it is a phenomenon that occurs wherever there is the opportunity to scrutinise the work.

As a sound recording may be subject to considered attention over a period of time recording personnel are concerned to present a finished work that is as good as they feel they are able to put together with all the technical resources at their disposal. Recording personnel also put a high premium on the technique and musical competence shown in a recording, feeling that musical 'errors', sounds that are incompatible with our cultural expectations and understandings of what is musical, tend to become prominent over a period of repeated listening. The end result is, in Sennett's phrase,[8] a 'collage of perfect details'.

Although the constructed recording may have the appearance of a performance, comprising as it does a sequential beginning, middle and end, it does not have the substance of one, that is, an uninterrupted sequence by the same musicians from start to finish and held together by a musical and emotional flow rather than by musical logic. It offers, therefore, an illusion that it is a reproduction of a real event.

Illusion

Illusion is fundamental to studio recording. We have referred to the illusion of the recorded 'performance' constructed out of perfected fragments. There are other, minor, illusions which attempt to persuade the listener he is hearing something other than what was recorded in the studio, and in different locations and spatial relationships to those actually existing there.

From the early acoustic days, recording personnel have relied on audial illusion for aesthetic effect. The following eye witness account of an orchestral recording session at Columbia's London studio in about 1911 illustrates a number of pertinent points.

> In the recording room . . . there were a number of small platforms of varying heights, each large enough to hold a chair and a musical stand. The piano, always an upright, had its back removed. The Stroh violins were nearest to the horn. Muted strings were never mentioned. The French Horns, having to direct the bells of their instruments towards the recording horn, would turn their backs on it, and were provided with mirrors in which they could watch the conductor. The tuba was positioned right back away from the horn and his bell turned away from it; he also watched in a mirror. The big drum never entered a recording room.[9]

It is evident from this account that even then recording personnel were not solely concerned with the reproduction of reality. Their adaptations of musical instruments and orchestral lay-out were not solely intended to minimise the limitations of the rudimentary recording equipment but also to create an illusion, to give an impression of what an orchestra might have sounded like. They were using their expertise at two levels, first, to store as faithfully as possible the sounds made in the recording room, and second, to adapt these sounds at source so they would project an impression about what was actually being recorded. In this example, it seems that it was being pretended that a small orchestra was being recorded.

In contemporary recording practice electronic enhancements or synthesisers may be used to imply the presence of musicians or instruments that were not actually present when recording took place.

Recordings also incorporate illusions about location and spatial relationships. In acoustic, mechanical recording, sound was gathered at one point in a recording horn and transferred mechanically on to a storage medium – a soft disc or cylinder on which a moving stylus made indentations corresponding to the sound energy. The procedure was reversed for replaying, with the sound diffused through another horn. Hence as sound was both collected and distributed from the one point, there were no practical or perceptual difficulties about location.

The introduction into sound recording of electrical broadcasting microphones had two important consequences. First, it meant that the sound source could be remote from the recording unit, and second, that more than one microphone could be used to gather the sounds, which could be fed into the one storage medium.

The essence of electrical recording is that changes in sound pressure caused by sound energy are transformed into changes in electrical current which are relayed by wire from the collecting source to the point where, like the acoustic techniques it replaced, they were transferred to a storage medium. The essential difference between electrical and acoustic reproduction was that in the latter the sounds would be diffused from a speaker connected electrically rather than physically with the storage medium.

The gathering of sounds by spatially separated microphones and their reproduction from one point overturned the single focus of acoustic recording. Electrically recorded sound is now a synthesis, which on replaying projects an illusion.

A synthesis is created of sounds collected at different points but recorded together so that on 'reproduction' they are heard as if they were all collected at the same point. As each sound is collected separately, and can be amplified if necessary, it need not even be of such a sufficient volume to be heard above other sounds when recorded, for it can be amplified electronically before being added to the other sounds. The most important factor for the final recording is the putting together of the varying sound sources, and the relative volume of each sound in that synthesis. An arbitrary sound balance has to be created, its task being to support the suggestion of performance it purports to represent.

The illusion is that the synthesised sound is one that existed in its own right and that a listener could have heard had he gone to the right place. Indeed part of the illusion is that a recording unit had gone there on the listener's behalf and had recorded what it had heard. We have called it an illusion, because it is physically impossible for this to have happened.

Stereo reproduction aims to project an illusion of a preferred spatial relationship between recorded sound sources as each sound, whatever the location of its source, is individually located on a two-dimensional plane. The use of stereo may be justified for marketing reasons on the grounds of greater fidelity, but its practical use is to enhance the illusion of recordings and make them more attractive to purchasers/listeners.

A related locational illusion is the ambience of a recorded sound which is used as a convention to indicate the type of environment in which the recorded sound is purported to have been heard.

One of the consequences of being able to record and reproduce the whole range of audible sound is that the location of the recording becomes a distinguishable component in the recorded sound of a musical instrument or voice. The ambience of a sound, that is, those qualities of the sound which derive from the acoustic environment in which it is made, are not easily distinguishable in the natural state, but once recorded and then 'reproduced' in a different acoustic environment, they become very clear. Thus, while offering a number of aesthetic opportunities, the ambience also introduced problems for recording personnel. For if the ambience and timbre of a sound source are recorded, it is indissolubly 'placed' in a specific environment. A piano, for example, will sound different in a small carpeted and curtained room, than in a large hall where there is likely to be reverberation or other extraneous sound intermingled with 'pure' piano sounds.

In the mid-1920s, under the influence of contemporary radio broadcasting, recording personnel began to use their ability to incorporate the ambience of the recording room into recordings. It was no accident, therefore, that an aesthetic was developed that 'in the guise of science [presented] the illusion of hearing as though in a distant concert hall . . . as a great advance in the technics of sound reproduction'.[10]

To achieve this, music was recorded in large halls, in some cases with an audience present. The impression deliberately created was that the listener was hearing a radio broadcast, with the advantage of choosing the musical programme. (Radio sound quality was, for a long time, much superior to the quality of recorded sound.) Radio, itself, at that time pretended that the listener was a witness to the original event.

Clearly, this is not the only way to present recorded music. An alternative aesthetic was developed later that suggested an intimacy between musician and listener, performer and audience, by emphasising the proximity of the musical source to the listener by virtually cutting out ambient sound. When first developed in opposition to the 'radio' aesthetic, the style it incorporated was known as 'crooning'. Subsequently, it has become the basis for the preferred sound in popular music. The use of multi-track magnetic tape has reinforced and sustained this aesthetic as it is more difficult to manipulate recorded sounds incorporating various ambiences in a way that sounds credible.

Today, most popular music recording in the studio is routinely undertaken in a non-ambient environment which may be almost total, as a 'dead' sound is regarded as a base from which other sounds may be more easily treated and adjusted and to which fragments may be added. The illusion fostered is that the listener is in the same room as the person(s) making the recorded sounds. It is an aesthetic that has become strengthened by its osmosis into the working practices of musicians and sound engineers in the recording industry.

A 'live' ambience, either real or electronically created, is conventionally used to suggest recordings apparently made in a concert hall. Much 'classical' music is contemporarily recorded in a way that aims to suggest that the music is 'heard' in a concert hall. If actually recorded in one, its natural ambience will not be disguised. Alternatively, large recording studios will be used where musicians can play together and all sounds can be collected by a small number of microphones, together with any ambience.

The illusion of the 'live' recording

There is a genre of popular music recording which does have the elements of a real performance. The 'live' recording is ostensibly based on actuality, typically a concert, and claims to offer a reproduction of that event yet, even here, the finished recording offers only an illusion of a reproduction, neatly illustrating some of the technical compromises that must be made.

First, there are technical biases in the recording equipment interfering in the reproduction of actuality. In practical terms, any item of recording equipment, be it microphone, recording medium, amplifier or speaker, cannot exactly reproduce original sound, as it will have various strengths, emphases and weaknesses related to the technical parameters of the material used in its construction. Recording engineers may be able to make choices about the equipment they use, and the way they use them. This has always been the case in recording. Moore quotes a sound engineer with knowledge of acoustic recording: 'Acoustic techniques were personal and subjective: recorders used their own favourite "sound boxes"; they might even have several, one for each sort of assignment – piano, voice, orchestra etc.'[11]

Microphones do not work in the same way as the human organ they attempt to copy, and therefore, in the presence of the same aural phenomena, may not 'hear' in the same way as the human ear. Similarly, in visual recording, the camera will 'see' things in different ways to the human eye. Human eyes are not uniformly the same. Some are short-sighted, for example, while others are colour-blind. We are perhaps more familiar with the mechanical biases incorporated in the camera than we are with those of sound recording. Our culture accepts that these biases do not necessarily render the camera inferior to the human eye, for in a number of ways, even without the intelligence that supports the human eye, it has superior sight. Scharf has pointed out,[12] for example, that the freezing of the image, while losing the fluidity and wholeness of movement, has enabled observation of the previously unobservable, inaccessible or unrepeatable. Different camera lenses offer varying perceptions and insights that can extend our knowledge of conventionally observed phenomena.

Second, by using more than one microphone to collect the sound its 'real' balance is inevitably destroyed. Sound sources are isolated as far as possible, to enable electronic enhancement and sound balancing to take place, and are thus not as they would be heard by a listener at the event. Additionally, the microphones set at arbitrary distances from the sound sources permanently 'place' that sound in an acoustic environment. Multi-microphone techniques imitate the physically impossible by 'hearing' simultaneously in more than one place. A new and artificial synthesis will be created in its place.

A further dimension of artificiality arises from expectations that sound recordings available in the market should not include extraneous noises, and should be of a consistently clear quality. In order to achieve this, sound recordings are normally 'posed' and undertaken in special places to isolate sound sources from possible interference. Hence, the actuality that the recording seeks to represent is not a real event, but a 'pseudo-event',[13] existing only for recording.

These technical reasons preventing a recording from being a reproduction of a performance are not the only reasons why a performance cannot be properly reproduced. A live performance in front of an audience is not only made up of musical notes, but also includes the aura of a performer, the rapport that he establishes with his audience, and the overall sound impression created. Musical 'errors' are overlooked in the context of the piece as a whole. Indeed, it is likely that listeners will not notice errors in technique as any errors will be outweighed by their impression of the piece considered as a whole. As performed music disappears as it is played, there is no chance of returning to confirm or refute an error. Sennett has commented on this aspect of live performance, 'the essence of live performance is that no matter what mistakes one makes one keeps going. Unless one has great presence and great public esteem, to stop in the middle of a piece and begin again is an unforgiveable sin.'[14]

There is excitement and tension at a live performance before an audience, felt both by the performer and, to a lesser extent, by the audience. The performer may be concerned to maintain a reputation, and may be worried about his ability to tackle a difficult piece, or to retain the sympathy of an audience. The audience may share these concerns, hoping to avoid embarrassment and any disturbance to their image of the performer. There may be an element of trade-off between a performer's technique and his ability to win over and enthrall an audience, but a performer is generally judged to be successful or not, good or bad, by the reaction of an audience.

Technological innovation in recording

The technique of the production of recording is clearly dependent on industrial technology. We have referred in passing to some of the major technical innovations in recording. They have had a profound effect not only on the cultural artifact, the recording, but also on the practice of the production of recording. At the same time, it is equally evident that the general pace and direction of innovation has been set, as we would expect, by social and political interests, and recording personnel have only exerted a smaller influence in choosing from a limited range of pre-selected options.

Until comparatively recently, the recording industry was so small, in commercial terms, that technological development of the equipment it used was dictated by the needs of other industries, such as public and commercial broadcasting, the military, and the cinema, and the recording industry adopted their techniques when it was convenient to do so. It seems clear that part of the impetus behind technological developments was economic, as innovations were adopted as a means of furthering inter- or intra-industry competition by enhancing the attractions of recordings in the face of competition likely to threaten profitability.

The two major technological innovations which have had the most profound impact on the production of recordings and the aesthetics of recorded music were both developed for totally different reasons by other industries, and in both cases appear to have been introduced into the recording studio for these economic reasons. While the basic technology of electrical recording had been developed during the First World War, and derived from wireless telegraphy and the discovery of the thermionic valve, the specific impetus for introducing the electrical microphone into sound recording came in the US from declining market performance in competition with radio offering 'free' entertainment and much better sound quality.

We have already noted the much improved sound quality of electrically recorded discs. Electrical techniques also widened the range of recordings possible by, for example, allowing recordings to be made with mobile recording units standing outside concert halls or other buildings, an innovation that obviated the need for performers to go to a studio to make recordings, or for companies to build studios suitable for all the types of recordings they wanted to make.

Magnetic tape was developed into a usable form for sound recording by the military during the Second World War for radio propaganda and intelligence purposes, having been originally developed, although not really applied, for round-the-clock broadcasting. It was also brought into the recording studio for production work primarily as a means, again, of improving the attractions of gramophone records by a wider range of sound reproduction and a lengthier period of recording. However, as we shall note, it also had a number of other advantages over the methods it replaced, being more manageable and robust, requiring fewer expert technicians to operate, and saving costs on performers.

In more recent years, the size, resources and expectations of the recording industry have multiplied, and it has been able to finance technological inventions in recording which have had few applications outside the recording studio. Innovations such as increased multi-track facilities, computer-assisted mixing, and a myriad of electronic means to enhance sounds have been introduced into studios as part of the competition between capital groupings, between studios competing for customers for their recording services.

Technology and the social relations of recording

The choice and design of productive technology is in the hands of capital, and we should, therefore, expect technology to be shaped to meet its needs. Not only can it be a powerful tool in reinforcing the control of capital, but in doing so it makes clear the real social relations of production which may have been concealed.

Technological innovation in the recording studio has been consistent with the argument that the introduction of new technology is invariably for the purposes of increasing control over the workforce.[15] The workforce in recording has never been large, and so controlling it has not been perceived as a major problem but may nevertheless be thought desirable.

The technology of recording makes more easily apparent the real social relationships of production. A clear indicator of where effective control lies in the studio is seen in the design of the recording console; one noticeable feature of recording has been the gradual consolidation of its control over recording sessions. Situated in the aptly named control room, it has been developed from a device used in early broadcasting to balance sounds from different microphones, and has now become the focus of recording activity as all information is routed through it, and peripheral equipment directed from it. Hence, effective direction of a recording session is inevitably in the hands of the operators of the console, the engineer and producer, and through them, capital.

The modern console is also designed to minimise labour costs by enabling one person, normally the engineer, to operate it. Within the last decade, the installation in some studios of computer-assisted mixing has enabled one operator to carry out highly sophisticated procedures which would otherwise require assistance.

Magnetic tape, too, while generally rationalised as offering improved technical reproduction and a wider range of aesthetic possibilities, also had the useful effect of enhancing the control of capital over performers, musicians and engineers. First, it became possible to isolate individual contributions, and therefore substitute them if necessary; second, less specialist engineering skills were required to achieve an acceptable result; and third, it was potentially much less costly, because disruptions such as a cough or unacceptable musical technique could be simply edited out without the necessity to repeat the whole 'performance'. This greatly reduced the opportunity of performers to influence events in the studio.

Many recording personnel appear to have an ambivalence towards the recording technology provided by capital for their use, and the associated recording techniques which are most suited to the idea of perfection, what we might call a 'recording' aesthetic. This aesthetic conveniently justifies the various technical innovations, a primary purpose of which has been to increase the control of capital over other recording personnel. It also has the useful secondary attribute of encouraging consumer investment in more complex and sophisticated 'reproduction' equipment.

In contemporary recording practice we can discern an alternative, competing 'performance' aesthetic which stresses the values of expression and emotionality or 'feel', emphasising the performance aspect. It allows recording personnel to regard a recording, notwithstanding the technology, as a form of performance which is creative and artistic, rather than as a commodity constructed for the marketplace at the behest and under the direction of capital.

Conclusion

We have argued in favour of the view that technology is unavoidably shaped by social, political and economic interests. It seems to us clear that, although some technological developments are sequential and dependent on preceding work, the specific technology used for any one application is *chosen* by particular social interests. Within a capitalist socio-economic system, the priorities will inevitably be those of capital. The application of any one technology must, therefore, be recognised as a social construct depending, among other things, on a partisan analysis of both the problem and acceptable solutions, and on choices about costs, resource inputs, and aims. The apparent 'naturalness' of technology is no more than a reflection of the familiarity of its form, and its definitions of problems and solutions.

This general case is confirmed in the example of recording. The technology of the finished recording is entirely appropriate for the role of the recording in a competitive marketplace for commoditised leisure. On the production side, the technology maximises the control of capital over other participants in recording, while minimising direct money costs. These priorities have become manifest in the particular way of hearing that recordings represent, as the chosen technology has become embedded in recordings through the acceptable constraints of various technical parameters, and through the effect of the development of different aesthetics which are intimately linked to it.

We highlighted three rival aesthetics of recorded music, competing answers to the questions of what a recording, and valid musical experiences, are, or should be. In the early days of recording, the dominant aesthetic was that a recording should aim to be a reproduction of reality, and aesthetic success was measured against this yardstick. This aesthetic became increasingly untenable as successive technical developments widened the range of recorded sounds and highlighted the role of illusion at the expense of realism, and a rival aesthetic emerged that celebrated technical and musical 'perfectionism' in recorded music. In opposition to this emphasis on technical sophistication and control, a third aesthetic which emphasised 'performance' values and the unique contribution of the performer, was distinguished.

We should note also that recordings, and their mass reproduction, have simultaneously led to both a standardisation of aesthetic experience, for all listeners are exposed to the same sounds, and a widening of aesthetic experiences, by making available to a public representations of existing sounds which were formerly inaccessible, as well as new ways of hearing sounds.

Epilogue

In the last few years, digital methods of recording and reproduction have been developed and made available. In terms of the production of recordings, the main impact of digital techniques on sound recording is to offer recording personnel increased control and flexibility in their use of recorded sounds. Fidelity is greater (notwithstanding the problems we referred to); it is less prone to such mechanical interference as noise, distortion, and variations in speed. It is a technology which supports, therefore, those recording personnel for whom the 'recording studio' values of perfectionism and technique, as opposed to 'performance' values of musicianship, have priority. It will again favour capital, those companies and individuals with access to extensive resources.

Associated with digital recording has been the introduction of the digitally based sound reproduction system now familiarly known as the 'compact disc'. The compact disc itself is essentially simply a different medium on which to market finished recordings. It, therefore, has no impact on the fundamental question we addressed, of what a recording is. Indeed, although many compact discs incorporate new digitally recorded material others simply represent old analogue recordings in a new finished form.

The technology fits into the general pattern of developments in recording we outlined, where periodic advances are used as successful marketing tactics, and help protect established companies from new entrants to the market and, in this case, from the consumer, as it reinforces the social division of labour between producer and consumer.

Notes

1. It is claimed that in the UK the recording industry 'failed to reach its full potential and achieved sales of only ⅔ of the level which could have been expected'; and that 'lost sales' would have had a retail value of over £200m. per annum (BPI, 1982, p. 41)
2. See Berger (1972), p. 84.
3. This chapter relies heavily for information about technical developments on Borwick (1977a and 1977b); Gelatt (1956); Lane (1975 and 1977); Moore (1976); Read and Welch (1959); Rust (1977); Townsend (1976).
4. See Borwick (1970) for example.
5. Read and Welch (1959), p. 237.
6. Ibid., p. 238.
7. See Benjamin (1970c).
8. Sennett (1977), p. 291
9. Herbert C. Ridout in 'The Gramophone' (1940), quoted in Gelatt (1956), pp. 134–5.
10. Read and Welch (1959), p. 238.
11. Moore (1976), p. 175.
12. Scharf (1974), chapter 9, pp. 212 ff.; also Benjamin (1970c), p. 387.
13. Boorstin (1963), p. 21.
14. Sennett (1977), p. 291.
15. See Dickson (1974).

Bibliography

Anderton, W.E., 'Professional sound recording', *Wireless World*, 1974, 80, 1462, 211–14.

Anthony, M., 'How to ruin a good recording', *Studio Sound*, 1974, 16, 4, 38.

Benjamin, W., 'Paris – capital of the nineteenth century', *New Left Review*, 1968, 48, 77–88.

Benjamin, W., 'The author as producer', *New Left Review*, 1970a, 62, 83–96.

Benjamin, W., *Illuminations*, London, Jonathan Cape, 1970b.

Benjamin, W., 'The work of art in the age of mechanical reproduction,' in Benjamin, W., *Illuminations*, 1970c.

Berger, J., *Ways of Seeing*, London, BBC, 1972.

Boorstin, D.J., *The Image*, Harmondsworth, Penguin, 1963.

Borwick, J., 'A record of success', *Esso Magazine*, 1970, 20, 1, 20–3.

Borwick, J., 'EMI at 75: the technical story', *Gramophone*, 1973, 51, 604, 608.

Borwick, J., 'A century of recording: part 1, the first 50 years', *Gramophone*, 1977a, 54, 647, 1621–2.

Borwick, J., 'A century of recording: part 2, the second 50 years', *Gramophone*, 1977b, 54, 648, 1761–5.

Briggs, A., *Mass Entertainment: The Origins of a Modern Industry*, Adelaide, Griffin Press, 1960.

Briggs, A., *The History of Broadcasting in the United Kingdom* (3 vols), London, Oxford University Press, 1961, 1965.

British Phonographic Industries, *1982 Yearbook*, London, BPI, 1982.

Buck-Morss, S., 'Walter Benjamin – revolutionary writer', *New Left Review*, 1981, 128, 50–75 and 129, 77–95.

Crabbe, J., 'Some technical and aesthetic barriers on the road to perfect sound reproduction', *British Kinematography*, 1965, 46, 42–4.

Cross, N., Elliott, D. and Roy, R. (eds), *Man-made Futures*, London, Hutchinson Educational, 1974.

De Bono, E. (ed.), *Technology Today*, London, Routledge & Kegan Paul, 1971.

Dickson, D., *Alternative Technology and the Politics of Social Change*, Glasgow, Fontana/Collins, 1974.

Drucker, P.F., 'Work and tools', in Kranzberg, M. and Davenport, W. H. (eds), 1972.

Eaves, M., 'Blake and the artistic machine', *Annals of the Modern Language Association of America*, 1977, 92:5, 903–13.

Ellul, J., *The Technological Society*, London, Jonathan Cape, 1965.

Faith, A., *Poor Me*, London, Four Square, 1961.

Gelatt, R., *The Fabulous Phonograph*, London, Cassel & Co., 1956.

Gillett, C., *Making Tracks*, London, Panther, 1975.

Harries, D., 'The economics of multi-track recording', *Studio Sound*, 1976, 19, 1, 30–4.

Haug, M.R. and Dofny, J. (eds), *Work and Technology*, London, Sage, 1977.

Heilbronner, R.L., 'Do machines make history?', in Kranzberg, M. and Davenport, W.H. (eds), 1972.

Houlton, R. 'The process of innovation: magnetic recording and the broadcasting industry in the USA', *Bulletin of the Oxford University Institute of Economics and Statistics*, 1967, 29, 1, 41–60.

Kranzberg, M. and Davenport, W.H. (eds), *Technology and Culture*, New York, Shocken Books, 1972.

Lane, B., '75 years of magnetic recording' (5 parts), *Wireless World*, 1975, 81, 1471, 102–5, 1472, 161–4, 1473, 222–5, 1474, 283–6, 1475, 341–2.

Lane, B., 'The thin brown line', *Studio Sound*, 1977, 18, 6, 72–8.

McLuhan, H.M., *The Gutenberg Galaxy*, London, Routledge & Kegan Paul, 1962.

McLuhan, H.M., *Understanding Media*, London, Routledge & Kegan Paul, 1964.

Melman, S., 'The myth of autonomous technology', in Cross, N. *et al.* (eds), 1974.

Moore, J.N., *Elgar on Record*, Oxford, Oxford University Press, 1974.

Moore, J.N., *A Voice in Time – the Gramophone of Fred Gaisberg*, London, Hamish Hamilton, 1976.

Read, O. and Welch, W.L., *From Tinfoil to Stereo*, Indianapolis, Howard Sams and Co. and Bobbs-Merrill Co., 1959.

Rust, B. 'The development of the recording industry' (2 parts), *Gramophone*, 1977, 54, 647, 1521–3 and 648, 1675–6.

Scharf, A., *Art and Photography*, Harmondsworth, Penguin, 1974.

Sennett, R., *The Fall of Public Man*, Cambridge, Cambridge University Press, 1977.

Times Literary Supplement, Walter Benjamin, 1968, 22 August, no. 3469, 885–7.

Tilsley, D., 'Computer assisted mixing', *Studio Sound*, 1975, 17, 10.

Townsend, K., 'From mono to multitrack', *Studio Sound*, 1976, 18, 8.

Williams, R., *Television: Technology and Cultural Form*, London, Fontana/Collins, 1974.

Wood, A., *The Physics of Sound*, London, Methuen, 1961.

Yeadon, T., 'Multi-track and studio practice', *Studio Sound*, 1975, 17, 3, 24.

Coda: making musical sense of the world

John Blacking

Although I had agreed to write a foreword to this volume, I found it impossible to do so when confronted by the completed manuscript. All that I might have wished to say specifically about the sociology of music seemed to have been well covered in the introduction and succeeding chapters. I was therefore left with the options of citing and endorsing points which had been adequately made by the authors, or of discussing new problems that have been raised by ethnomusicological research but are not really germane to the purposes of this volume. Since the first option would have seemed unnecessarily patronizing and the second irrelevant, I asked to be excused from my obligation to contribute a foreward and I have contributed the following postscript.

I want to discuss very briefly some issues in social analysis which have been suggested to me by ethnomusicological studies of musical traditions as cultural systems. I hope that they might stimulate new explorations in sociology, in much the same way that 'musical' behaviour has recently become the focus of interesting research in psychology and cognitive science. (I have placed 'musical' in inverted commas because researchers in these fields tend to use restricted definitions of music and musicality that must ultimately be challenged.)

The basic problem here is the status of music-making as a special kind of social action, and my approach to it can be caricatured by inverting some of the phrases in this volume. Thus I am interested in 'the musical character of society', 'ritual as musical performance and the symphonic nature of social life', 'a popular musical interpretation of modern social groups', and 'a musicology of social structure'. This approach could be summed up with the sentence: 'People talk about music as they talk about social life, because social life can be organized musically'. In other words, just as art can reflect and challenge society, so social life can be modelled on art. Musical symbols need not always be secondary, and the reality of social life can be constructed with musical intelligence.

I distinguish 'musical intelligence' from 'musical thought' in the same way that I distinguish 'music' as an innate human capacity from 'musics' as cultural systems. 'Musical thought' is a culturally defined process involved in composing, performing, listening to *and* talking about what members of different societies categorize as special ('musical') symbol systems and kinds of social action. 'Musical intelligence' is the cognitive and affective equipment with which people make *musical* sense of the world.

I argue that musical intelligence is not the only source of 'music-like' sounds and activities, and that it may be used for non-musical activities. Thus, musical structures can be derived from patterns of body movement applied to instruments,[1] and musical intelligence may be used for organizing cultural phenomena that might not be described as 'musical', such as architecture, mathematics (especially Boolean algebra), rhetoric and poetry.

This definition therefore differs in some respects from that of Howard Gardner[2], who identified musical intelligence as one of seven 'frames of mind' but conceived of it exclusively in acoustical, rather than more general symbolic, terms. I do not disagree with Gardner's basic arguments about modular intelligence or about the identity of musical intelligence. I want only to extend the notion of musical intelligence beyond specifically musical parameters to include a more abstract system of ordering human thought and action.

This is because of the results of ethnomusicological research. They have provided convincing evidence that the ability to make music is as innate and as species-specific as the capacity for speech; but at the same time the discovery of many different processes and products that are culturally defined as musical has made it necessary to disassociate musical intelligence from specifically 'musical' characteristics. Musical intelligence cannot usefully be defined in strictly acoustical terms, as A. J. Ellis reported in 1885 after measuring the musical scales of several Asian traditions: 'the Musical Scale is not one, not "natural", nor even founded necessarily on the laws of the consitution of musical sound so beautifully worked out by Helmholtz, but very diverse, very artificial, and very capricious'.[3]

It may be objected that the biological foundations of music-making should not be invoked in a discussion of the sociology of music. But I would defend this approach on the following grounds: first, a science of society cannot be scientific if it does not take into account the biology of the actors; secondly, sociologists are in fact making assumptions about human biology and psychology when they analyse decision-making or economic activity, and I see no reason why aesthetic behaviour should not be accepted as a basic human propensity no less than sexuality, language, or food-gathering; thirdly, satisfactory explanations of the processes of musical composition and improvization, and of the ability to 'think in motions', as Victor Zuckerkandl described it, to use intuitive modes of thought and to make sense of nonverbal behaviour without any cultural preparation, all presuppose abilities that require more than the efficient learning of skills; and fourthly, if there are biological foundations of music-making, a fuller understanding of them should, as Claude Lévi-Strauss has claimed, provide the key to progress in the human sciences.[4]

I shall not discuss further the biological foundations of music or the relationships between a hypothesized musical intelligence and the structures of musical systems and musical composition. I shall be concerned only with their implications for the study of social relationships and cultural change. The importance of aesthetic communication has been stressed by the biologist, J. Z. Young:

> 'There is no body of facts that yet enables us to understand the origins of aesthetic creation or religious beliefs and practices. Presumably both sorts of activity were somehow of assistance to Palaeolithic man in the business of getting a living. This does not mean that carving, or painting, or offering prayers for the dead were crudely of "practical" value, for instance, by improving hunting technique. Yet there is a case for saying that creation of new aesthetic forms, including those of worship, has been the most fundamentally productive of all forms of human activity. Whoever creates new artistic conventions has found methods of interchange between people about matters that were incommunicable before. The capacity to do this has been the basis of the whole of human history'.[5]

It is precisely because the creation of aesthetic forms has been such a productive human activity, and because this capability was so dramatically externalized with the appearance of *Homo sapiens*, that it can be argued that nonverbal, aesthetic communication has been crucial not only for the development of societies and cultural forms, but also for the very evolution of *Homo sapiens* and the capacity for verbal language.[6] Although this is pure speculation, there is plenty of evidence in contemporary and recent traditional societies of the aesthetic foundations of social life.

In an early study on 'The Impress of Personality in Unwritten Music', Percy Grainger wrote of country folk that

> 'their lives, their speech, their manners, even their clothes all show[ed] the indelible impress of a superabundance of artistic impulses and interests . . . . . their placid comments upon men and things so often preferred to adopt the unpassionate formal and patterned habits of "art" (so familiar to us in rural proverbs) rather than resemble the more passionate unordered behaviour of inartistic "life" '.[7]

What Percy Grainger described, and what ethnomusicologists and anthropologists have since found in several different societies, is that some people not only place artistic activities at the centre of their social life, but that they construct their social world with artistic modes of thought. These facts do not conflict with Kurt Blaukopf's view that the basis of all music sociology is the sociology of sound-systems, or with Howard Becker's concept of art-worlds: in fact, they help to explain how such musical and social phenomena can emerge and why there should be structural relationships between music and society. Whether or not early prehistoric societies were constituted without verbal language as we know it, musical thought and action can be, and in many societies are, primary modelling systems of thought and part of the infrastructure of social life.

What is sociologically most interesting about music-making are situations in which people associate with, participate in, or affiliate to, music groups because they are primarily attracted by the sounds that they create or reproduce. There is no doubt that music can be used as a quasi-totem and focus for the interests of groups of the same age, similar political persuasions, social aspirations, and so on; but in all these cases a straightforward *sociological* explanation is possible, and the musical element is not of special significance.

What is important and unusual, and presents a challenge to sociology, is the fact that music-making can be more than a totemic emblem: it can be a means of transforming individuals and social groups, and hence can have unexpected social consequences. Although we may agree that artistic production is never entirely an 'action autonomous', as Siegfried Nadel argued, we can see that there is a sense in which aesthetic activity, even as a social fact, can generate new social movements whose significance is far more than a mere reflection of other social actions. We may generalize and say that aesthetic activity can be the source of social formations and of social change. In studying the sociology of the imagination, therefore, we need to be aware of the imagination of new abstract realities which can create their own sociology. I have described elsewhere how in South Africa special kinds of musical performance helped people to feel their way towards new social and political realities.[8]

The best attempt to understand this aspect of the sociology of music is Alfred Schutz's article on 'Making music together',[9] but the full implications of this have not really been pursued. Schutz argued that 'music is a meaningful context which is not bound to a conceptual scheme. Yet this meaningful context can be communicated'.[10] 'The peculiarity of the musical process of communication consists . . . . in the fact that both the flux of the musical events and the activities by which they are communicated, belong to the dimension of inner time'.[11]

Schutz was suggesting that music-making was a kind of archetype of the communicative process which underlies all social relationships, a ' "mutual tuning-in relationship" upon which alone all communication is founded. It is precisely this mutual tuning-in relationship by which the "I" and the "Thou" are experienced by both participants as a "We" in vivid presence.' Schutz hoped that his analysis would 'in some measure contribute to the clarification of the structure of the mutual tuning-in relationship, which originates in the possibility of living together simultaneously in specific dimensions of time. It is also hoped that the study of the particular communicative situation within the musical process will shed some light on the non-conceptual aspect involved in any kind of communication'.[12]

There is, therefore, a research programme in the sociology of music which needs to be pursued, and one whose results could revolutionize contemporary thinking about decision-making and social action. Hitherto, the emphasis has been on the ways in which people make sense of their social worlds with music, and make sense in music with the world. These approaches contribute respectively to sociology and to musicology. I have argued that ethnomusicological research confirms Schutz's view that some kind of tuning-in relationship is at the heart of all effective (and affecting) social organization, and that the ideal model for studying it is the situation of making music together.

It seems that individuals have the capacity for making *musical* sense of the world and that they can, through certain kinds of musical performance and tuning-in with others, transform abstract structures of cognition and affect into social and cultural forms. Musical intelligence is a social intelligence which enables people to organize their bodies in mutually agreeable and intelligible ways without the need to rationalize or to try and fix the experiences. How mutual tuning-in becomes conceptualized and can be reproduced in other contexts, with other meanings, is a major problem for social theory. If we understood better how people make musical sense of the world, and how this relates to making sense of the world with music and sense in music with the world, we might make some interesting advances in sociology. Above all, those who hope to change the world in significant ways might be able to understand better how the cheapest and most available form of energy, aesthetic energy, could be harnessed for greater social and political benefit, as it was in many pre-industrial societies.

Notes

1 See, for instance, John Blacking, *How musical is man?* (Seattle, University of Washington Press), 1973, pp. 12–19, and 'Patterns of Nsenga *kalimba* music', *African Music* 2(4), 1961, pp. 26–43.
2 Howard Gardner, *Frames of Mind: the theory of multiple intelligences*, (London: Paladin Books), 1985.
3 A. J. Ellis, 'On the musical scales of various nations', *Journal of the Society of Arts*, 33, 1885, pp. 485–527.
4 Claude Lévi-Strauss, *Le cru et le cuit* (Paris: Librairie Plon), 1964, p. 26.
5 J. Z. Young, *An introduction to the study of man* (Oxford: Clarendon Press), 1971, p. 519.
6 See, for example, John Blacking, 'Dance, conceptual thought and production in the archaeological record'. In Sieveking, G. de G., I. H. Longworth and K. E. Wilson (eds) *Problems in Economic and Social Archaeology* (London: Duckworth), 1976.
7 Quoted in John Blacking, *'A commonsense view of all music': reflections on Percy Grainger's writings in ethnomusicology and music education* (Cambridge University Press), 1987.
8 See John Blacking, 'Political and musical freedom in the music of some black South African churches'. In Holy, Ladislav and Milan Stuchlik (eds) *The Structure of Folk Models* (London: Academic Press), 1981.
9 Alfred Schutz, 'Making music together', *Social Research* 18(1), March 1951, pp. 76–97. Reprinted in *Collected Papers II.* Studies in Social Theory, Ed. and introduced by Arvid Brodersen (The Hague: Martinus Nijhoff), pp. 159–178.
10 op. cit., p. 76 or 159.
11 op. cit., p. 92 or 173.
12 op. cit., p. 79 or 162.